To N
Thanks for
me to set it in gear
at LSU

Tim 10-12-00

DO827388

The Political Right in Postauthoritarian Brazil

The Political Right in Postauthoritarian Brazil

Elites, Institutions, and Democratization

Timothy J. Power

The Pennsylvania State University Press
University Park, Pennsylvania

An earlier version of Chapter 5 appeared as "Parties, Puppets, and Paradoxes: Changing Attitudes Toward Party Institutionalization in Postauthoritarian Brazil," *Party Politics* 3, no. 2 (April 1997): 189–219. Reprinted by permission of Sage Publications, Ltd. Copyright © 1997 Sage Publications, Ltd.

An earlier version of Chapter 6 appeared as "Elites and Institutions in Conservative Transitions: Ex-Authoritarians in the Brazilian National Congress," *Studies in Comparative International Development* 31, no. 3 (Fall 1996): 56–84. Reprinted by permission of Transaction Publishers. Copyright 1996 © Transaction Publishers.

Library of Congress Cataloging-in-Publication Data

Power, Timothy J. (Timothy Joseph), 1962– .
The political right in postauthoritarian Brazil : elites, institu-
tions, and democratization / Timothy J. Power.
    p. cm.
Includes bibliographical references and index.
ISBN 0-271-02009-1 (cloth : alk. paper)
ISBN 0-271-02010-5 (pbk. : alk. paper)
    1. Conservatism—Brazil. 2. Brazil—Politics and govern-
ment—1985– . 3. Right and left (Political science).
I. Title.
JC573.B7 P68 2000
324.28104'09'045—dc21   99-056473
                                                          CIP

It is the policy of The Pennsylvania State University Press to use acid-free paper for the first printing of all clothbound books. Publications on uncoated stock satisfy the minimum requirements of American National Standard for Information Sciences—Permanence of Paper for Printed Library Materials, ANSI Z39.48-1992.

For Joseph Stephen Power and Barbara Jane Power

Contents

Figures and Tables

Acknowledgments

Many persons and institutions in the United States and Brazil assisted me with my work on this book, and it is my pleasure to acknowledge them here.

For financial support in my field research, I thank the Institute for the Study of World Politics, the Helen Kellogg Institute for International Studies at the University of Notre Dame, and the Council on Research at Louisiana State University. Special thanks go to the Fulbright Commission in Brasília, which supported me with two grants, first as a doctoral student in 1989–90, and later as a visiting lecturer at the University of Brasília in 1994. While in Brazil, I was extremely fortunate to be placed in the good hands of the Comissão Fulbright, which for a decade has been my home away from home. I am grateful to Dr. Marco Antônio da Rocha, executive director of the Comission, and to his marvelous staff for their friendship and support.

At Louisiana State University, where I taught from 1992 to 1999, I benefited from the mentorship of my department chair, Dr. Cecil L. Eubanks. His strong commitments to teaching, research, and professionalism set an example for me to follow. At LSU I also profited greatly from interaction with my friend and colleague Mark J. Gasiorowski, with whom I collaborated on several projects that enriched my understanding of democratization.

In Brazil, I thank the Department of Political Science and International Relations at the University of Brasília. My friends David Fleischer and Luiz Pedone, both former chairs of the department, have been teaching me about Brazil for many years, and are always generous with their time and assistance. Among the many other Brazilian scholars who have helped me along the way, I would like to single out José Álvaro Moisés, João Paulo Peixoto, Francisco Weffort, and Jorge Zaverucha for their contributions. Also, many current and former colleagues at IUPERJ, CEDEC, IDESP, and CEBRAP have lent helpful assistance in the past, and in lieu of thanking them all by name I would like to draw attention to the significant contributions of these four institutions to Brazilian and comparative social science. Foreign scholars of Brazil are greatly indebted to the faculty of these research institutes and to the work that they produce.

My research in the Brazilian Congress was facilitated by numerous current or former members and employees of that institution. I especially thank three former deputies, João Gilberto Lucas Coelho, Nelson Jobim, and Antonio Carlos Nantes de Oliveira. I respect them not only for their intellectual skills and their encyclopedic knowledge of the National Congress but also for the parts they played in Brazil's transition to democracy. Among Congressional employees I thank in particular Jales Marques, João Eustáquio da Silveira, and Samir Machado, along with the staff of the Centro de Documentação e Informação (CDI) of the Chamber of Deputies. I am also grateful to those members of Congress who agreed to be interviewed for this book.

The data collection for this book was greatly improved by suggestions from colleagues. Professor Juan Linz put me in touch with two of his former students, Michael Coppedge and the late Charles Gillespie, who graciously permitted me to reproduce questions from their elite surveys in Venezuela and Uruguay, respectively. Maria D'Alva Gil Kinzo, Scott Mainwaring, and Leôncio Martins Rodrigues did the same for questions they used in Brazil. I also learned much from Barry Ames, who collaborated with me in building a portable dataset on Brazil's constitutional convention of 1987–88. In creating this dataset, which subsequently has been used by several other scholars, Barry and I were assisted by the late Patrícia Soares de Carvalho, my friend and later my sister-in-law. Patrícia's untimely death in October 1997 was the saddest of losses.

I could not have completed the survey data analysis without the kind assistance of Etelvina Maria de Souza Rocha at the University of Brasília, Jim Stukas at Notre Dame, and Mark Gasiorowski and Kit Kenny at LSU. Also at LSU, David Huxsoll, Scott Wilson, and David Gauthier provided research assistance. I thank all of these individuals for their contributions.

One of the most rewarding aspects of my work, both in Brazil and in the United States, has been the opportunity to develop a wonderful network of friends and peers with similar interests and experiences. My fellow graduate students at Notre Dame—in particular Nancy Powers, Volker Frank, and David Dixon, with whom I haunted the hallways of the Kellogg Institute in the 1980s—made the supposedly dehumanizing experience of graduate school very human indeed. In and around Brazilian studies, I have benefited greatly from my friendships with Jeffrey Cason, Wendy Hunter, Peter Kingstone, J. Timmons Roberts, Kenneth Serbin, and Kurt Weyland, all of whom conducted their doctoral dissertation research in Brazil at the same time as I did. For a Brazilianist political junkie like myself, there was nothing quite like sharing an apartment with Kurt Weyland in Brasília during Brazil's first presidential election in twenty-nine years. I will never forget our many late-night conversations while seated on piles of newspaper clippings, comforted by Cerveja Antárctica and the catchy political-ad jingles emanating from the TV.

This book originated as a dissertation in the Department of Government and International Studies at the University of Notre Dame. Committee members Michael J. Francis, Guillermo O'Donnell, and J. Samuel Valenzuela were careful readers of the dissertation, which was written under the direction of Scott Mainwaring. Much of what I have learned over the past decade and a half—about political science, about Brazil, and especially about scholarly citizenship—I have learned from Scott, who since 1986 has supported my professional development with wisdom and patience. I am grateful for his mentorship and for his thoughtful criticisms of my work, which he has been asked to read far too many times. I am also indebted to Guillermo O'Donnell, whose pathbreaking work on authoritarianism and democracy has inspired so many scholars of Latin American politics, including myself. In particular, I thank him for the many nocturnal seminars in South Bend in which he patiently taught me "English" (of the billiards variety, that is). My mentors deserve credit for whatever is praiseworthy in this book, and are absolved from any responsibility for its defects.

I owe a great deal to Jeffrey Cason, William C. Smith, and Kurt Weyland, who read the entire manuscript and provided many excellent comments and criticisms. John Carey and Matthew Soberg Shugart generously commented on an early draft of Chapter 6, and Octávio Amorim Neto contributed a thoughtful critique of Chapter 7. The manuscript profited greatly from these diligent critics, as well as from the helpful suggestions of Sandy Thatcher, the director of Penn State Press and a strong supporter of young scholars in Latin American studies. I have done my best to incorporate their insights, and again, I bear responsibility for any errors or omissions that remain.

My wife, Valéria Carvalho Power, has been enriching my life since we first met in Brasília, her hometown, in 1990. Although she indulges my irrepressible fascination with her native country with good humor, she still cannot comprehend why, out of all the many *maravilhas* of Brazil that I could have chosen as an object of study, I chose its politicians. I am grateful to Valéria for her love and support. She knows that sainthood is guaranteed for spouses of dissertators and tenure-track assistant professors. Also, I extend my gratitude to Valéria's family—particularly her parents, Alípio Moreira de Carvalho and Neuza Miranda Soares de Carvalho, and her cousin,

Júlio César Moreira—for their strong support of my ongoing work in Brazil.

Finally, I thank Joseph Stephen Power and Barbara Jane Power. They first introduced me to Latin America when we moved from snowy Hudson, Massachusetts, to the beautiful colonial city of San Juan, Puerto Rico, in February 1975. What was supposed to be a six-month stay in Latin America turned into eighteen wonderful months for them and into a career for me— the least of their many gifts to their son. This book is dedicated, with love and gratitude, to my parents.

Continuities in Political Democratization 1
Politicians and Institutions in Postauthoritarian Regimes

Introduction

Are conservative transitions to democracy conducive to eventual democratic stability? As the renaissance of democratization studies completes its second decade, the jury remains out on this question. One reason for this sense of inconclusiveness is that in retrospect, the astonishing advance of global democracy in the 1980s overwhelmed the capacity of comparative political scientists to interpret events and processes. In a classic example of the "moving target" syndrome in comparative politics, scholars were called upon to interpret one set of unexpected transformations just as another set of transitions was rapidly unfolding in another part of the globe. This analytic overload seemed to short-circuit a number of promising theoretical constructs and streams of literature. When the lights came back on, as it were, the study of democratic transition had already been largely abandoned in favor of analysis of regime consolidation. Thus, despite its reputation as a dynamic locus of comparative political analysis, the study of democratization accumulated a backlog of unfinished business.

Among the more intriguing questions in the study of democratization, one that is often posed but little explored, remains the relationship between former authoritarian regimes and the democratic regimes that replace them. Several analysts have emphasized the fact that there are different routes from dictatorship to democracy, and that transition processes vary considerably. Some scholars have made these processes the dependent variable, developing typologies of transitions and tracing the various "paths to democratization" (Stepan 1986; Share and Mainwaring 1986). Other scholars have conceived of these paths as possible independent variables for explaining differences among nascent democratic regimes, as in the "modes of transition" approach to democratic consolidation (Karl and Schmitter 1991; Linz and Stepan 1996). Still others look more directly and retrospectively to specific features of defunct authoritarian regimes, drawing connections to suspected "legacies" in democratic successor regimes (O'Donnell 1992; Jowitt 1992). To date, the majority of these studies have been tentative and speculative; the relationship of the past to the present has generally been hypothesized, not tested.

Given all these proposed typologies and hypothesized outcomes, it is surprising how little empirical research has been conducted on discrete modes of transition from authoritarian rule. Few if any case studies—whether of the hypothesis-testing or hypothesis-generating variety—have scratched the surface of authoritarian legacies.[1]

This lacuna is unfortunate, given the fascinating question that legacies raise. Consider the following dilemmas of a recent transition to democracy in Latin America. First, a military government establishes a partnership with a group of conservative politicians. In return for defending the authoritarian regime and its policies, the civilian politicians are given numerous positions of power, and they establish secure power bases. The military regime falters and eventually withdraws from power, but the cohort of right-wing politicians survives the transition to democratic rule. The country is then faced with the challenge of consolidating democracy, a task that clearly depends heavily on the performance of professional politicians. However, nearly half the country's political class has a proven twenty-year record of supporting military-authoritarian rule. Where is the critical mass of elites necessary to move democratization forward?

Second, the country in question is saddled with phenomenal economic inequalities that now must be urgently addressed. The promise of democracy holds out the possibility for redistributive change. However, the country's political right has opposed almost all efforts to redistribute income or otherwise democratize the economy.[2] Surviving the democratic transition

1. For important exceptions in Latin American politics, see the work of Anita Isaacs on Ecuador (1993) and Frances Hagopian on Brazil (1996).
2. For the sake of argument, and here only, I am deliberately mixing two competing definitions of democratization. On the one hand, democratization signifies procedural change, meaning the establishment of democratic practices and the generalized growth of commitment to those practices. On the other hand, democratization may also imply substantive change,

intact, the right remains in a position to torpedo most progressive proposals. What, then, of the popular association of democracy with change? The country confronts a dilemma: without a minimum of participation by ex-authoritarians, *democracy* is not possible, but with too much participation, *change* is not possible. How is it possible to reconcile the two goals?

Third, the departing military regime was highly concerned with political appearances. Wherever possible, it maintained the formal trappings of a democratic regime, including democratic institutions such as political parties and a Congress. But under military rule, these political structures were stripped of their powers—in practice, they were only facsimiles of real, functioning institutions. They were handed over to civilian politicians to "inhabit" but not use. Paradoxically, in a country where representative institutions were "preserved" under authoritarianism, in the successor regime these structures now find themselves in crisis: their emasculation has ill prepared them for democracy. The political right, accustomed to weak institutions under authoritarian rule, shows little interest in building stronger ones under the new regime. Where is the political capital necessary to drive the democratic rebuilding of representative institutions?

These dilemmas, tradeoffs, and paradoxes tell us something about the country in question. They tell us that the country has undergone a process of democratization characterized by a high degree of continuity from one regime to the next. They also hint at what kind of democracy the country might expect to have, at least in its early years. It will be a conservative regime. It will feature a political landscape in which personnel and practices from one kind of regime are superimposed upon another, implying major challenges to the potential consolidation of democracy. It will be a regime whose initial survival and eventual consolidation will—again, paradoxically—depend upon those who long opposed its birth: former authoritarian elites, in this case the political right. It will be a democracy where the right's importance in political life will be magnified for years to come.

The country inspiring these propositions is contemporary Brazil. Brazil presents all of the conundra suggested above, and indeed suggests many more. It is a case from which we might learn a great deal about political continuities in the aftermath of dictatorship. Now familiar as a textbook case of a "conservative" transition to democracy, Brazil is an excellent case

meaning progressive or redistributive advances in the socioeconomic sphere. It is to the former and not the latter definition that I subscribe, as I demonstrate later in this chapter, but for the moment let both stand.

to learn about what we might expect in the aftermath of other such transitions.[3]

This book is an appraisal of Brazilian democracy, focusing specifically on implications of certain political continuities in the postauthoritarian era. In general terms, it addresses the tensions between authoritarian legacies and democratic institution building in Brazil's "New Republic" (1985–). It considers the juxtaposition of continuity and change as reflected in the world of professional politicians and in the institutions that politicians inhabit. I depart from an observation often made about Brazilian politics: many politicians in positions of power and influence in the New Republic—a democratic regime—also held similar positions in and supported the 1964–85 military dictatorship. This continuity is perplexing and immediately raises some interesting questions. How is it possible for politicians to have so skillfully survived a political transition? How do formerly pro-authoritarian politicians behave during a period of increasing political democratization? And what are the implications of their behavior—and attitudes—for the possible consolidation of democracy?

This book attempts to provide some answers to these questions, based on a case study of the Brazilian political right since 1985. These questions, and others that will be posed alongside them, are relevant both theoretically and comparatively. From a theoretical perspective, we know little about what it means for a new democracy to have inherited a significant portion of its political class from an outgoing authoritarian regime. While we have some basic, intuitive orientations on how to think about this problem—such as the contributions by Robert Dahl (1971) on the beliefs of political elites, and Juan Linz (1978) on elite loyalty and disloyalty to democracy—the body of theory is underdeveloped because of the paucity of relevant case studies.

In comparative perspective, Brazil is a paradigmatic case of a conservative transition from authoritarianism. While most often compared to the case of Spain—a country that today enjoys consolidated democracy—in the early post-Franco era, Brazil also shares important similarities with other "continuist" transitions in varying stages of completeness.[4] Two broadly similar transitions—also from authoritarian capitalism, also with high con-

---

3. The theme of continuity is well established in the literature on the Brazilian transition. For representative contributions, see Share and Mainwaring (1986), Smith (1987), and especially Hagopian (1986, 1990, 1992, 1996).

4. The similarities between the Brazilian and Spanish transitions are reviewed by Share and Mainwaring (1986). The differences are emphasized by O'Donnell (1992).

tinuity in elites, and occurring roughly at the same time as Brazil's—were those in Turkey after 1983 and South Korea after 1987. Beginning in 1989, the world began to witness a second wave of conservative transitions. These were no longer in the South but now in the East; no longer from authoritarian capitalism but from totalitarian socialism; no longer privileging the right but former Leninists. In cases such as Albania, Bulgaria, and Romania, former Communists won the first contested elections; and in nearly every Eastern European case where Communists did not win the first round of elections, they were victorious in the second round. These events generated intense speculation on the long-term effects of the surprising survival of ex-authoritarian elites (e.g., Higley, Kullberg, and Pakulski 1996).[5] The present study is an exploration of the Brazilian case and is not explicitly comparative, but it is intended to generate concepts and hypotheses that may be employed in cross-national analysis of conservative transitions to democracy. The relevance and generalizability of the concepts presented here are conditioned by the specific historical circumstances of Brazil and the most-similar cases; they may also undergo modification as other countries experience conservative transitions from authoritarian or totalitarian rule.

The Right and Democracy in Latin America

With the important exception of Nicaragua, all recent Latin American transitions to democracy have been away from authoritarian capitalism. In practical terms, this means that former authoritarian elites are nearly always coterminous with the political right. In examining recent political science literature on the subject of the right, Edward Gibson (1992, 1996) concluded that the comparative study of conservative political action is woefully underdeveloped. This observation is especially relevant to the literature on Latin American politics, where the right as a political actor has been almost entirely overlooked. Latin Americans and Latin Americanists seem to have invested much effort into researching the political behavior of progressive forces (i.e., social movements, the popular Church, organized labor, and working-class parties), while the political actors that often seek to *retard* social change (the military and the right, for example) are less under-

---

5. Most literature on the return of ex-Communists to power has raised concerns about the future of democracy. However, Samuel Huntington has recently suggested a less alarmist view of the "red return," arguing that "perhaps all that the red return signifies is that people who have the political talent to rise to the top in communist systems also have the political talent to rise to the top in democratic systems" (Huntington 1996: 8).

stood. Such a bias was understandable during the period of democratic transition in the late 1970s and 1980s, when progressive actors were at the forefront of the anti-authoritarian struggle and the "resurrection of civil society" (O'Donnell and Schmitter 1986). But in the democratic era of the 1990s, would not the advent of increasingly inclusionary regimes—which have now incorporated many such progressive actors, and more important, large numbers of voters—seem the to reduce the proportional influence or salience of conservative actors in Latin America? After all, the political right's privileged social constituencies are necessarily a minority segment in any society in the world, and their influence may well diminish when a society opts to allocate power via the institution of universal suffrage. Why, then, is it important to study the right under democracy?

The Right as a Segment of Society. First, at the most basic level of democratic citizenship, the right is a social sector like any other. Rightist politicians and their conservative constituents must have basic citizenship and voting privileges for political democracy to exist in the first place (Dahl 1971). It is possible to study the right in the same way that many popular and progressive actors are often analyzed, that is, in terms of the variable of political inclusion or exclusion. Such a perspective is frequently obviated by the practical realities of Latin American political systems, where the social and political right usually rank at the very bottom of the list of potentially excludable actors. However, it is important to recall that sustainable democracy demands the political incorporation of *all* major social sectors, even those that supported authoritarian regimes in the past.[6]

The Right and Democratic Legitimation. At the level of political elites, the right should be incorporated as an agent of legitimation of the democratic system. This observation is central to Linz's (1978) important comparative study of the processes of democratic breakdown. Following Max Weber, Linz proposed that legitimacy—which he defined (1978: 16) as "the belief that in spite of shortcomings and failures, the existing political institutions are better than any others that might be established, and that they therefore can demand obedience"—is a factor of controlling importance in the consolidation of democratic regimes. The actions and posturing of elites are central to the legitimation process. Elite actors may contribute to legitimation by "adherence to the rules of the game" (ibid., 20); conversely, they

---

6. Some nascent competitive regimes have limited the participation of former authoritarians and yet managed to qualify as polyarchies, as in early postwar Germany or Japan. Yet such proscriptions have generally been selective, conditional, and nonpermanent.

can withdraw legitimacy from the regime by practicing disloyal or semiloyal opposition. Insofar as the political right occupies a highly visible and central role in virtually every Latin American political class, and insofar as in many cases the right lent support to the recent authoritarian regimes, the right arguably ranks second only to the armed forces in terms of overall importance to democratic legitimation in postauthoritarian situations.

The Right as Dominant Economic Actor. Although this observation does not refer to the *political* right per se, it would be inexcusable to overlook the overwhelming economic centrality of the social sectors represented by the Latin American right. All of the new Latin American democracies can be classified as capitalist systems, and all reflect the tremendous concentrations of wealth and capital typical of the region. With its effective control over the investment function, the right often enjoys de facto veto power as new democratic governments implement stabilization or redistributive policies. The political right can be expected to take action to defend the interests of its constituents during periods of democratic redrawing of the laws governing the economy, a phenomenon clearly visible in Brazil's Constituent Assembly of 1987–88 (Dreifuss 1989; Nylen 1992; Payne 1994; Martínez-Lara 1996; Kingstone 1999).

The Right and the Development Model. Drawing on the preceding observations about the right's influence within the political elite and in the economy, we may also perceive its importance to the definition of the national agenda. One need not rely upon a concept like "hegemony" to acknowledge the right's importance in the formulation of national goals, perceived interests, and development models in Latin America. In most countries, the right reaffirmed its political presence during democratization by adopting a neoliberal discourse and mounting an unprecedented attack on the postwar developmentalist state. Neoliberalism was identified with a number of prominent postauthoritarian presidents.[7] In the 1990s, a number of authors studied the right by examining the emergence of neoliberalism and its relationship to the survival and possible democratic incorporation of the right (Borón 1992; Gibson 1990, 1992, 1996; M. Souza 1992; see also Weyland 1996b). One assumption that these authors share is that changes within the right will imply some change at the level of the political system, an assumption also shared by this author. The new conservative discourse vis-à-vis neoliberalism is certainly an object worthy of study, as is

---

7. These include León Febres Cordero in Ecuador (1984), Carlos Menem in Argentina (1989), Fernando Collor in Brazil (1989), and Alberto Fujimori in Peru (1990).

any major shift in elite orientations toward state structures and macroeconomic policy. However, the *electoral* and *political* potency of the neoliberal "revolution" can easily be exaggerated.[8] The right is doubtless important in setting the public agenda; whether the right ultimately realizes its policy goals is a matter for empirical study.

The Right as an Organized Political Force. The history of twentieth-century Latin America shows that where the political right is not effectively incorporated into democratic systems, the probability of military intervention and system breakdown increases dramatically. From the time of oligarchical republics to the present day, the political right has repeatedly urged the armed forces to intervene when it has perceived a threat to its interests. The perceived need for effective political participation by the right is so great that it led Guillermo O'Donnell and Philippe Schmitter (1986: 62–63) to speculate that successful transitions from authoritarianism are more likely if the right wins the first free elections under democracy. Institutional vehicles, such as effective party systems and dynamic parliaments, can draw the right into political arenas where negotiation and democratic competition discourage the use of the "military card" as a legitimate power currency. Where the right has *not* been represented in or by political institutions—as Torcuato di Tella argued with regard to the tragic case of twentieth-century Argentina (cited in Gibson 1990)—conservative forces have resorted to invoking military protection, with disastrous results for almost all political actors, sometimes even for the right itself.

Of all the reasons listed here for studying the political right in the new Latin American democracies, this final reason is the most important. While not detracting from the important factors of legitimacy and economic success in the new regimes, a focus on the *institutional incorporation* of the right has the virtue of drawing our attention to the fragile nature of postauthoritarian politics. Simply put, more than any other actor in political society, the right has the capacity to bring the regime down. With this factor in mind we can observe a great number of potential conservative strategies

---

8. In countries where political survival depends heavily on politicians' access to state resources, politicians' endorsement of neoliberalism is often partial, contradictory, or simply opportunistic—as in the case of Nylen's (1992) Brazilian interviewee, who propounded "liberalism for everyone, except me." Also, neoliberalism is weakly grounded in mass opinion, and thus its successes in the electoral arena have usually been achieved by charismatic populists rather than by programmatic parties. The postelection about-faces of Menem and Fujimori can be taken as evidence that politicians are also aware of the acute difficulty of popularizing economic liberalism. For analysis of the relationship between personalism and the neoliberal coalition, see Weyland (1996b).

under democracy. Where relations between the right and the military remain warm (the historical pattern), institutional incorporation of the right should be an objective of the nonrightist forces in the political class. Where these relations are cool or even conflictual—perhaps because the postauthoritarian right no longer sees the armed forces as a credible ally—then institutional incorporation is likely to be an objective of the right itself.

These issues revolve around the fundamental and universal objective of new democracies, which is simply to avoid breakdown (O'Donnell 1985). Although, as of this writing, only in Peru has the civilian political right actually reversed a process of democratization, there are still excellent grounds for privileging the study of this actor. The Latin American right needs to be analyzed not only to correct a glaring imbalance in the regional literature, but also to provide comparative perspective on the trajectories of ex-authoritarians in Eastern Europe and elsewhere.

Conservative Democratization: Transition and Consolidation

Transitions and Typologies

In the 1980s, as political democratization deepened in Latin America and other regions of the world, the literature on democracy and regime transformation (which later forged onward into the phenomenon of democratic consolidation) became ever more rich and diverse.[9] This literature not only sharpened our awareness of historical and comparative issues in the saga of Latin American democracy but it also carved out at least a modest place in intellectual history. The democratization research program signified scholars' disengagement from the economic and structural modes of explanation that were dominant in the 1960s and 1970s, and their turn toward more eclectic and less deterministic methodologies. While dependency and Marxism have by no means disappeared from intellectual life, it is clear that the dominant trend in the study of Latin American politics has been toward assuming a higher degree of autonomy for politics and actors than was the case two decades ago.[10]

9. This literature is now so massive that even the review essays are too numerous to list in this space. Two "cumulative" works that draw on two decades of amassed wisdom of the democratization literature, and that cite the relevant bibliography throughout, are Przeworski et al. (1995) and Linz and Stepan (1996).

10. In the case of the transitions literature, Levine (1988) testily makes the point that some of the same scholars played important roles in these two different intellectual eras, as if their personal and scholarly evolution somehow disqualified their newer research and findings. My own view is that such evolution ultimately makes the establishment of newer perspectives more rather than less convincing.

The study of regime transition combined with a new respect for the autonomy of the political generated new kinds of contributions on Latin American politics. First came actor-oriented studies employing "distinctly political concepts"[11] and focusing on such topics as the military, political elites, and social movements; later, as democracy took root, came the "new institutionalism" centering on parties, legislatures, electoral laws, and other elements of the institutional architecture of nascent polyarchies. This book—a study of political elites and representative institutions in Brazil—is equally indebted to both of these waves of literature.

For the purposes of this book, a comprehensive review of the recent literature on transitions to democracy is not necessary. It is, however, necessary to revisit typologies of transitions to democracy—to consider how best to distinguish among various patterns of transition and specifically ask where to place the Brazilian case. Surveying the literature, it is apparent that the degree of continuity from the preceding regime is a crucial variable in transitions and in the new democracies which they produce; this variable has in fact been the main taxonomic tool in most typologies. A distinction has commonly been made between transitions to democracies that evince sharp breaks with previous patterns of authoritarian rule and those that retain important elements of the ancien régime. These two ideal types have been given various names in the literature. The distinction made by Luciano Martins (1986) between "continuous" and "discontinuous" transitions is a typical example of this basic twofold typology. Let us adopt this simple, intuitive distinction as a starting point for our discussion.

In this typology, the dichotomous variable concerns the fate of authoritarian regime elites. In the "discontinuous" ideal type of democratic transitions, the authoritarian elites—for whatever reason—cease to dominate the political process, and a democratizing coalition takes power that effects a sharp break *(ruptura)* with the policies and practices of the past. Examples include cases as different as Costa Rica in 1948, Argentina in 1983, and

11. O'Donnell and Schmitter (1986: 4) provide a concise justification for such an approach in the specific case of democratic transitions:

> When studying and established political regime, one can rely on relatively stable economic, social, cultural, and partisan categories to identify, analyze, and evaluate the identities and strategies of those defending the status quo and those struggling to reform or transform it. We believe that this "normal science methodology" is inappropriate in rapidly changing situations, where the very parameters of political action are in flux. This includes transitions from authoritarian rule. . . . We believe, therefore, that this type of situation should be analyzed with distinctly political concepts, however vaguely defined and difficult to pin down they may be.

Czechoslovakia in 1989. In contrast, in "continuous" transitions, authoritarian elites initiate the process of liberalization, control the pace of the political transition, and retain substantial power in the subsequent democratic regime, often dominating the political agenda. While recognizing that no single case will correspond perfectly to this ideal type, we may still recognize that Spain between 1975 and 1982, Brazil after 1985, Turkey after 1983, and South Korea after 1987 were or are incipient polyarchies with important political continuities from their authoritarian regimes: thus, they can be said to have resulted from "continuous" transitions. Because "continuous" is a synonym of "uninterrupted" and unwisely connotes unwavering linearity (these transitions varied widely in their degree of "smoothness"), I prefer to substitute the term "conservative." Henceforth, I shall use the terms "conservative transition" and "conservative democratization" to refer to situations of regime transformation and consolidation where levels of political continuity remain high.[12]

The proper characterization of the Brazilian transition to democracy is made clearer if we take the ideal type of conservative transition and break it down further into two subsidiary ideal-type versions. In the first version of conservative transition, the transformation of regime is governed by the terms of a political pact. O'Donnell and Schmitter define a pact as an

> explicit, but not always publicly explicated or justified, agreement among a select set of actors which seeks to define (or, better, to redefine) rules governing the exercise of power on the basis of mutual guarantees for the "vital interests" of those entering into it. . . . They are often initially regarded as temporary solutions intended to avoid certain worrisome outcomes and, perhaps, to pave the way for more permanent arrangements for the resolution of conflicts. (1986: 37)

An example of a "pacted" conservative transition is that of Spain in the late 1970s (Maravall and Santamaría 1986). In the second form of conservative transition, no *explicit* pact is ever articulated, yet, for a time, politics is played out "as if" there were one (note that if government and opposition both adopted maximalist strategies, then a conservative transition would not be possible in the first place). An explicit pact is in essence replaced by

---

12. What I have lumped together as "conservative transitions" are known by countless other names in the literature: "elite-led transition," "pacted transition," "transition from above," "transition without rupture," *reforma pactada,* and so on. Important theoretical contributions have been made by Rustow (1970), Levine (1973), Lijphart (1977), Peeler (1985), and Burton and Higley (1987), among others.

an ill-defined spirit of accommodation or understanding, a tenuous element that endangers the transition process precisely because it can evaporate at any moment. If, alternatively, political accommodation is enshrined in institutions or through a process of political learning, as authors such as Dankwart Rustow (1970), Daniel Levine (1973), John Peeler (1985), and Anita Isaacs (1993) have pointed out, then the possibilities for sustainable democracy are enhanced.

Brazil corresponds to the second type of conservative transition, where a political pact was never made explicit.[13] Thus, a proper characterization of the Brazilian transition must emphasize the specificity of the Brazilian case as an unpacted affair while still accounting for its basic conformity with the model of conservative transition. The typology of democratic transitions proposed by Donald Share and Scott Mainwaring (1986) is capable of such a characterization. Their threefold typology of "transition through [authoritarian regime] collapse," "transition through extrication," and "transition through transaction" is more sophisticated and more sensitive to nuance than the traditional twofold typology alluded to above. Share and Mainwaring's ideal type of "transition through transaction" emphasizes two factors, control and continuity: elite control over the timing of political change and the great continuity of political elites throughout the transition process. The authors hold that the conditions for a successful transition through transaction are five.

First, the outgoing authoritarian regime must be long established and have earned some popular support. Second, the authoritarian regime must be capable of containing "subversive threats" that could derail the transition process. Third, the democratic opposition must accept the "rules of the game" as laid down by the authoritarian elites. Fourth, mass mobilization must be limited. Fifth, transitions through transaction require skillful leadership (Share and Mainwaring 1986: 193–201). In this broad characterization, the ideal type of transition through transaction is sufficiently flexible to include both Spain of the late 1970s, where political and social pacts were central to the transition process, and Brazil of the 1980s, where they were not. The first four of the five conditions specified by Share and Mainwaring are illustrative of the basically conservative nature of these two transi-

13. If in fact—as rumor has long had it—Tancredo Neves had outlined a secret pact with the military during the final months of the authoritarian regime in 1984–85, the issue became moot when the alleged pact died with him in April 1985.

tions.[14] The fact that these conditions obtained in Brazil place the 1974–85 transition squarely in the category of transitions through transaction, which may be understood as a subset of conservative transitions in general.

Outcomes of Conservative Transitions: Some Questions

Ideal types are intended to not only stress similarities across cases but also point up differences that stimulate interesting research questions. Thus, the characterization of the Brazilian transition as a transition through transaction or, more generally, as a conservative transition, is useful to provide some comparative perspective to our discussion, but to ask the right questions we must look to where such a characterization is less useful.

Transitions to democracy are generally understood to begin with political liberalization under authoritarian rule and to end with the inauguration of a successor democratic government. Thus, they are really the intervals between two different forms of political domination. Excessive focus on transitions as independent political processes can cloud our understanding—or recollection—of the regimes that are bridged by transitions (Levine 1988). An analytical category such as transition through transaction, intended to capture the dynamics of an interval between two regimes rather than those of the regimes themselves, is incapable of fully addressing two issues that are central to our analysis: the specificities of the outgoing authoritarianism and the legacy of that authoritarianism as it impacts the construction of a new democracy.

Democratic development in postauthoritarian settings is conditioned not only by the nature of the transition process just concluded but also by the political structures and processes of the preceding regime (Valenzuela 1992). In sum, "legacies" are a crucial issue. Authoritarian legacies matter in all outcomes of transitional processes, but for obvious reasons they matter most in situations of high continuity from one political regime to the next. In light of this observation, it is important to state some propositions about the legacy of the Brazilian authoritarian regime of 1964–85.

14. The fifth condition, skillful leadership, was far more relevant in the Spanish case, where King Juan Carlos, Adolfo Suárez, and later Felipe González all played salutary roles. For an excellent overview of elite statecraft in the Spanish transition, see Gunther (1992). As Share and Mainwaring acknowledge, observers tend to associate skillful leadership with *successful* transitions through transaction; thus we may overlook cases of failed transitions in which strong leadership was nonetheless overwhelmed by other factors. In any case, the leadership variable is difficult to measure, and only unusually high or low values on this variable receive attention in the literature.

In comparative perspective with other Latin American experiences, the anatomy of Brazil's military regime was unique. In contrast to the recent bureaucratic-authoritarian regimes in Argentina, Chile, and Uruguay, Brazil's generals welcomed the cooperation of civilian professional politicians. Shortly after the 1964 coup, military rulers helped establish a progovernment party (known as ARENA [Aliança Renovadora Nacional] until 1979, and PDS [Partido Democrático Social] thereafter), assisted it in electoral competition, and afforded party politicians positions of power in the executive branch, especially at the levels of state and local government. Also in contrast to their counterparts in the Southern Cone, Brazilian leaders chose to preserve the national legislature. The ARENA/PDS leadership was thereby guaranteed domination of an emasculated but still visible political institution. Equipped with a government-sanctioned political party and control of a symbolically important forum (the Congress), the civilian political right fared far better in Brazil than in the countries of the Southern Cone.

Outside of Latin America, other authoritarian and totalitarian regimes have attempted to incorporate and adapt the democratic institutions of parties, elections, and parliament (Hermet, Rose, and Rouquié 1978). The Brazilian experiment was distinctive, however, in that these institutions assumed greater importance over time, and played a central role in the demise of the military regime. While several scholars have studied the "hybrid" nature of Brazilian authoritarianism and stressed the significance of the retention of parties and Congress between 1964 and 1985 (Linz 1973; Kinzo 1988; Lamounier 1989), few have considered the implications of these factors for democratic sustainability in the postauthoritarian era. The preservation and perversion of formal political structures such as parties and the legislatures—institutions that should occupy central roles in any consolidated democracy—created a postauthoritarian legacy that has three principal manifestations.

First, Brazil's professional politicians were able to cling to the representative institutions held over from the vanquished democracy, inhabiting them and dominating them, and thus survive an era that for the Latin American political class in general could only be described as disastrous. Second, the political institutions themselves—corrupted, restructured, and emasculated at the hands of the generals—were thrusted into the postauthoritarian era with neither the strength nor the adaptability necessary for democratic politics. They were—and mostly still are—only facsimiles of their institutional counterparts in consolidated democracies. Third, the intentional marginalization of Congress was brought about by stripping it of its decision-making functions, which reduced federal legislators to little more than go-betweens in the relationships among federal, state, and local executives. While this kind of clientelistic politics existed in Brazil long before 1964, the political structures of the military regime exacerbated it. In sum, the legacy of Brazil's conservative transition from authoritarianism is threefold: it involves (1) *continuity in political personnel,* (2) *weakness of political institutions,* and (3) *the intensification of anti-institutional political practices.*

This book departs from the assumption that these unique characteristics of the Brazilian military regime have profound consequences for the quality and sustainability of democracy in the New Republic. This assumption and the nature of democratic consolidation itself are discussed in the following chapter. For now we can preface that discussion by posing two sets of questions that orient much of the analysis to follow.

Given the existence of authoritarian legacies, the first set of questions that we must ask concerns the degree of their importance. To what extent do the continuity in political personnel and the weakness of political institutions influence the process of democratic consolidation in Brazil? In what specific ways have these postauthoritarian traits manifested themselves since the advent of democracy in 1985? How does democracy "feed back" upon authoritarian heritages—in other words, how has increased political pluralism affected the political class and the main representative institutions in Brazil? Most important, how have politicians—especially those who consistently lent their support to the authoritarian regime—responded to the imperative of democratic institutionalization in the New Republic? These questions draw our attention toward the actors and processes of conservative democratization, and attempt to tease out their interrelationships in the Brazilian case.

The second set of questions is addressed to what a case study of Brazil can contribute to our understanding of conservative democratization. Are conservative transitions conducive to democratic stability? Which forms, if any, of conservative democratization are viable or desirable? A dominant hypothesis of the literature on democratization—mostly implicit, but sometimes stated explicitly, as by Levine (1988)—is that conservative transition processes lead to resilient democratic regimes.[15] A corollary to this hypothesis is the idea that the political right, usually but not always meaning forces

15. In Levine's words, "[C]onservative transitions are more durable" (1988: 392).

loyal to the outgoing authoritarian regime,[16] should retain a privileged role throughout the transition process—perhaps, for good measure, winning the first free elections (O'Donnell and Schmitter 1986: 62–63). Even authors hostile to conservative transitions for the substantive sacrifices they entail (Peeler 1985; Karl 1986) have argued for the importance of such processes in establishing the procedural norms that are the defining characteristics of democracy. Political continuities are often decried, but are still widely believed to be stabilizing forces in the consolidation of democratic regimes.

These hypotheses and arguments cannot account for the experience of Brazil since 1985. Conservative democratization in Brazil has not facilitated but rather hindered the process of democratic consolidation (O'Donnell 1992; Hagopian 1992), if by democratic consolidation we refer to the construction of a political regime with effective representative institutions. Elsewhere, in other cases of conservative democratization, the existence of "negative continuities" has been effectively addressed through pact making and the growth of parliamentary or other institutional norms. In Brazil, the legacy of authoritarianism has militated against both of these possible solutions—against pact making, because most political forces in Brazil do not have the vertical representative linkages necessary to make pacts stick, and against institutionalization, because a generation of politicians was socialized to politics in a system where representative institutions were simultaneously weakened, marginalized, and instrumentalized. This book calls into question some of the dominant hypotheses about transitions and continuities, as it examines the tensions, paradoxes, and drawbacks of the Brazilian variant of conservative democratization.

Baseline Propositions and Hypotheses

In examining the prospects for democratic consolidation in Brazil, this book focuses on the interrelationships among three postauthoritarian political continuities: continuity of personnel, of political practices, and of weak institutions. It accompanies the response of a certain subset of Brazilian politicians—the civilian political right, which I define in Chapter 2—to the challenges, inherent in any incipient democracy, of strengthening political

16. Before the breakdown of the totalitarian regimes in Eastern Europe began in 1989, the literature on transitions to democracy was restricted to the demise of right-wing capitalist regimes, as occurred in Southern Europe and Latin America in the 1970s and 1980s. When I refer generically to the "right," I refer to the latter pattern, to forces supporting conservative military regimes.

institutions and establishing widespread commitment to democratic practices. It is necessary at an early stage to disaggregate some of these phenomena and processes and to set out some basic propositions that can be tested
in the empirical analysis that follows.

The level and units of analysis can be specified. The bulk of this book
concerns Brazilian party politicians who served in the first three democratically elected legislatures (1987–91, 1991–95, and 1995–99) in the New Republic. Thus, one unit of analysis is individuals, as the research examines
Brazilian elites *in their institutional roles* as members of political parties and
the National Congress. Second, and conversely, these institutions themselves also constitute units of analysis, as I document their trajectory during
a period of regime transformation. Third, the attitudes and behaviors of
politicians vis-à-vis parties and Congress, which are measurable and can be
classified along a continuum from pro- to anti-institutional, together can be
understood as elements of what Marcelo Cavarozzi (1986) and Guillermo
O'Donnell (1992) have referred to as the "predominant style of politics."
The category *style of politics* can be further disaggregated, as it is really the
sum of discrete political practices, but it remains a heuristically useful category in and of itself. Finally, the most abstract level of analysis is that of
political regime. Politicians, institutions, and political practices are all important systemic elements whose specific interrelationships to a certain extent define the contours of the regime. Below, I offer some hypotheses about
how these elements interact in postauthoritarian Brazil.

As the foregoing implies, the emphasis here is on politicians and institutions at the *national level*. Is such an approach justifiable in federal Brazil,
where political machines are organized regionally and locally, and where
political life is often nakedly parochial? In her excellent recent study of the
impact of regime change on regional elites in Minas Gerais, Frances Hagopian (1996: 27) warns that "[n]ot to disaggregate research on the Brazilian
state, territorially *as well as* institutionally, is to presume erroneously, or at
least without any means of confirmation, that the hypothesized shift in
power from decentralized points of the system to a single national center
has already taken place" (italics in original). This caveat is amply justified
when the units of analysis are traditional elites and political machines,
which in Hagopian's work are correctly identified as the ultimate sources of
political continuism in Brazil. However, it is also legitimate to reverse the
angle of Hagopian's analysis. Rather than examine the effect of regime
change on regional elites, this book *assumes* the (subnationally generated)
elite continuity so well documented by Hagopian, and traces its significance

and repercussions at the national level. Of the iceberg that is Brazilian political power, only the tip appears in Brasília, but for democratic consolidation the tip of the iceberg is arguably more crucial than the five-sixths submerged in federalism. Empirical analysis of national-level elites and representative institutions is essential to any macropolitical understanding of regime change and democratization.

This book departs from the proposition that politicians, institutions, and practices have combined in unusual and interesting ways in recent Brazilian political history. Under the 1964–85 military regime, democratic institutions were uniquely superimposed on an otherwise authoritarian political landscape. In the post-1985 democracy, authoritarian-era political practices are etched in relief in a political system that is intended to maximize accountability. Throughout both regimes, the minimal criteria for political survival have remained constant to the degree that many politicians have held prominent roles under both systems. As subsequent chapters illustrate, the retention of representative institutions between 1964 and 1985 paradoxically exacerbated anti-institutional orientations of certain political elites; this paradox assumed crucial importance after 1985, when numerous supporters of the military regime successfully survived the transition to democratic rule.

These speculations about the legacy of authoritarianism have Weberian origins. Eighty years ago, Max Weber's brilliant essay on "Parties and Parliament in a Reconstructed Germany" pondered the prospects for democracy in the nascent Weimar Republic (Weber 1978). Surveying the post-Bismarckian authoritarian legacy, Weber observed that where parliaments are weak in the face of strong bureaucracies and monarchs, the recruitment of leadership and the quality of the political class are likely to suffer. In recent works, both Eli Diniz (1989) and O'Donnell (1992) have stressed the relevance of Weber's arguments for contemporary Brazil. Both cited Weber in pointing out that the marginalization of parliament has dire consequences for politicians' behavior, and thus for democracy. Diniz argued that legislators without serious responsibilities turn their attention to patronage issues, thus abdicating power to the bureaucracy; O'Donnell speculated that politicians socialized to politics under authoritarianism are likely to remain clientelists with weak loyalties to institutions. These observations are consistent with my understanding of obstacles to democratic consolidation in the New Republic. Building upon these contributions and upon Weber's enduring insights, we may conclude this chapter by formulating a set of tentative propositions about politicians, institutions, and political practices in the aftermath of the authoritarian regime of 1964–85.

(1) Regarding *politicians*, we can begin by making the simple observation that a substantial segment of the political class until recently owed its loyalties to a nondemocratic regime. Brazil had democracy before 1964 and began slowly returning to it in 1974, yet many politicians openly defended the military dictatorship. Thus, it is reasonable to assume that such politicians have weak loyalties to the democratic regime.

(2) Regarding *institutions*, the principal representative institutions manipulated by the military regime—parties and Congress—are likely to show the scars of their experience. In order to become fully functional under democracy, they must rid themselves of certain attributes acquired via military intervention. The crucial early years after a transition to democracy constitute a "critical juncture"—a window of opportunity—in which to achieve institutional redesign.

(3) Regarding *practices*, politicians who lost decision-making powers under authoritarianism had to develop some other activities. Party building was neither viable nor rational. The continuing availability of political opportunities in the executive branch, combined with the emasculation of Congress, made legislative careers less desirable. It would seem that politicians who remained in the legislature had few alternatives but to practice clientelism. But the incentives toward individualistic clientelism did not operate uniformly throughout the political class. Clientelistic inducements were stronger among those who supported the military and benefited from privileged access to state resources, and weaker among those who—excluded from the circles of power and patronage—instead devoted their energies to opposition activism.

(4) The political elites propelled into the New Republic are likely to have brought their learned behaviors—practices—with them. To the extent that the rules of the game allow it, they will continue the practices that brought them success in the past.

(5) The subset of politicians socialized to weak institutions and patronage politics is likely to resist institution building, because stronger representative institutions would increase political accountability and sharply reduce the spaces available for individualistic clientelism. (This proposition is based on the Weberian hypothesis suggested by O'Donnell [1992], which he did not test empirically.) Depending on the size of this cohort and its degree of internal unity, its resistance to institution building should "feed back" upon

parties and Congress, thus reinforcing the baseline weaknesses alluded to in proposition 2 above. The resistance to institution building should be empirically verifiable precisely during the "critical juncture" immediately after the transition to democracy.

(6) Returning to the overarching concern with democratic sustainability, the postulated feedback loop between propositions 5 and 2 now takes on theoretical significance. When a powerful cohort of politicians has good reasons for resisting institution building and increased accountability—and when the window of opportunity for institutional redesign is therefore missed—the prospects for sustainable democracy are bleak.

Definitions and Concepts **2**
Consolidation, Institutions, and the Right

Toward an Analytic Framework

In the preceding chapter, I used a number of terms associated with the study of political regimes and political institutions. In the interest of clarity, it is well to state explicitly and early on in this study my understanding of a few key concepts, including that of the political right in Brazil. This chapter reviews the key concepts and definitions that structure the empirical analysis in the remainder of the book.

Political Regime Types

A *political regime* encompasses the set of rules, practices, and linkages that structure the relationships between state and society. The notion of regime speaks to the nature of macropolitical *decision making*: it describes the rules of access to public authority, the characteristics of actors that may legitimately bid for such authority, and the conditions under which these actors may exercise such decision-making authority when they finally acquire it (O'Donnell and Schmitter 1986: 73). The category of regime type—a three-fold typology of democratic, authoritarian, and totalitarian is widely accepted—points to the ways in which widely understood rules, practices, and linkages affect state decision making, state-society relations, and the toleration of opposition to the government. For example, in ideal-type democratic regimes the government is held highly accountable to the citizenry, while in ideal-type totalitarian regimes this equation is reversed.

Authoritarian regimes represent a common form of political system in the modern world, and were the norm in Latin America in the 1970s. The classic definition of authoritarian regimes was developed by Juan Linz in his work on Franquist Spain. According to Linz, an authoritarian system: (1) permits a limited amount of political pluralism, but does not recognize rulers as accountable; (2) does not have an official ideology, but rather a "mentality"; (3) forgoes the totalitarian strategy of popular mobilization; and (4) effectively concentrates power in one person or a small group, who exercise it "within formally ill-defined limits but actually quite predictable ones" (Linz 1976: 165). The first of these conditions (in Linz's words, "limited, [but] not responsible, political pluralism") was especially relevant in the recent Brazilian authoritarian regime, whose governments permitted elections (some of which they lost) to take place at several levels of government, but never held direct presidential elections, which certainly would have brought the regime to an earlier end. The perceived need of the Brazilian authoritarian governments to preserve a semblance of pluralism led to their preservation of parties and parliament; this in turn generated the principal "legacy"—a postauthoritarian cleavage within the political class—that stands at the core of this book.

Democratic regimes represent the regime type with the most powerful appeal to legitimacy in the postwar world (Diamond, Linz, and Lipset 1989). Historically, democracy has been defined both in terms of its normative/substantive connotations and in terms of its procedural characteristics. However, in recent political science the latter notion, as championed by Joseph Schumpeter, has all but eclipsed competing definitions (Huntington 1989). Schumpeter (1947: 269) argued that *political democracy* is a method of decision making whereby "individuals acquire the power to decide [for the collectivity] by means of a competitive struggle for the people's vote." Expanding upon Schumpeter's procedural definition, Dahl (1971) held that a political regime is democratic or "polyarchic" to the extent that it permits both participation by citizens and organized opposition to the government. By virtue of Schumpeter's and Dahl's emphasis on procedural variables, we can usually know a political democracy when we see one, and this book follows the recent thrust of the literature by defining democracy procedurally. Democracy exists when citizens have the basic rights (civil liberties, freedom of organization) that are essential to participation and opposition, when all adult citizens can vote, and when periodic elections are held that hold out the possibility of an alternation in power.

The Consolidation of Democratic Regimes

Democratic consolidation is a contested concept, and one that requires a significant amount of caveats, disclaimers, and modifiers before it can be employed in this book. After democracy had returned to most of South America by the mid- to late 1980s, Latin Americanists began to direct themselves away from the study of transition and toward the analysis of the conditions under which fledgling democracies might endure. In their efforts, they were inspired by a companion literature focusing on Southern Europe, where countries that had transited to democracy in the 1970s seemed to have achieved sustainability by the mid-1980s.[1] From its inception, however, the consolidation literature has been controversial. Navigating what is arguably more slippery terrain than the previous regime-oriented literatures that preceded it (concerning democratic breakdown and transition, respectively), the emerging research on consolidation has been plagued by controversies over how best to define and measure the dependent variable. Most analysts tend to agree—as is usually the case with classifications of political regimes—that they "know it when they see it." Statements to the effect that Swedish democracy is consolidated, that Russian democracy is not, and that the Czech Republic is somewhere in between these two cases would hardly raise eyebrows. Thus the tendency in the consolidation literature has been to develop ideal types against which the empirical cases in question—nearly always described as "unconsolidated"—can be juxtaposed and compared. A representative example of the ideal-type approach is drawn from the important comparative study by Juan Linz and Alfred Stepan, who see consolidated democracy as a political situation in which democracy has become "the only game in town."

> Behaviorally, democracy becomes the only game in town when no significant political groups seriously attempt to overthrow the democratic regime or secede from the state. When this situation obtains, the behavior of the newly elected government that has emerged from the democratic transition is no longer dominated by the problem of how to avoid democratic breakdown. Attitudinally, democracy becomes the only game in town when, even in the face of severe political and economic crises, the overwhelming majority of the people believe that any further

---

1. The early efforts at cross-regional comparisons are reviewed in Mainwaring (1986a) and Power and Powers (1988).

political change must emerge from within the parameters of democratic formulas. Constitutionally, democracy becomes the only game in town when all the actors in the polity become habituated to the fact that political conflict will be resolved according to the established norms and that violations of these norms are likely to be both ineffective and costly. In short, with consolidation, democracy becomes routinized and deeply internalized in social, institutional, and even psychological life, as well as in calculations for achieving success. (Linz and Stepan 1996: 5)

This rendering of the concept is highly insightful, and it clarifies the issues by breaking down consolidation into discrete behavioral, attitudinal, and constitutional components. Yet the definition's shortcomings are symptomatic of consolidation's slippery slopes. While pointing helpfully to the substantive content of consolidation in each one of three hypothesized subcomponents, Linz and Stepan typify extant approaches in declining to supply criteria for operationalization and measurement that would permit the observer to know when the threshold of consolidation has been crossed.

In their own review of the literature, Linz and Stepan point to two broad approaches to consolidation that are related but analytically distinct. The first is the one that they adopt and that is embodied in the definition cited above: an approach geared toward understanding the processes by which *nascent* democracies avoid breakdown and achieve consolidation.[2] To use a word of which Linz and Stepan are fond, the first approach focuses on the *crafting* of democratic consolidation. A second approach in the literature is to "enumerate all the regime characteristics that would improve the *overall quality* of democracy" (Linz and Stepan 1996: 5; italics in original). Case studies have often employed the latter framework, illuminating shortcomings of new democratic regimes and prescribing various correctives—e.g., stronger parties, more proactive parliaments, smoother executive-legislative relations, less corruption, more accountability, constitutional frameworks, and various social and economic policies—that would presum-

---

2. The implication is that challenges to nascent democracies and to consolidated democracies necessitate different approaches; these approaches can be appreciated by comparing the consolidation literature of the 1990s with the breakdown literature of the 1970s. Linz and Stepan are careful to note that consolidated democracies are not immune to future breakdown. But they argue that "such a breakdown would not be related to weaknesses or problems specific to the historic process of democratic consolidation per se, but rather to a *new* dynamic" of unsolvable problems, antisystem actors, or disloyal or semiloyal behaviors (Linz and Stepan 1996: 6).

ably improve the quality of democratic performance and facilitate eventual consolidation. The distinction between the "crafting" approach and the "quality" approach is not a clean one: in practice, many scholars work with a foot in each camp. But the fact that both variants of the literature claim to address "democratic consolidation"—and that virtually every case study of postauthoritarian politics, whatever the topic, at least *invokes* this ubiquitous term—led to some conceptual and methodological entanglements in the first decade of this research program.

By the late 1990s, some serious criticisms had been lodged against the consolidation literature, even by some of its originators. One criticism was that the concept of consolidation was a minefield of tautology (Schneider 1995): democratic consolidation was sometimes defined as the absence of breakdown, and democracies that broke down were ergo not consolidated. Another criticism was that the consolidation literature failed to deal very well with "unconsolidated democracy," denoting postauthoritarian regimes that fall in the "excluded middle" between transition and consolidation, and that may indeed be the "most probable [outcome] under contemporary circumstances" (Schmitter 1995: 16).[3] A third criticism was that the study of consolidation was increasingly teleological, as if analysts were impatiently expecting all new democracies to evolve institutions and practices mirroring those in the long-standing democracies of Europe and North America (O'Donnell 1996). Underlying all of these criticisms was a growing frustration with consolidation as an object of inquiry, and a sensation that the reach of this literature may have exceeded its grasp.

Since democratic consolidation is a highly abstract dependent variable that has proven difficult to handle, it is not surprising that the most successful and persuasive approaches to this problem have been those that have "disaggregated" consolidation in order to understand its various components and dimensions. For example, in the definition cited earlier, Linz and Stepan (1996) see consolidation as entailing the three dimensions of behavioral compliance, mass legitimacy, and constitutional norms. While none of these domains alone can capture the dynamics of consolidation, each is a discrete and legitimate area of inquiry that adds to the understanding of the whole process.

Similarly, Philippe Schmitter (1992) has argued persuasively that demo-

---

3. In a classic essay, Douglas Chalmers was far ahead of his time in conceiving of uninstitutionalized and yet "democratic" regimes in Latin America, and in my view originated a framework that at least partially addresses the current theoretical inadequacies cited by Schmitter (1992). See Chalmers (1977).

cratic consolidation is a multidimensional process that operates at different speeds in different arenas. His proposed method of inquiry is one that disaggregates the category of regime into several "partial regimes," each of which is organized around the representation of different social actors and the resolution of their conflicts: the electoral regime, the pressure regime, the representation regime, and so on. This line of thinking has several virtues. One is that it recognizes that there is not a single type of "democracy" to be consolidated in postauthoritarian regimes but rather (via various combinations of partial regimes) different types of "democracies." Highlighting the various combinations and outcomes not only addresses O'Donnell's concerns over teleology, but also gives theoretical and taxonomic life to the "excluded middle" between authoritarianism and ideal-type democracy. A final advantage of Schmitter's framework is that it provides a sober and practical approach to *empirical research* on consolidation, one that can organize the middle-range research program for some reasonable time into the future. Rome was not built in a day, and a comprehensive theory of democratic consolidation is likely to elude scholars for a good while hence.

Based on this brief review of the evolving consolidation literature, at the present juncture it seems wise for the analyst to do two things. The first step is to *disaggregate the concept of consolidation* by undertaking solid empirical studies—of "partial regimes," relevant actors, processes, and institutions, etc.—and thus advance the body of existing knowledge about postauthoritarian regimes. These types of studies—on party systems and democratization (Kitschelt 1992; Mainwaring and Scully 1995), on legislatures and democratization (Longley 1994), on civil-military relations (Agüero 1995; Hunter 1997), and on numerous other topics—are not only empirically "doable," but can be successfully informed by existing middle-range theory. To the extent that they observe the twin admonitions about potential tautology and teleology, they represent the most promising research agenda at present.

The second step is to *use explicit standards of the "quality of democracy"* in evaluating the functioning of partial regimes. The notion of democratic quality should be coaxed from the closet of consolidation. Such an "honest" strategy negates the common (and often tellingly accurate) criticism that the consolidation literature has an empirical facade and a normative core. Not only is it intellectually legitimate to specify normative standards of the quality of democracy—inclusiveness, competitiveness, accessibility, responsiveness, accountability, and so on—but it is also analytically compelling, insofar as such standards provide rapid, no-nonsense shortcuts to the macropolitical appraisal of regimes. This openly normative strategy was the approach adopted by Robert Dahl in his classic work *Polyarchy: Participation and Opposition*. Before explicating the conditions under which polyarchies might emerge, Dahl first told us why polyarchy mattered (Dahl 1971, chaps. 1–2). More recently, Guillermo O'Donnell's work has focused on the quality of democracy in Latin America, particularly with regard to the rule of law and "low intensity citizenship" (e.g., O'Donnell 1993).

In its empirical dimension, this book disaggregates the problem of democratic consolidation in Brazil by concentrating on a crucial partial regime, that of national representative institutions. Parties and parliament are the twin arenas in which ex-authoritarian elites are observed. But actor- and institution-centered research, for example in the middle-range empirical studies cited above, should not shy away from reflections on the ultimate theoretical goal: an adequate understanding of democratic consolidation. Therefore, in its theoretical dimension, this book subsequently examines the contribution of the part to the whole; that is, it assays the contribution of the institutional partial regime to the *kind* of democracy that is emerging in Brazil, principally by focusing on the quality of democracy in the partisan and legislative arenas. The question posed in the Brazilian case is whether conservative transitions to democracy are conducive to a successful democratic regime. For the moment, however, it is important to address a more immediate question: why choose the "partial regime" of national representative institutions? Why adopt an institution-building approach to democratic consolidation?

Political Institutions: Parties and Parliament

Political institutions are often invoked but seldom defined. In his classic analysis of Third World politics, Huntington drew on Parsonian sociology to define institutions as "stable, valued, recurring patterns of behavior" (Huntington 1968: 12). More recently, Huntington's behavioral definition of institutions has given way to definitions focusing on incentives, constraints, and the overall structuring of political action. For example, for Peter Hall, institutions are "the formal rules, compliance procedures, and standard operating procedures that structure the relationship between individuals in various units of the polity and economy" (Hall 1986: 19). For Douglass North, institutions are "the rules of the game in a society or, more formally . . . the humanly devised constraints that shape human interaction" (North 1990: 3). Institutions often take the shape of formal organizations, such as legislatures and political parties. But they may also be simply iterated procedures or actions, such as the tradition under which Brazilian presidents declare open the United Nations General Assembly. *Political institutionalization,* in the Huntingtonian formulation, refers to "the process[es] by which organizations and procedures *acquire* value and stability" (Huntington 1968: 12; emphasis added). To put this same idea into Hall's or North's language, political institutionalization would be the process by which "operating procedures" become "standardized," or by which the "rules of the game" become widely accepted and practiced. If institutions are "compliance procedures," then institutionalization denotes the convergence of actors toward a self-regulating equilibrium of compliance.

Political institutions are important to polyarchy because direct democracy is no longer possible in mass societies—it has been replaced by *representative democracy.* Modern society recognizes the need for some mediating structures between rulers and ruled, and all forms of political regime, whether democratic or nondemocratic, have innovated political structures to address that need. Contemporary, representative democracy—as in the Schumpeterian formulation outlined earlier—is defined by the presence of elections, by which certain citizens are designated and authorized to make decisions for the collectivity. Although elections by definition constitute the single most important political institution in democratic regimes, in and of themselves they are not sufficient to make democracy work.[4] Elections, as Schumpeter (1947) argued, are the method through which a democratic regime produces a political class. However, in order to conform to the democratic ideal, political elites must remain responsible to the electorate—they must be tethered to the citizenry through formal links of accountability. Representative democracy, in other words, *depends* on political accountability. Without elections, representation cannot be democratic; without accountability, democracy cannot be representative.

This book focuses on two institutional channels that link state and society in democratic regimes: parties and parliament. These institutions are in fact creations of modern representative democracy; no democracy is known to be without them. Parties and parliament are considered so important to legitimation and domination that almost all political regimes—even totalitarian regimes—have either appropriated these structures or fashioned others in their image. In nondemocratic regimes parties and legislatures have

4. For a critique of the "electoralist fallacy" in democratization studies, see Schmitter (1995).

played varying roles, but in political democracy there are some clear expectations as to what these institutions are supposed to do. They are expected to carry out representation and decision making while observing the specifically democratic imperative of accountability. For effective democracy, parties and parliament must be widely perceived by major political actors as successfully performing the function of accountable representation.[5] What follows are some further observations on these institutions' role in political democracy.

Political parties. In democratic theory, parties have long been thought to constitute the central mediating structures between state and civil society. Parties have numerous functions. The most obvious, as Giovanni Sartori (1976) pointed out, is the competitive function. Parties create political alternatives: they place candidates at elections, and structure the voters' choice. They are also essential to the process of political representation—parties aggregate and advance the interests of groups and individuals. Parties also organize political recruitment—in a consolidated democracy, parties are normally the principal channels through which individuals rise to positions of power (Valenzuela 1992). Finally, parties are also clearly agents of domination: if parties can command the allegiance of a significant segment of the electorate, they can provide the basis for stable government (Mainwaring and Scully 1995; Mainwaring 1999). This is an observation relevant to Latin America, where recent economic and social crises have drawn much attention to the issue of governability.

Parties do not always succeed at the tasks that democratic theorists have assigned to them. Parties have always had rivals in the game of representation, but today these rivals are more visible and vibrant than ever before. This fact has led some scholars to de-emphasize a party-centric view of democracy and to stress the alternative channels of representation—interest groups, social movements, corporatist arrangements, and the like—

---

5. I say "major political actors" because I do not believe it is necessary to satisfy *all* political actors—although clearly this is the most desirable situation for any regime. In all democracies there are political sectors that claim that the representative institutions do not function well enough, and quite often this is a valid claim. Likewise there are political forces that, despite guarantees of their rights and the opportunity to compete in elections, will always lose out in a given democratic polity. When the definition of democracy involves procedural and not substantive variables, the analytical question is to determine whether actors have opportunities for participation and opposition, and to assess—independently of the claims of allegedly excluded actors—whether polyarchy exists or not. This is not a simple determination, just as it is not easy to define democracy or consolidation in the first place; but that does not mean we should avoid trying.

commonly found in modern polities (Schmitter 1992). Moreover, the nature of parties and party systems varies widely. In Latin America, there is impressive variation in the importance and strength of parties in political systems (Mainwaring 1988, Mainwaring and Scully 1995), but there is undoubtedly a relationship between the effectiveness of parties and the possibilities for democracy. The few cases of unequivocally long-lived democracies in Latin America—Chile, Costa Rica, Uruguay, and Venezuela—all shared the common trait of prominent, effective, and valued parties.

So how essential are strong parties to *new* democracies? Strong parties are clearly not a sufficient condition for the long-term survival of democracy.[6] But there is no doubt that under conditions of democracy, certain functions of parties—the structuring of electoral choices, the performance of the representative function, and the promotion of political accountability—assume paramount importance, and even more so in the critical early years of an untested regime. To the extent that they successfully exercise these functions, parties can provide the linkages between elites and masses, or between the state and civil society, which are so critical to citizen assessment of political life and therefore to democratic legitimacy. And it is democratic legitimacy that young democracies desperately need to generate. As Herbert Kitschelt writes:

> Electoral party competition has been supplemented and, in some instances, even displaced by other modes of political involvement and collective decision making, especially corporatist and plebiscitarian forms of interest intermediation. Nevertheless, universal suffrage, competing political parties, and legislative bodies *remain central distinctive features of modern democracy.* For this reason, the configuration of party systems and their stability profoundly influence the effectiveness and popular acceptance of a democratic order. (Kitschelt 1992, 7; italics in original)

This line of argument directs our attention to the quality ("effectiveness") and legitimacy ("popular acceptance") of democracy, recognizing

---

6. It is evident that a heavily party-centric political system may foster systemic rigidities that make impasses more likely, as occurred in Chile from the late 1950s to the early 1970s (A. Valenzuela 1978). It is also possible that strong parties may "crowd out" other forms of interest representation and lead to resentment of an oligarchical *partidocracia*, as occurred in Venezuela in the late 1980s and early 1990s. In both cases, excessively strong parties have been cited as a source of "deconsolidation" of established democracies. For an excellent case study with valuable theoretical reflections on the costs of "partyarchy," see Coppedge (1994).

that the party system remains the crucial axis of political change in new regimes. Although scholars may disagree about exactly how "strong" or "important" parties should be, this should not distract us from recognizing the alternative—there are strong reasons to believe that *weak* parties are prejudicial to democracy. Weak parties lessen the possibilities for negotiation and compromise among political actors and increase the likelihood that demands will be presented in confrontational fashion. Weak parties also normally signify that popular interests are underrepresented in the political system, whereas elites will likely continue to have easy access to decision makers (Mainwaring 1992–93). Finally, weak parties diminish democratic accountability. As Chapter 5 will demonstrate, Brazil's extraordinarily weak party system has enabled politicians to circumvent normal democratic channels of accountability with surprising ease.

Parliament. Many of the observations made above about the role of parties in a democracy also apply to parliament. Like parties, legislatures provide channels for political recruitment and for the representation of societal interests, and they are important in securing legitimate domination. However, there are some important differences between the two institutions. Legislatures always enjoy a constitutional mandate (whereas in some systems, like the United States, parties do not), and thus have a formal role in the decision-making process. Also, where parties often incorporate a diverse set of actors within the institution, as reflected in their usually hierarchical internal organization, legislatures often remain the domain of political elites.

The elite variable is important to this book. In most democracies, national legislatures are obvious magnets of political recruitment, and in practice they constitute the principal political terrain upon which political elites interact with one another on a consistent basis. Thus, in both popular and scholarly associations, the concepts "legislature" and "political class" have considerable overlap. If we allow that citizen assessment of the political class is an important factor in determining the legitimacy of a democratic regime, then it follows that the national legislature—including its recruitment patterns, internal politics, and performance/output—is a key entry point to the study of democratic consolidation.

As in the case of parties, legislatures in democracies are often assessed by their capacity to carry out the function of representation. This does not mean that the composition of parliaments should necessarily reflect the distribution of societal groupings—in practice, this never happens (Dahl 1971: 20–23). What it does mean is that democratic legislatures, the outstanding symbols of popular sovereignty under democracy (Blondel 1973), should strive to guarantee accountability. This implies not only the obvious imperative of making the legislature itself accountable to the voters who gave it a mandate—an issue of enormous sensitivity in Brazil—but also the unique role of the legislature in supervising *other* elements of the state apparatus and making them perform on behalf of the citizenry as well. Presidential systems, which are a minority among democratic systems but are the rule among political systems in Latin America, assign a special role to the legislative branch in overseeing the activities of the executive. Assessing a Latin American legislature's capacity for representation, then, requires attention to both the vertical linkages between citizens and legislators and the horizontal power relations among the branches of government.

The lack of a significant body of research on legislatures is one of the most serious lacunae in the study of Latin American politics.[7] Prior to the wave of democratization in the 1980s, this shortcoming may have been justified due to the perceived fragility or outright irrelevance of the majority of elected assemblies in the region—and the few studies did emerge were mostly driven by the "weak-legislature hypothesis" that has traditionally oriented most political science research on Third World parliaments (Mezey 1985; see also Close 1995a, Needler 1995). The collaborators in Weston Agor's (1971) edited volume did identify some Latin American exceptions to this pattern—Chile, Costa Rica, and Uruguay (notably, the same countries cited above as having effective political parties)—while nevertheless demonstrating that parliaments in the region play less important decision-making and policy-making roles than their counterparts in consolidated democracies. Empirically we still know little about Latin American parliaments, but comparatively we may still observe that when legislatures lack decisional and policy input into the political system, the representation that they provide is usually representation in name only.

In Latin America in general and Brazil in particular, there are critical interrelationships among *representation, accountability,* and the *expansion of legislative influence.* This proposition is an intuitive one to scholars familiar with democracy and political and institutions in the region, but it is also grounded in Weber's early analysis of legislatures in democratization. Like post–World War I Germany, the regime that inspired Weber's hypothesis,

---

7. For a recent survey, see Close (1995a). A major step forward in this regard will occur with the publication of the edited volume by Scott Morgenstern and Benito Nacif (forthcoming).

postauthoritarian Brazil confronted a situation in which the outgoing regime had thoroughly undermined and debilitated the national legislature. The challenge both regimes faced was how to fortify and incorporate parliament in a new democracy. In Brazil's Constituent Assembly of 1987–88, this challenge was foremost in the minds of many politicians. The response of the Brazilian political right to legislative institutionalization is dealt with in detail in Chapter 6.

In summary, parties and parliament are representative institutions, closely linked to the origins of polyarchy. And although their role may have diminished in many political systems, and newer representational forms have emerged alongside them, parties and parliament remain indispensable to the functioning of modern democracy. Political democracy is already present in Brazil, but the consolidation of that regime means making it more functional and effective—thus the attention to the "partial regime" that revolves around parties and parliament. Subsequent chapters of this book will show that concern about the viability of Brazilian institutions is prevalent even among those elites who shape and dominate them.

Formal Versus Informal Institutions. Although the institution-building framework has emerged as a key approach to the comparative study of democratic consolidation, O'Donnell (1996) has cautioned against some potential complications therein. One analytical pitfall is to concentrate only on formal institutions to the exclusion of informal ones. O'Donnell's conception of political institutions encompasses not only complex organizations but also "practices" that are fundamental to the operation of the polity. These include particularism, clientelism, and other nonuniversalistic relationships that function outside the formal legal-constitutional framework (O'Donnell 1996: 40).

These sorts of nonformalized political practices are the consistent and predictable behaviors of political elites by which they interact either with each other or with segments of the nonelite population. To professional politicians, they are the norms that are generally understood as promoting political survival. These behaviors occur both inside or outside complex organizations, and may have the effect of either strengthening or undermining formal representative institutions. Although theoretically there is an infinite number of informal practices, within any particular political system the number of "viable" behaviors is actually quite limited. The options available are quite well known to individuals, since normally it is the successful exercise of these practices that determines both initial access to the political class and the probability of continued survival. This emphasis on the relationship between individual rationality and the generalization of practices does not deny the possibility of political practices that are highly altruistic or normatively oriented, nor does it preclude the possibility of politicians' deliberately challenging the system with consciously nonconformist practices. It simply intends to highlight the degree to which prevailing political practices are norms, approximating "rules of the game" which must be observed by all actors: politicians who ignore them risk marginalization. In O'Donnell's view, students of democratic consolidation have been insensitive to these practices. An ill-advised "fixation" on formal institutions has rendered scholars incapable of building typologies of the kinds of polyarchies that *are* emerging, as opposed to the kind that "should be" emerging based on the existing models of Europe and North America.

It is tempting to classify informal practices along the same lines as political regimes—as democratic, authoritarian, totalitarian, and so on—but real-world political systems almost always incorporate practices that do not "correspond" to the prevailing regime type. Elements of clientelism may exist under democracy; populism under totalitarianism; personalism under bureaucratic-authoritarianism. In processes of regime transition and consolidation, such as the process of democratization under way in Brazil, it is possible to witness a spectacular coexistence of countervailing political practices. One approach to democratic consolidation has been to view it as occurring when one style of politics is supplanted, though not necessarily eliminated, by another style more in accord with the legal trappings of the regime—in other words, when the informal "rules of the game" begin to approximate the formal ones. O'Donnell (1996) notes that in certain polyarchies this may never fully occur—as it has not in several notable regimes (India, Japan, Italy) that are commonly cited as consolidated democracies.

O'Donnell is right that informal, extraparty, extraparliamentary practices are in fact political institutions in their own right, and that the study of consolidation should not ignore these factors. But it is also correct to insist on the enduring importance of formal institutions. The reason for this is one that O'Donnell himself has often emphasized—political accountability (O'Donnell 1992, 1994). Elections are the fundamental, definitive institution of any polyarchy, and their purpose is to empower certain individuals to decide in the name of others (Schumpeter 1947). In democracy, the relationship between rulers and ruled presupposes the transparency of political elites and their subjection to a system of rewards and punishments: citizens may reward elites by reelecting them, or punish them by removing them from office. Where both elections *and* accountability exist, we have democracy; to focus only on the former is to commit the "electoralist fallacy" (Karl and Schmitter 1991). Although some fragmentary, nonuniversalistic mechanisms of political accountability can sometimes be embedded in informal practices, these can never be the main avenue of accountability in a political system based on democratic citizenship and competitive elections. As long as the regime is centered on electoral and representative principles, the *primary* mechanisms of accountability must logically rest on the formal institutions that organize political competition (parties) or that symbolize popular representation (parliaments). This is the justification for the institution-building approach employed in this book, wherein "institution" denotes formal, complex organizations: national representative institutions.

Authoritarian Veterans and the Brazilian Political Right

To this point I have outlined some of the concepts, definitions, and propositions to be employed in an analysis of political elites and institutions in Brazil's conservative transition to democracy. In concluding this chapter, it is now essential to specify the elite segment to be studied, which I have referred to as the Brazilian political right. The use of the term "right," which I have not yet defined, raises some difficult conceptual questions.

What is the right? Robert Kaufman suggested that

> when the term "right" is used without modifiers, it is used to mean those sectors of the social system—rural and urban upper-class individuals, families, cliques, interest groups, and political parties—that tend to defend their advantageous position in . . . society and advocate conservative social and economic policies. The term is not used without some misgiving . . . on the other hand, the term, with all of its problems, does reflect a certain reality in . . . Latin American politics. (Kaufman 1967: 1)

Since Kaufman does not define "conservative," his definition is tautological. Yet Kaufman's definition is useful in a heuristic sense: he recognizes that when social scientists speak of the Latin American right (or, alternatively, "conservatives"), we are alluding to some typical connotations. Patrimonialism, clientelism, elitism, authoritarian mindsets, resistance to social change, defense of privileges, resistance to various forms of popular political participation, disregard for constitutional procedure or support of military intervention, ambivalence or outright hostility toward political democracy—these are all characteristics that have been associated with the Latin American right.

Under such a loose, connotative definition, the Brazilian right appears as exceedingly large and diverse. Painting an accurate portrait of conservative forces in Brazil is no easy task. But any attempt to do so would likely be directed at the following social sectors: the armed forces, large and medium-sized landowners, and elements of the industrial bourgeoisie, as well as smaller segments of the Catholic hierarchy, the middle classes, and the media. All of these are crucial actors in the political system, and have justifiably elicited scholarly attention. Yet this book is about one component of the right on which very little research has been done: the political right.

The political right is understood here as that segment of the right found in the political class (taking the political class as the universe of civilian professional politicians). It is the segment of the right that competes in elections for the privilege of holding public office; it is the segment we observe in parties and in parliament. Although the political right may see itself as the legitimate representative of the larger right, it must be kept analytically distinct.[8] The right has segments and factions, diverse modalities of power articulation, and many arenas in which it operates. Parties and parliament, it should be emphasized, are only two of those arenas in which the right pursues its interests simultaneously. But if democracy is to be consolidated in Brazil—and to ensure the quality of democracy in the "partial regime" of representative institutions—then these arenas must be privileged and fundamental.

To proceed to the empirical analysis, we need a clear working definition of the political right in Brazil. The instinct of a comparativist is to begin by identifying the right in the party system. In the Brazilian context, however, this method is problematic. Brazilian political parties are historically weak, and their ideological character limited and uneven (Lamounier and Meneguello 1986). The closest Brazil has come to a party system based on stable and easily perceptible lines of ideological conflict was during the "artificial" two-party system of 1966–79, when the military obligated politicians to

8. In this sense, the approach in this book is somewhat different from that of Edward Gibson's insightful work on Argentina, in which the author places greater relative emphasis on a sociological understanding of the right's "core constituencies" in upper-class society (Gibson 1996). Both Gibson and I acknowledge the organic relationship between these social sectors and the political right, but we assign them different analytical weights due to fundamental differences in our respective research questions. Gibson assays the representational requirements of privileged social segments and how these are needs are (or are not) met, whereas this book examines the political right as embedded in specific institutional contexts: the party system and the national legislature. Thus, our divergent operational definitions of the right naturally reflect our differing empirical and theoretical agendas.

join either the progovernment party (ARENA, later PDS) or the officially sanctioned Brazilian Democratic Movement (MDB). During the two-party period, the MDB, while not a left party itself, sheltered most of the remaining active left sectors. ARENA, on the other hand, harbored no progressive actors—the party was clearly perceived as the right. But the fragmented post-1985 multiparty system has seen the dispersion of the conservative ARENA/PDS cohort into several parties. The 1986 elections returned to Congress some 219 veterans of the ARENA/PDS party structure, elected by seven different party labels. By 1989 these politicians were found in five more parties, some of their own creation. This dispersion is in sharp contrast to the situation before 1984, when these politicians were unified in the official government party of the military regime.

This book is centrally concerned with the quality and sustainability of democracy in Brazil. Thus, for the purposes of the present study, it is less important which party labels these politicians choose *now*, in a period of seemingly limitless partisan options, than where they stood *then*, under military authoritarianism. My overarching concern with the question of political democracy has drawn me to a classificatory scheme that weighs individual and institutional commitments to authoritarian rule. In the period from 1966 to 1985, there was always one government party (first ARENA, then PDS from 1979 to 1985) that supported and attempted to legitimize the military regime. Since I am interested in the current behavior of civilian politicians who supported an authoritarian government, my sample is confined to those politicians who had an ARENA or PDS party affiliation prior to 1985. These individuals are *veterans of an authoritarian power structure* who remain active in the post-1985 democracy. This cohort of politicians is the subject of this book. Again, the cohort of interest is derived *experientially*, and not via ideological, class-based, or functionalist definitions of the political right.

The criteria for inclusion in this cohort begin with an examination of the membership of the federal parliament, the primary national locus of interaction of professional politicians in Brazil. A conservative estimate is that more than 1200 different individuals have served in the National Congress since the first indisputably democratic elections for this body occurred in November 1986, some twenty months after the transition. Examining the political biographies of these legislators, I included an individual in the ARENA/PDS cohort if he or she: (1) was a candidate, either successful or unsuccessful, for elective office on the ARENA or PDS ticket between 1964 and 1985; (2) was nominated to serve the ARENA/PDS party in one of the public offices for which direct elections were suspended at various times between 1964 and 1985 (president, vice president, senator, governor, vice governor, or mayor of a capital city or "national security" municipality); or (3) served on the National Executive Committee of either ARENA or PDS between 1964 and 1985 (see Appendix A). (When politicians responded anonymously to my survey questionnaires, described in Appendix B, they themselves reported their pre-1985 party affiliations.) These criteria focus on the political class, and from within this class they isolate individuals who made an open, public, and institutional commitment to the military regime. (The selection criteria actually underestimate the extent of support for military rule among political elites, because they do not include many onetime or future politicians who served the regime in technocratic or bureaucratic roles; nor do they include the regime's many vocal sympathizers among retired or future politicians). Today's active politicians who meet these criteria can be described as authoritarian elites who survived into a democratic regime. This cohort, which Chapter 3 examines in more detail, represents ARENA in its "afterlife."

To what extent does the cohort generated by these contextually specific decision rules—which are based on party identification under the military regime—overlap with other possible understandings of the "political right?" Certainly some members of MDB (the opposition party) were politically conservative and tolerant of military government, and no doubt some ARENA/PDS politicians were politically more centrist and supported a military withdrawal. Yet between 1966 and 1979, ARENA was perceived as the "authoritarian" party and MDB as the "democratic" party, and party identification would predict a politician's stance vis-à-vis military rule in the overwhelming majority of cases. Thus, authoritarian-era party identification, while not a perfect reflection of the left-right cleavage in the first decade of democracy, was as good as any available. Moreover, an experiential operationalization of the right is consistent not only with the theoretical orientation of this study, but also with Brazilian academic, journalistic, and to a certain extent, popular usages of the term. In contemporary (post-1985) political discourse, to refer to "the right" is normally to refer to the constellation of social forces that participated in and lent support to the military *sistema* of 1964–85. To refer to the *political* right is logically to single out the professional politicians—meaning civilians—who were part and parcel of the authoritarian power structure. Thus, throughout this book the terms "political right" and "ARENA/PDS cohort" are used interchangeably; the terms "ARENA/PDS veterans," "ex-authoritarians," "electoral right," "legislative right," and "conservative political class" are used to refer to the same subset of politicians.

Defining the right in this way is useful for the present study, but it has an obvious temporal restriction: Brazilian political recruitment will eventually render it inoperable. Through intergenerational population replacement of politicians, the ARENA/PDS cohort will vanish, with most of the losses likely to occur in the second decade of the coming century. This is a central problem with all experiential definitions in political analysis. It was once possible to define the Spanish left as those who personally struggled against Franco, though it is no longer feasible to do so; it is still possible to define the Cuban right as those who personally struggled against Castro, but it will not be for much longer. Such definitions eventually expire, but during their analytical "shelf life" there is no doubt that they provide vivid, revealing, and compelling entry points into the travail of political life. The temporal coverage of this book, which examines the first three legislative sessions (1987–99) under Brazilian democracy, ends comfortably prior to any conceivable "expiration date" of the ARENA/PDS cohort. When the relevance of an experiential focus on the right declines—as it did with a Civil War focus on the Spanish left, as mentioned above—analysts should and will seek new definitions of the Brazilian right. These definitions will presumably derive from a future political context whose contours are presently undefined, a context that will certainly be "post-postauthoritarian" (but hopefully not neo-authoritarian). But in the present political context of the 1990s, and in the empirical coverage of this book, the authoritarian-era experiential cleavage within the Brazilian political class remains of the utmost relevance. Veterans of the ARENA/PDS power structure played major roles in the first four governments of the New Republic.

Having explicated the cohort to be studied, it is also important to specify the logic of the comparative analysis to be employed. What is the control group of politicians against which the ARENA/PDS cohort should be compared? Many new individuals have been recruited into Brazilian political life since 1985, and increasingly one comes across politicians who either had no party affiliation under military rule or who were simply too young to have been politically active. Comparing these politicians to the ARENA/PDS cohort would make it difficult to isolate the hypothesized effects of authoritarian legacies. Therefore, to provide for a cleaner analysis, politicians minted after 1985 are "censored cases"—that is, they are excluded from the study. The attitudes and behaviors of the ARENA/PDS veterans will be compared to their *contemporaries*, politicians active in 1964–85 who did *not* endorse the authoritarian regime but rather struggled against it. This group, the mirror image of the ex-authoritarians, is the "opposition cohort." Politicians belong to the opposition cohort if they possess the reverse characteristics from those embodied in the decision rules for defining the right. They are included if they were members of the MDB between 1966 and 1979, or if they were members of the PMDB or any of several other opposition parties during the liberalized multiparty system of 1979–85. In sum, the analysis provides for a controlled comparison by examining only veterans of the military era, whether of progovernment or opposition vintage.

The handful of politicians who, at different times between 1964 and 1985, belonged to *both* the government party and the opposition are assigned to the ARENA/PDS cohort. The reason is that in terms of the underlying theoretical rationale for the classification—whether politicians cast their lot with authoritarianism—such politicians clearly belong to the category of interest. Without exception, these were ARENA politicians who deserted the regime near its end, joining the opposition in a rational bid for political survival. I am aware of no cases involving the opposite trajectory.

Chapter 4 will provide a detailed sketch of the ARENA/PDS cohort, and Chapters 5 and 6 will compare the cohort with the opposition veterans in terms of the imperative of democratic institution building in the New Republic. Chapter 7 examines the right's collective action over the past dozen years. Chapter 3, however, steps back in time to look at the political ancestry of today's ARENA/PDS cohort.

ARENA and Its Ancestors　**3**
The Brazilian Political Right, 1946–1985

Introduction

The purpose of this book is to assess the role of the political right in Brazil's post-1985 democracy. However, an adequate understanding of the contemporary right cannot be achieved by focusing only on the past decade and a half. The following two chapters provide detailed information about the Brazilian right—not only about its present-day characteristics, but also about its recent ancestry and trajectories.

The task of this chapter is primarily a historical one, examining the political right before 1985. I focus mainly on the post–Estado Novo period (from 1946 onward), during which Brazil developed national politics, mass politics, and (sometimes) competitive politics. Only after 1946 can we say that the Brazilian political right experienced a political environment even remotely resembling the one that exists in the New Republic. The right's insertion into a modern polity, and especially its experimentation with democratic institutions and practices in the first postwar democracy (1946–64), will prove instructive as we later examine similar processes of adaptation in the 1980s and 1990s.

In the first part of this chapter, I discuss the elitist political tradition in which the right is situated. Although Brazil is correctly described as a conservative, patrimonial polity with a strong elitist tradition, this tradition has been weakened by strong challenges during recent experiments with polyarchy. The position of the right within this tradition defies easy description. If on the one hand the right has been the historical hegemon within this context of an elitist political culture and weak representative institutions, on the other hand it is clear that the right's political space (at least in the electoral arena) has occasionally diminished in the postwar experiments with political pluralism. But the Brazilian right has never suffered an outright political defeat that would cut it off from its lifeblood, the patrimonial state—though this came perilously close to happening in 1989. In two subsequent sections of this chapter, I develop these observations by reviewing the role of the electoral right in two contrasting political regimes: the democratic Second Republic (1946–64) and the period of military authoritarianism (1964–85).

The Elitist Tradition and Recent Transformations

This study privileges several specific continuities in Brazilian politics from the 1960s through the 1990s. However, continuity has been a prominent feature of Brazilian politics from day one. Historians and social scientists have often noted the surprising ease with which Brazilian elites[1] have navigated the country's various transitions: from colony to empire, from empire to oligarchical republic, and from military-authoritarian rule to mass democracy.

The contours of Brazilian politics are often seen as molded by the patterns of interaction and realignment within a privileged class of politically influential individuals. While there is a diversity of approaches to the study of social domination in Brazil,[2] there is also consensus regarding a number of features that characterize the elitist Brazilian political tradition. Among the elements most commonly diagnosed are the following:

1. *Political conservatism*, understood in its most general sense as a drive to preserve the political and economic status quo as well as *paz social* (social peace), and to limit the possibilities for popular participation.

---

1. "Elites" is an ambiguous term, so a few words of clarification are necessary. The sense here is not of social or economic elites but rather of *political* elites. Political elites need not necessarily belong to the privileged classes, though (even with the social complexity of today's Brazil) they usually do. While other authors have defined Brazilian political elites broadly—so as to include generals, bishops, and union leaders, for example (compare McDonough 1981)—my focus is on professional politicians. In any case, the very idea of an "elitist tradition" in Brazilian politics suggests that the social, economic, and political elites may often intermingle and overlap.

2. A review of some of the specifics mechanisms of social control is provided by Flynn (1974).

2. *Clientelism*, or a kind of social, economic, and political interaction based primarily on the exchange of favors between individuals of unequal status (Leal 1977; Cammack 1982; Geddes and Ribeiro Neto 1992).

3. A *patrimonial* or *"cartorial"* state (Faoro 1958; Schwartzman 1982; Nylen 1992; O'Donnell 1992) that is powerful, centralized, and bureaucratic par excellence, and that elites penetrate and turn to their advantage in profoundly antirepublican style through practices such as *empreguismo* (the use of public employment for political ends), nepotism, and other forms of corruption.

4. *Collaboration among elites* at various levels, under which central elites grant considerable privileges to regional and local elites in return for their assistance in maintaining social control (Leal 1977, Cintra 1979, Hagopian 1996).

5. An *enduring or static quality* (hence the name sometimes given to elite politics, *o sistema*[3]), resulting from:
   (a) a political culture predicated on the foregoing factors;
   (b) rules and institutions designed to preserve the political dominance of conservative regions and social sectors, and
   (c) continual military intervention to preserve the system. (The historical importance of this final factor can hardly be underestimated.)

The foregoing is a description of a political *tradition*, but says little about its protagonists: Brazilian political elites. A characterization of Brazilian political life emphasizing its basic conservatism (with a few historical exceptions, for example the contentious years of the early 1960s) would essentially be accurate. However, such a view must take care to avoid determinism and a monolithic view of the power structure. If we argue that conservatism has always held the upper hand, we run the risk of conflating the concepts "political elite" and "political right." But are these sectors really identical? Are there no segments of the elite that do not also belong to the right? The answer to this question depends largely upon the historical period that one is examining.

Certainly in the Old Republic (1889–1930) there was no significant left/right cleavage within the national political elite. In this period, a comfort-

---

3. The properties of *o sistema* are elaborated by Schmitter (1971, conclusion). See also the work of Leeds (1977).

able, unified elite managed the affairs of state, giving a predictable—albeit undemocratic—flavor to the politics of Brazil. Political contestation was an elite affair between the "ins" and the "outs," with minimal popular participation, and with ideological divisions that were readily apparent only to the players themselves. This was the heyday of the "politics of the governors," in which a handful of notables, mostly drawn from the populous states of São Paulo and Minas Gerais, alternated in power.

The tranquillity of oligarchy eroded in the 1920s, and was shattered in the 1930s by the emergence of Getúlio Vargas and the rise of urban populism in Brazil. The Vargas years sparked national debate about issues of popular participation and redistribution, and his person and policies combined to introduce a new cleavage (for or against *getulismo*) within the national elite. The 1946 Republic permitted free elections and the expansion of suffrage, mobilizing huge numbers of new voters into the system and opening up spaces for new and diverse political appeals and alternatives. Because of this fundamental change in the logic of winning political power, for the first time members of the national elite—in their incarnation as professional politicians—fanned out across the political spectrum, with many leading populist attacks on the very system of power and privilege that had produced them, and with a few even endorsing socialism. Populism in Brazil, as elsewhere in Latin America, had the twin effects of introducing modern mass politics and a newly disunified elite.[4]

The post-Vargas pluralization of elite politics did not signify the outright defeat of traditional rightist forces. Though conservatism suffered a steady electoral decline during the Second Republic (as is described below), only in the period immediately prior to the 1964 military coup did the "traditional" wing of the national elite really lose the upper hand. For example, despite a steady erosion in its support, the largest conservative party of this period (the Partido Social Democrático, or PSD, the vehicle of right-wing *getulismo*) remained the largest party in the Chamber of Deputies until 1963. The political realignment that occurred in the wake of the coup reinforced the impression that elites would forever maintain the so-called *sistema*: the majority of the political class warmly embraced military-authoritarian rule, which quickly restored preexisting patterns of domination. Conservative political elites demonstrated their instinct for survival by

4. On this period, and especially on the multiclass nature of populism, see the two essays by Conniff in his (1982) edited volume. For a comparative perspective on how populism shaped the modern party systems in eight Latin American countries (including Brazil), see Collier and Collier (1991).

backing a regime that was exclusionary, repressive, and lacking in international legitimacy. But the democratic interlude of 1946–64 showed the first clear evidence of a pluralization process taking place within the political class: new alternatives to conservatism and traditionalism, although failing in the end, had at least been placed on the national agenda.

The 1964–85 regime institutionalized an intraelite cleavage that had been taking shape since 1930: authoritarians versus democrats. The minority of professional politicians who dared to challenge the post-1964 military governments willingly forsook most access to state power and resources, arguably the primary means by which the Brazilian elite has reproduced itself. Those who backed the so-called Revolution remained firmly entrenched within the state, thus having ample opportunities to construct durable political machines (Hagopian 1996). Thus was born the contemporary political cleavage at the heart of this book: the distinction between the ARENA/PDS cohort, which supported military rule, and the remainder of the political class, which struggled for a return to political democracy. As argued in the previous chapter, this distinction is not perfectly reducible to the left/right cleavage, although the two overlap closely. By and large, the ARENA/PDS party structure was the preserve of the political right, while the organized opposition united the "nonright" elements—a heterogeneous category, to say the least. The electoral successes of the opposition MDB after the pivotal liberalization of 1974, which are discussed in a subsequent section of this chapter, demonstrated that conservative elites could no longer expect unchallenged hegemony in a polity where popular votes began to count for something. But if the experience of the last two decades shows anything, it is that conservatives have proved remarkably successful at adapting to changing political conditions.

Since its inception in 1985, the New Republic has ratified many of the postwar changes in the nature of conservative domination. There is greater pluralism within the political class. Conservatives still plainly dominate— the coalitions that supported the early postauthoritarian presidents drew heavily on the military regime's base of support—but now they have to fight for it. The best evidence of this was found in the 1989 presidential election. In the first round, three of the top four finishers were progressive candidates and longtime opponents of the authoritarian regime. In the runoff, the conservative political class closed ranks around Fernando Collor, who was seen as their only hope to head off the victory of the socialist candidate, Luis Inácio Lula da Silva of the Workers' Party (Partido dos Trabalhadores, or PT). The right funded Collor heavily, and generally mobilized all of its existing social and political networks throughout the country, but Collor still nearly lost the election. After the victory of Collor—the seventh consecutive president to have been a member of ARENA/PDS—many veterans of the military regime settled in for another five comfortable years in government, which Collor was unable to deliver (he was impeached in September 1992 and ultimately removed from office). In any case, the narrow margin of its candidate's victory in 1989 can hardly have been comforting to the former authoritarian coalition. This helps to explain why in 1993–94 many of the same conservative elites, determined to block Lula's path to the presidency, this time cast their lot with a moderate social democrat, Fernando Henrique Cardoso, who easily defeated Lula and brought several leading ARENA/ PDS veterans into his government. This alliance was reproduced in the 1998 presidential election, when Cardoso became the first Brazilian president to win immediate reelection to office.

Therefore, while the Brazilian political system is still colored by a strong tradition of elitism, it is no longer possible simply to equate the political elite with political conservatism. A diversity of ideologies has come to exist within the political elite. However, as Peter McDonough showed in his study of the authoritarian coalition in the 1970s, intraelite pluralism does not necessarily make the world of Brazilian politics any less elitist in its practice and outcomes. McDonough argued that Brazilian elitism is perpetuated in part by its own labyrinthine and inchoate nature. Cleavages within the elite have become multiple, cross-cutting, and less predictable; more important, these cleavages do not find expression in institutions and organizations. According to McDonough, "this is what gives Brazilian politics its unideological, experimental gloss" (1981: 236).

Subsequent chapters of this book will lend empirical support to McDonough's observation about the uninstitutionalized nature of the Brazilian polity. At this point, it is worthwhile to note some of the tensions sparked by the clash of an elitist tradition with contemporary political democracy. Democracy, as defined in the preceding chapter, is based on a competitive struggle for the people's vote. The existence of political democracy, therefore, should logically provoke division and fierce competition among elites, since there are more elites than there are positions of effective power. However, some scholars have argued that the weight of Brazil's past—which encompasses the fragility of political institutions, an elitist political culture (the *sistema*), and the circumstances of the most recent transition from authoritarian rule—attenuates the emergence in Brazil of the vigorous intraelite contestation that democratic theory would predict. As one strong advocate of the "patrimonialist" interpretation of Brazilian politics wrote during the political liberalization of the early 1980s, "[E]lites are divided on a wide range of issues, but are united in a desire to preserve their power. . . . The sharing of power is acceptable; the hogging of power is not" (Roett 1984: 20).

Similarly, a number of authors have commented on how the lack of a sharp break between the 1964–85 authoritarian regime and the New Republic encouraged the perpetuation of elitism and patrimonialism. Frances Hagopian (1992, 1996) provided rich evidence that during the democratic transition, elites in the state of Minas Gerais—both those that supported military rule and those that supported democratization—made every effort to arrive at a pact that would guarantee participants continued access to power. The muddled politics of the transition was described by Maria do Carmo Campello de Souza as "invertebrate centrism," which she saw as "characterized by a vast center whose boundaries and backbone are unknown, an ideological and political arena in which everyone seems to be in alliance with everyone else, yet each is actually alone" (M. Souza 1989: 355). Guillermo O'Donnell has expressed a similar idea: "The Brazilian transition was channeled through an accord of 'all for all' to *not* resolve the transition by competing electorally with one another" (O'Donnell 1992: 31; italics in original). As mentioned above, a victory by Lula in the 1989 presidential election would have marked a sharp break with the nebulous coalition politics of the first democratic ruler, José Sarney, but this did not come to pass.

If this discussion of contemporary conservatism seems inexact, then that is an accurate reflection of its subject. To recapitulate, I have argued that Brazilian politics is characterized by a conservative, elitist tradition but that this legacy has been weakened by strong challenges in the two democratic regimes since 1946. Still, based upon an examination of the progovernment coalitions of the first four presidents in the New Republic, it is clear that conservative political elites—the vast majority of whom supported the move against democracy in 1964—have navigated recent political transitions with success, and have not yet been dislodged, en masse, from positions of effective power. Their posture vis-à-vis democratic institutions is traditionally ambiguous. But before we address the question of post-1985 institutionalization, it is necessary to preface the analysis by reviewing the recent electoral history of the Brazilian right.

The Right in the Second Republic

Conservative Parties Under Democracy

To discuss the electoral right in the democratic regime of 1946–64, we need an operational definition of the right. The definition cannot be strictly comparable with my operational definition of the post-1985 right (see Chapter 2), because this period antedates the foundation of the ARENA/PDS party structure in 1965–66. Therefore, with some misgiving, I shall follow other authors (Soares 1973, Lima 1983) in using a party-based definition of the political right: the right is defined simply as politicians who belonged to political parties widely viewed as "conservative." Because it is reputational, and due to the catch-all nature of most Brazilian parties, this operational definition is imperfect, but such an approach has been widely used in studying the politics of the 1946–65 period.

Following Glaucio Ary Dillon Soares (1984: 44–55), there were six identifiably conservative parties in the Second Republic.[5] Two were highly influential and competitive throughout Brazil; the others were limited by regional concentration or personalistic domination. A few observations are in order for each one.

The Partido Social Democrático (PSD, the Social Democratic Party) was the dominant political party of the Second Republic.[6] Despite its name, it bore little resemblance to European social democracy. The PSD was one of two parties that were created by Getúlio Vargas in 1945 in order to preserve the extensive political machine he had built during his Estado Novo dictatorship (1937–45). Unlike its urban junior partner, the Partido Trabalhista Brasileiro (PTB) engineered by Vargas's Labor Ministry, the PSD was interwoven with long-established networks of rural domination in the less developed regions. Born of the Estado Novo bureaucracy—most of the early leaders of the PSD had been Vargas-appointed *interventores* in state govern-

5. Scholars differ over the ideological classification of the 1946–64 parties. For example, Kinzo (1988: 19–20), in what she termed a "very loose ideological division," classifies Adhemar de Barros' Partido Social Progressista (PSP) as a conservative party, whereas Lima (1983) placed this party alongside the PTB in the category of "populist-reformist." Kinzo also classified the old Christian Democratic Party (PDC) as "*trabalhista*-reformist," whereas Soares (1973) viewed it as conservative. I have followed the Soares classification, mainly because it was replicated in Lima's (1983) critique of his work. In any case, Kinzo's own disclaimer applies equally well to her predecessors' analyses and to mine: "This is a very rough classification, since the parties of the period 1945–64 were far from being clearly oriented ideologically, undermined as they were by clientelism, populism, and regional politics" (1988: 19).

6. The PSD should not be confused with the Partido Democrático Social (PDS), the successor of ARENA founded in 1979.

ments and capital cities—the party always had a close relationship to the state apparatus. Patronage was the bread and butter of PSD politics: in return for delivering votes, local PSD notables won access to state resources and the right to make appointments in the state bureaucracy. The party was pragmatic, with a reputation for moderation and conciliation. Because of these attributes, and because the PSD's impressive penetration throughout the interior of the country made it an ideal vehicle for generating support for governments, the party was seen as a major stabilizing force in electoral politics. In her authoritative study of the PSD, Lucia Hippolito argued this position very strongly, affirming that the role of the PSD "center" was crucial for the survival of the multiparty system and therefore for democracy itself; as the PSD waned, so did the Second Republic (Hippolito 1985). While the PSD did lose ground to other parties over time, its electoral record remained impressive. The party did not lose a presidential election until 1960, and it maintained a plurality in Congress until 1963.

The União Democrática Nacional (UDN, National Democratic Union), the other major conservative party, was the second strongest electoral force for the greater part of the 1946–64 period. The UDN was an umbrella party for sectors of the national oligarchy that opposed Getúlio Vargas and his populist policies. At the outset of the democratic regime the UDN's social base was similar to that of the PSD, being concentrated in rural areas and small towns. Over time, however, the UDN began to do better in urban areas and to capture middle-class voters, especially in what is today the state of Rio de Janeiro (Soares 1973: 217–18). But the party's lack of access to state resources meant that its potential for further growth was limited; despite its participation in the first two PSD governments and its support for Jânio Quadros, winner of the 1960 presidential election, the UDN never truly dominated the national executive.

The UDN's ideology was vaguely liberal and antistatist, though plagued by contradictions. Its proclaimed support for democratic freedoms did not prevent it from twice supporting military intervention in the presidential succession process. Nor did the UDN's opposition to Vargas's arbitrary rule prevent it from endorsing an authoritarian solution in 1964. In her study of the UDN, Maria Victoria de Mesquita Benevides (1981) argued that these contradictions typified the "ambiguities of Brazilian liberalism." After the coup of 1964, the heavy participation of former UDN leaders in military governments led then-deputy Tancredo Neves (PSD–Minas Gerais) to call the authoritarian regime the "*Estado Novo* of the UDN" (Wesson and Fleischer 1983: 105).

While the PSD and UDN parties dominated in the early years of the Second Republic, they lost ground steadily to the third major party, the PTB. By the time of the 1964 coup, the three parties' delegations to the federal Chamber of Deputies were roughly comparable in size (Fig. 3.1).

In the orbit of the two large conservative parties operated several smaller ones. The Partido Republicano (PR) was a holdover from the Old Republic, having been founded before the turn of the century. It was highly personalistic, organized around its leader Artur Bernardes, who had been president of the Republic in the 1920s. The PR was based mainly in Minas Gerais, Bernardes's home state, and faded after his death in 1955. The Partido Libertador (PL) was similarly limited by regional and personalistic appeals: it was the political vehicle of Raul Pilla, a leading figure in Rio Grande do Sul. The PL was a conservative anti-Vargas party that championed the parliamentary system of government. Easily the most ideological party on the right, the Partido de Representação Popular (PRP), led by Plínio Salgado, was the remnant of a brown-shirt movement of the early 1930s and propounded functionalist representation à la Mussolini's Italy. Finally, the center-right Christian Democratic Party (PDC), while less successful than most of its counterparts in South America, began to grow significantly in the years before the Second Republic collapsed in 1964.

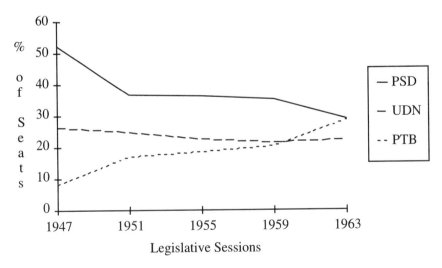

Fig. 3.1
Party strength in the Chamber of Deputies, 1946–1963 (percentage of seats)
SOURCE: Wesson and Fleischer 1983: 94.

The Political Overrepresentation of the Right

Conservative parties in the Second Republic tested the waters of a political system more democratic and competitive than any Brazil had yet experienced. Nonetheless, the electoral right entered democracy with tremendous advantages. One was a constant throughout Brazilian history: the close relationship of conservative elites to the state apparatus. In the Second Republic, this factor privileged the PSD—a party born of the state clientelism of the Vargas era—over the UDN, a party with a similar social base yet with less access to state resources, especially at the federal level. The electoral competition between these two parties has been characterized by Maria D'Alva Gil Kinzo as "a product of the struggle between oligarchical factions over control of the government machine" (Kinzo 1988: 10). Simply by virtue of being contenders in this struggle, the conservative parties were in a favorable position already.

Without minimizing the importance of bureaucratic control, there was another factor at work that guaranteed the political centrality of the right. I refer here to the rules and institutions that promoted then—and continue to guarantee today—the overrepresentation of the right in Brazilian politics. Brazil has a federal political system, and like all federal countries it has struggled to find an acceptable distribution of power among the subnational units. In practice this has meant that the less populous, less developed states—where traditional forms of political domination prevail—have been overrepresented in national politics, whereas the more populous states (i.e., São Paulo), where industrialization and urbanization are very advanced, have had their influence severely curtailed. The underdeveloped states, which are located in the North, Northeast, and Center-West regions of Brazil, are numerically far superior to the modern states, which are located in the South and Center-South. Thus, in the Federal Senate—where, just as in the United States, each state has an equal number of senators—the backward regions enjoy a built-in advantage. But unlike U.S. bicameralism, which bases representation in the lower house of Congress strictly on population, the Brazilian system also overrepresents the less developed states in the Chamber of Deputies.

In the Constitution of 1946, this was achieved by establishing a minimum number of deputies per state (seven), and then by employing strict proportionality (one deputy for each 150,000 inhabitants) only for states with a population of less than three million. Thus, a state with three million inhabitants would have twenty federal deputies. However, above the level of twenty deputies the ratio of legislators to inhabitants would change from 1:150,000 to 1:250,000. This was a clear attempt to punish the larger states. In 1962, this constitutional provision afforded São Paulo twenty-seven fewer deputies than it would have had under strict proportionality. Similarly, Minas Gerais was penalized by seventeen fewer representatives. The state of Bahia lost eight; Rio Grande do Sul seven, Paraná and Pernambuco three each, and Rio de Janeiro and Guanabara one each (Souza 1983: 25). Similar electoral systems were established by the constitutions of 1967 and 1988.[7] The political overrepresentation of the right, then, occurs via a distortion of representation in the National Congress, which overwhelmingly favors the states and regions that make up the electoral base of Brazilian conservatism.

Thus, the democracy of the Second Republic produced a national legislature that was probably more conservative than the Brazilian electorate. As Robert Packenham observed, presidential elections in this period—which were national, direct elections based on the principle of "one person, one vote"—consistently produced executives who were more "change-oriented" than the National Congress (Packenham 1971). Packenham's "conservative legislature" hypothesis is one frequently cited explanation for the political impasse of the early 1960s. His observation is also relevant to politics in the New Republic, because as we shall see in subsequent sections, the formal overrepresentation of the right has been maintained to this day.

Decline and Crisis of the Right

A general tendency in Brazilian politics between 1946 and 1964 was the decline of the electoral right (Soares 1973, 1984). Despite some minor exceptions—for example, the late surge of the Christian Democrats—the trend was secular. In the federal Chamber of Deputies, the share of seats held by the three largest conservative parties (PSD, UDN, and PR) declined from 84.3 percent in 1945 to 67.1 percent in 1950, 63.5 percent in 1954, 62.6 percent in 1958, and 52.1 percent in 1962. Soares's linear regression estimated that conservative parties were losing 1.66 percent of congressional seats with each passing year; at this rate, the right would disappear from Congress in 1993 (Soares 1984: 49). He attributed this decline to three fac-

---

7. In the Constitution of 1988, the distortion of representation is achieved by establishing a minimum number of eight deputies and a maximum of seventy deputies per state. Unlike the rules of the 1946–64 period, the current provisions are directed at limiting the power of of only one state: São Paulo, which today contains nearly a quarter of the national population.

tors: the Second Republic's expansion of suffrage,[8] structural changes such as urbanization and industrialization, and improvements in the organizational capacity of leftist and populist parties (Soares 1973, 81; Lima 1983, 89–91).[9] Figure 3.2 illustrates graphically the decline of the right, including all six conservative parties described above.

The decline of conservatism as an electoral force was only one element of a major transformation of the Brazilian political system in the Second Republic. Political changes took place against a backdrop of accelerated socioeconomic development. Gross domestic product more than doubled

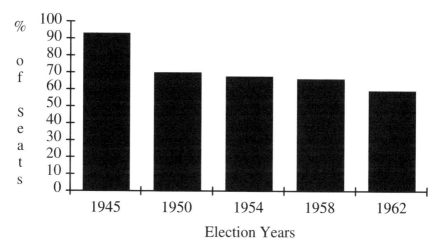

Election Years

Fig. 3.2
Decline of the electoral right in the Second Republic, 1945–1962 (size of the conservative bloc in the Chamber of Deputies, by percentage of seats)[a]
SOURCE: Calculated from Santos, Monteiro, and Caillaux (1990).
[a] Conservative parties are defined following Soares (1973, 1984): PSD, UDN, PR, PL, PRP, PDC.

8. Though expanded, suffrage was still not universal: illiterates were not granted the vote until 1985.
9. A decade later, Olavo Brasil de Lima Jr. argued that Soares had oversimplified these trends, and that in fact the changes in relative electoral strength were much more complex, since all parties had experienced fluctuations at different levels of competition. The large parties, which happened to be conservative, were gradually eclipsed by small parties, whose strength varied greatly from state to state and among levels of government (Lima 1983: chap. 4). While I acknowledge Lima's criticisms of Soares, my focus here is on the strength of the political right at the level of *national* politics, and its relationship to political democracy. Therefore, I prefer to emphasize the trend of rightist decline first noted by Soares (1973). For a critical review of Lima's position, see Pereira, Caropreso, and Ruy (1984: 102–5).

from 1950 to 1960, and the population was growing at a 3 percent annual rate. The urban population was growing even faster, by an astonishing 5.15 percent yearly (Santos, Monteiro, and Caillaux, 1990: 37). The process of urbanization was accompanied by breathtaking increases in industrialization, literacy, life expectancy, and practically all other indicators of development. These transformations were reflected in the political system in the form of a dramatic rise in support for populist and progressive parties and candidates. This secular trend was evident within the dominant pro-Vargas coalition (PSD-PTB) itself. While in 1945 the conservative PSD's congressional delegation was roughly seven times the size of that of the labor-based PTB, by 1963 the PTB could claim to be the senior partner. The PTB's success in the 1962 elections, combined with defections from other parties, had made it the largest party in the Chamber of Deputies, and it was already the second largest in the Senate. More important, an unexpected historical twist—the resignation of Jânio Quadros in August 1961—gave the presidency to a PTB politician for the first time. João Goulart, the populist former labor minister and a protégé of Vargas, was widely distrusted by the right, which conspired with the armed forces to install a parliamentary system and reduce Goulart's presidential powers. When these powers were restored via a plebiscite in January 1963, Goulart's immediate opening to the left wing of his party only fueled conservatives' fears.

By early 1964, the Brazilian political right had clearly lost the hegemony that it had enjoyed throughout the entire Second Republic. The political initiative was perceived as belonging to the populist and progressive forces identified with President Goulart. Thus it was perhaps not surprising that the traditional "moderating power" of Brazilian politics, the armed forces, would intervene on April 1, 1964, to oust Goulart and reestablish a conservative governing coalition. Of course, the events and processes leading up to the 1964 coup were far more complex than has been indicated here, and authors have disagreed sharply over their relative importance.[10] But few would disagree that the coup constituted a conservative restoration after the crisis of the early 1960s.

The Right and Military Rule, 1964–1985

The Creation of ARENA

The military movement that ended democracy in 1964 differed from previous interventions in that the armed forces did not return power to civilians,

10. For a vivid description of the events leading up to the coup, see Skidmore (1967). For debate on its causes, see O'Donnell (1973), Stepan (1978), Serra (1979), Wallerstein (1980), and Soares (1986).

but decided to hold onto the reins of government indefinitely. The Brazilian presidency was occupied by army generals from 1964 to 1985. Therefore, despite the strong element of military-civilian cooperation under authoritarianism, it is important to stress that the April 1964 coup was indisputably a military initiative, and that for the next two decades the ultimate decision-making authority in Brazil rested with the army. But our concern here is the coup's effect on professional politicians, especially conservative ones.

The military coup was welcomed by the conservative wing of the political class. While it is difficult to measure the preferences of individual politicians immediately prior to the coup, it is clear that the first military president, General Humberto Castello Branco, had little difficulty in securing many politicians' subsequent endorsements of the so-called Revolution. In the first two years of his rule, Castello Branco governed with the support of a majority faction in Congress, the Bloco Parlamentar da Revolução, still based on the old political parties of the Second Republic. When Castello Branco signed the Second Institutional Act (AI-2) in October 1965, a decree that abolished all existing parties and imposed a two-party system, the extent of support for the Revolução was even clearer. AI-2 marked the beginning of a political cleavage that would characterize Brazilian politics for a generation or more: authoritarians versus democrats.

In the wake of AI-2, nearly two-thirds of federal legislators, and all twenty-two state governors (that is, those that survived the early *cassações*, or political purges), chose to join the progovernment Aliança Renovadora Nacional (National Renovating Alliance, or ARENA) rather than the opposition Movimento Democrático Brasileiro (Brazilian Democratic Movement, or MDB) (Jenks 1979: 106–26). A breakdown of the pre-1964 party preferences of the founders of ARENA and MDB, based on data collected by David Fleischer (Wesson and Fleischer 1983) shows more clearly the basis of government support: ARENA was built largely on the foundations of the defunct conservative parties. Table 3.1 illustrates the party affiliations of federal deputies not purged by the first two Institutional Acts. Overall, some 64.6 percent of the Chamber membership joined ARENA in 1965–66. Among legislators who had belonged to conservative parties in the Second Republic, 76.2 percent chose ARENA and only 23.8 percent chose the opposition MDB. Legislators who had belonged to other parties, most of which were populist or progressive in orientation, chose MDB over the progovernment ARENA by a margin of 55.6 percent to 44.4 percent.

An examination of the "afterlife" of the abolished parties sheds more light on the early composition of ARENA. The party most easily absorbed into the authoritarian coalition was the UDN. Fleischer found that some 90

Table 3.1 Pre-1966 party affiliations of federal deputies, 1966–1971

	1966–1967 Legislature[a]			1967–1971 Legislature		
Pre-1966 Affiliation	ARENA	MDB	Total	ARENA	MDB	Total
Conservative Parties[b]	189	59	248	218	60	278
All other parties	71	89	160	57	68	125
Unknown	—	—	1	1	5	6
TOTALS	260	148	409	276	133	409

SOURCE: Calculated from Wesson and Fleischer (1983, table 4.2).

[a] Does not reflect legislators purged (*cassados*) by AI-1 (1964) and AI-2 (1965–66).
[b] Conservative parties in the Second Republic: PSD, UDN, PR, PL, PRP, PDC.

percent of the UDN's deputies and 100 percent of its senators joined ARENA, making the ex-*udenistas* the largest single bloc within the new party. The former PSD experienced some division, but still mostly opted for ARENA, with 65 percent of its federal deputies and 74 percent of its senators affiliating. The PDC and PL had similar proportions, while the old PR and PRP joined ARENA in their entirety (Wesson and Fleischer 1983: 103–5). These migrations were complete by early 1966.

Given the partisan ancestry of its founders, it was clear that ARENA would be the new vehicle of political conservatism after AI-2. However, the nature of rightist politics had changed. Rather than belonging to several parties that competed with each other under democratic rules, the electoral right was now organized in *one* party in support of a military dictatorship.[11] The issue of *why* conservative politicians would endorse authoritarianism is of course critical to understanding the nature of the ARENA party. A first reason has already been revealed: the gradual electoral decline of the right in the preceding decade had led to a disenchantment with competitive politics. This effect was most pronounced within the UDN, which democracy had not treated kindly: the party was denied control of the national executive and legislative branches throughout the Second Republic. Therefore, it was less than surprising that the *udenistas* would applaud the coup of 1964 and participate heavily in subsequent ARENA governments.

A second reason for participation in ARENA was political rationality.

---

11. As was discussed in Chapter 2 and is evident from the data presented here, some conservative elements opted for the opposition MDB rather than ARENA; for example, somewhere between a quarter to a third of the old PSD migrated to MDB. The ideological dividing lines of two-party systems are never perfect, but the generalization holds that ARENA, not MDB, was the party vehicle for the political right after 1966. For a fuller discussion of this issue, see Kinzo (1988: 19–25).

ARENA was the party of the government. In Brazil, where the state has traditionally played an enormous role in development, where subnational governments depend heavily on the central power, and where interest groups and ordinary citizens alike routinely turn to politicians for favors, the rules of the political game exert strong pressures on individual politicians to support the federal executive. The forces that induce *governismo* are intimately related to the *sistema* and the concept of the patrimonial state discussed earlier. For many of the politicians recruited from the old PSD, their reasons for supporting the military government were the same that led them to support Getúlio Vargas and Juscelino Kubitschek—they wanted access to state resources, a fundamental source of political power in Brazil (Leal 1977; Souza 1983).

This interpretation of politicians' preference for ARENA suggests that ideological affinities between the conservative political class and military elites played a minimal role in their partnership. But it is difficult to gauge the actual importance of ideology, for two reasons. First, the large conservative parties of the 1945–64 period were only weakly ideological at best. Second, in accordance with Linz's (1976) classic characterization of authoritarian regimes, the Brazilian military failed to promote an official ideology after the coup. In fact, the military's discourse and policies showed considerable variation over time, from repressiveness to toleration in the political sphere, from orthodoxy to statism in the economic sphere, etc. The primary overlap in the orientations of ARENA politicians and their military sponsors might be characterized as a vaguely shared preference for "exclusionary" politics, of the kind associated with the rural wings of the UDN and PSD. But for politicians choosing between ARENA and MDB in 1965—and this emerged repeatedly in the recollections of informants interviewed for this book—the exigencies of local and regional politics were sometimes as important, if not more important, than the grandiose manifestos of the "Revolution." Both new parties (but especially ARENA) incorporated former rivals, especially in the interior of the country. To keep ARENA together, the military regime was forced to devise new electoral rules to permit "cohabitation" within the progovernment party, which will be discussed in Chapter 5.

Social and Electoral Bases of ARENA

The new conservative party had several clearly defined tasks in the military regime. As part of a larger strategy to maintain the trappings of a democratic system—which involved an opposition party, regularly held elections, and the retention of the National Congress—ARENA was expected to generate legitimacy for the new regime. But ARENA was also expected to assist in the work of governing Brazil, thus permitting the military to enact its policies and programs within the states. From its creation, ARENA did what the PSD and UDN had done so well in the Second Republic, which was to build political networks and clienteles within the vast, underdeveloped interior of the country. The first national elections under military rule, held in late 1966, established voting patterns that would endure until the return of political democracy in 1985. ARENA dominated in the less developed areas of Brazil, especially in the impoverished Northeast, whereas the opposition MDB had its best showings in the South and Southeast, the most developed regions of the country.

Figures 3.3 and 3.4 illustrate the variation of ARENA's electoral strength across regions. But as Kinzo pointed out in her study of the MDB,

> To assert that electoral support for the opposition party is particularly localized in the South and Southeast does not lead one to conclude that

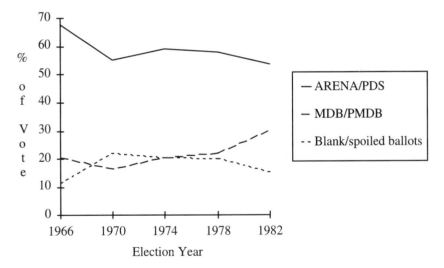

Fig. 3.3
Electoral results for the Chamber of Deputies, Northeast region, 1966–1982 (percentage of votes)[a]
SOURCE: Pereira et al. (1984: 55).
[a] Data for states of Alagoas, Bahia, Ceará, Maranhão, Paraíba, Rio Grande do Norte, and Sergipe. Results for 1982 reflect only PMDB vote, because votes for other opposition parties (PDT, PTB, PTB, PT) were negligible.

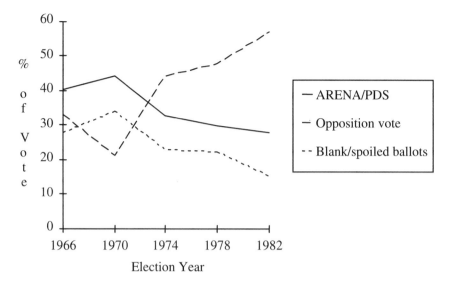

Fig. 3.4
Electoral results for the Chamber of Deputies, Southeast region, 1966–1982[a]
Source: Pereira et al. (1984: 59).
[a] Data for states of Espírito Santo, Minas Gerais, São Paulo, and Rio de Janeiro.
Results from 1966–1978 reflect vote for MDB; results from 1982 show all
opposition parties (PMDB, PTB, PDT, PT).

there simply exists a regional cleavage, upon which support for the
ARENA and the MDB is based. A cleavage certainly exists, but it is
based on the level of urbanization—and possibly industrialization—
which to a large extent influences voting behavior. (Kinzo 1988: 66)

Throughout the authoritarian period, support for ARENA varied inversely
with urbanization, as is illustrated by the results of the 1978 legislative elections (Table 3.2).

Why did ARENA dominate in rural and small-town Brazil? These are
areas where levels of political information are low and dependence on government resources is high, thus favoring the practice of patronage politics
and the establishment of rural clienteles. Wherever indices of development
were higher—and this includes the capital cities of poor states, which tend
to be islands of modernity in the less developed regions—ARENA performed poorly in elections. These patterns were so clearly defined that by
the early 1980s, when the opposition vote was surging rapidly, ARENA's
strength had become geographically restricted: the PDS, successor to

ARENA, could accurately be dubbed by the press as the "party of the Northeast."

Electoral Trends under Authoritarian Rule

The electoral battles between MDB/PMDB and ARENA/PDS from 1966 to 1985, and the relationship of this struggle to the processes of liberalization and democratization, have been well documented in the literature (Alves 1985; Kinzo 1988; Lamounier 1984, 1989; Lamounier and Meneguello 1986; von Mettenheim 1995). Rather than recapitulate the electoral history of this period, I shall restrict myself to outlining some important general trends.

Apart from the fact that the retention of elections by a military dictatorship is in itself noteworthy, two aspects of this period deserve mention. The first concerns the rules and limitations that the military imposed in order to maintain the hegemony of ARENA/PDS. Authoritarian measures known as *casuísmos*, which rewrote the rules of electoral competition to favor the government party, were employed from time as the military deemed necessary. The second interesting aspect is that despite their continual reworking of the electoral system, in the second decade of authoritarianism (1974–85) military strategists proved unable to stem the opposition tide. Over time, as elections became increasingly plebiscitarian, the ballot box became the outlet for popular dissatisfaction with military rule—as Bolivar Lamounier (1984) described it, elections were the "Achilles Heel" of the generals in an unprecedented process of "opening through elections."

The first elections under military rule showed the limits of military tolerance. Against the wishes of his more hard-line advisors, General Castello Branco decided to let the eleven gubernatorial elections scheduled for October 1965 go ahead as planned. The result was that opposition candidates won in the two most important elections at stake, those in Minas Gerais and Rio de Janeiro states. Confronted by angry hard-liners, Castello was forced to accede to some of their demands. He permitted the opposition governors to take office, but days later (October 27, 1965) decreed AI-2, which made all future elections of the president, vice president, and governors indirect. This was followed four months later by the Third Institutional Act (AI-3), which required that mayors of state capitals and dozens of other cities vital to "national security" be appointed by state governors.

Together, these two institutional acts formed the basis for ARENA/PDS dominance throughout most of the authoritarian regime. ARENA-controlled state assemblies would "elect" ARENA state governors, though in fact these were usually selected by military presidents. Then these ARENA governors would appoint ARENA mayors in all of the important municipalities in the state. To a certain extent, then, ARENA was "the party of the state governors" (Wesson and Fleischer 1983: 105). Direct elections for governors were not restored until 1982, and mayors of state capitals and vital cities were not directly elected until November 1985 (after the military had already withdrawn from power). This meant that in practice, meaningful executive power in Brazil was reserved exclusively for ARENA/PDS politicians for nearly two decades.[12] The major electoral barometer was provided by national legislative elections, which were held on their normal quadrennial cycle.

The trend in legislative elections was favorable to ARENA only until the pivotal 1974 balloting. The first authoritarian elections in October 1966 had produced a resounding ARENA victory across the board. The dominance of ARENA, along with heightened repression and censorship at the apogee of military rule, combined to produce widespread voter alienation in the 1970 contests. Resulting from apathy but also from an organized boycott of the election, invalid votes (blank and spoiled ballots) outnumbered the votes given to the opposition MDB (Table 3.3). But the MDB, in danger of imminent collapse, responded to the 1970 disaster with a process of internal renovation aimed at making the party a viable alternative to military rule. The party's 1971–73 reorganization, as well as a spirited protest candidacy in the indirect presidential election of January 1974, breathed new life into the MDB (Kinzo 1988, chap. 5). Its startling comeback in the November 1974 elections, in which the party won sixteen of the twenty-two Senate seats at stake, marked the beginning of the plebiscitarian phase of electoral politics. Protest voting began to be channeled through the MDB, such that after 1974, the MDB's vote total rose while the number of blank and spoiled ballots declined (Table 3.3). The MDB's strong 1974 performance could not be explained solely by its capture of voters who had spoiled their ballots in 1970; the increase in the MDB vote was greater than the decrease in blank and null votes. Therefore, ARENA suffered a real decline in support in the four years between the elections (Kinzo 1988: 154–55).

The military government's shock at the 1974 results prompted it to launch a strategy aimed at preventing MDB advances in subsequent con-

12. Only in what is today Rio de Janeiro state did the opposition MDB ever control a state government, and even then the incumbent governor was seen as a client of the military government.

Table 3.2 Urbanization and party preference in national legislative elections, 1978

City size	Senate (percentage)			Chamber (percentage)			Number of Votes Cast (x 1000)	Percentage Abstained
	ARENA	MDB	Blank and Spoiled	ARENA	MDB	Blank and Spoiled		
State capitals	21.9	58.5	19.6	23.6	55.7	20.7	9,913	14.3
Cities >30,000 pop.	25.7	54.3	20.0	30.9	47.3	21.8	9,456	14.8
Towns <30,000 pop.	47.1	35.7	17.2	53.8	26.1	20.1	18,079	22.0

SOURCE: Adapted from Kinzo (1988, table 3.6).

Table 3.3 Results of all legislative elections, 1966–1982 (percentages)

Year	Senate			Chamber of Deputies			State Assemblies		
	ARENA	MDB	Blank and Null Votes	ARENA	MDB	Blank and Null Votes	ARENA	MDB	Blank and Null Votes
1966	44.7	34.2	21.2	50.5	28.4	21.0	52.2	29.2	18.6
1970	43.7	28.6	27.7	48.4	21.3	30.3	51.0	22.0	26.8
1974	34.7	50.0	15.1	40.9	37.8	21.3	42.1	38.8	18.9
1978	35.0	46.4	18.6	40.0	39.3	20.7	41.1	39.6	19.3
1982[a]	36.5	50.0	13.5	36.7	48.2	15.1	36.0	47.2	16.8

SOURCE: Lamounier (1989, table 3).

[a] Results for 1982 show PDS votes in the ARENA column, and show votes for all four opposition parties (PMDB, PDT, PTB, and PT) in the MDB column.

tests. Basically, this consisted in rigging the rules of the electoral game through *casuísmos* in order to maintain ARENA majorities in legislative bodies. The *casuísmos* are worth reviewing here not only because they provoked major changes in the party and electoral systems, but because of what they indicate about the declining appeal of ARENA and the Revolução more generally. The necessity of arbitrary interventions in support of the government party constituted recognition of the changing nature of Brazilian politics in the second decade after the coup. The decline of ARENA and its successor party, PDS, is normally understood as a withdrawal of legitimacy from the military regime, yet this phenomenon—when viewed historically in light of electoral trends since World War II—could also be interpreted as another manifestation of the secular trend of the decline of conservative parties in Brazil (Soares 1984: 49–55).

Perhaps the most famous *casuísmo* occurred in the wake of the 1976 municipal elections, in which the MDB advanced again by winning control of city councils in the five largest cities. In April 1977, President Ernesto Geisel closed Congress[13] and issued a number of constitutional reforms known collectively as the April Package. Its effects were twofold. First, the decree permitted future constitutional amendments to be passed by a simple majority, which once again gave ARENA a free hand in this area. Second, the April Package guaranteed continued ARENA majorities in Congress by apportioning federal deputies on the basis of population rather than registered voters, and by giving each state a third, indirectly elected ("bionic") senator, which in nearly every state went to ARENA. These two changes slowed the advance of the MDB and guaranteed the continued overrepresentation of the right in Congress (Table 3.4).

In 1978 the MDB made another strong showing. In the proportional elections for the federal Chamber and for state assemblies, the party did even better than in 1974, but the effects of the April Package left ARENA with majorities in both houses of Congress. Still, after this close call military strategists decided that the two-party system—imposed by AI-2 in 1965—was no longer working to their advantage. General Golbery do Couto e Silva, chief political strategist for presidents Geisel and Figueiredo, opted to "divide and conquer" the opposition by ordering a return to a multiparty system. He expected that the progovernment coalition would remain intact

---

13. After 1974, ARENA no longer had the two-thirds majority in Congress necessary to amend the Constitution. Under the Fifth Institutional Act (AI-5) of 1968, the president could do so by decree, but only if the legislature were not in session.

Table 3.4 Overrepresentation of ARENA/PDS in Congress, 1966–1982 (percentage of vote obtained in elections and of seats held by ARENA/PDS at beginning of legislative sessions)

Year	Senate			Chamber of Deputies		
	Votes	Seats	Difference	Votes	Seats	Difference
1966	44.7	71.2	(+) 26.5	50.5	67.7	(+) 17.2
1970	43.7	89.4	(+) 45.7	48.4	71.9	(+) 23.5
1974	34.7	69.7	(+) 35.0	40.9	56.0	(+) 15.1
1978	35.0	62.7	(+) 27.7	40.0	55.0	(+) 15.0
1982	36.5	66.7	(+) 30.2	36.7	49.0	(+) 12.3

SOURCE: Lamounier (1989, table 4).

while the MDB would splinter into various factions; the 1979 amnesty law, permitting the return of exiles and *cassados* to political life, would facilitate the opposition split. Golbery's expectations were mostly correct. The MDB (reorganized in 1979 as the PMDB, Partido do Movimento Democrático Brasileiro) diminished in size, while four new, smaller opposition parties emerged in its orbit. These were the Partido dos Trabalhadores (PT), an independent socialist party; the Partido Popular (PP), a short-lived center-right party that merged with the PMDB in 1982; and two parties disputing the Varguist mantle, the Partido Democrático Trabalhista (PDT) of Leonel Brizola and the Partido Trabalhista Brasileiro (PTB) of Ivete Vargas. While the PDT eventually carved out a space as a self-styled "social democratic" party,[14] the rival PTB bore little resemblance to its *getulista* namesake in the Second Republic. By 1983 the PTB was in a tacit alliance with the progovernment PDS, and is today considered a conservative party. Meanwhile, the progovernment ARENA party, suffering fewer defections, simply changed its name to the Partido Democrático Social (PDS). The political system, having liberalized after 1974, became increasingly competitive in the early 1980s. In a major step toward political democracy, direct elections for state governors were scheduled for 1982.[15]

Despite the more open climate, the military proved unwilling to place ARENA/PDS in the electoral arena without protecting the party first. A study by the National Intelligence Service (SNI) indicated that the PDS was likely to win the gubernatorial elections only in the four Northeastern states

14. Although the PDT associated itself publicly with the major socialist parties of Western Europe, its social democratic credentials were never very convincing due to the suffocating weight of Brizola's cult of personality.

15. On liberalization and democratization in Brazil, see Mainwaring (1986b), Martins (1986), Smith (1987), and Skidmore (1988).

of Alagoas, Sergipe, Bahia, and Maranhão (cited in Alves 1985: 223). Thus, in November 1981 came yet another "package" of *casuísmos* designed to aid the PDS in the 1982 contests. President João Figueiredo's electoral reforms were designed to discourage collective action among opposition forces: party coalitions were prohibited, and parties were required to put up candidates for every office in a given municipality or else be barred from the ballot in that jurisdiction. No candidate was permitted to withdraw from a race unless his or her entire party withdrew as well. Finally, the November Package's most important feature was the institution of the *voto vinculado*, or the requirement of a straight-ticket vote, never before adopted in Brazil. By forcing voters to choose one party's candidates from the bottom of the ballot to the top, the military believed it could create a "reverse coattails" effect, turning PDS's domination of local-level politics into an national election victory (Fleischer 1984).

I draw attention to the military government *casuísmos* neither for their creativeness nor for their arbitrary nature—the manipulation of electoral legislation has a long history in Brazil—but for what they have to say about the electoral right as a political actor. The institution of measures blatantly designed to favor ARENA/PDS constituted explicit recognition by the military of the party's waning appeal: were the playing field kept level, ARENA/PDS would lose.[16] The outcome of the 1982 elections showed this beyond a doubt. Together, the opposition parties took 56.8 percent of the valid votes for the Chamber of Deputies, 57.9 percent of those for the Senate, and 58.5 percent of those cast for governors. The PMDB won nine governorships and the PDT one. The PDS won twelve governorships, but once again these were mostly the poorer states; the ten states won by the opposition were responsible for 75 percent of Brazil's total economic output (Alves 1985: 228–29). Also important was the failure of PDS to win an absolute majority in the Chamber of Deputies—the first time since 1964 that the progovernment party had lost control of a house of Congress. Combined with the loss of nearly all the prestigious state governments, this was a powerful blow to the PDS. Despite the elaborate *casuísmos* and the built-in advantages that come with controlling state resources in Brazil, a real redistribution of political power had taken place, and the last elections under military rule had confirmed the declining strength of the political right.

16. Likewise, had the military not instituted rules designed to keep ARENA/PDS together, it is likely that the progovernment coalition would have disintegrated. These rules and their relationship to the internal structure of ARENA/PDS are discussed in Chapter 5.

The Transition to Democracy and the Division of the PDS

From 1966 until 1984, the Brazilian electoral right was relatively cohesive, working within the ARENA/PDS party structure.[17] But in the wake of the political realignment brought about by the 1982 elections, strains began to become visible within the PDS. The fading legitimacy of the authoritarian regime, the reduced electoral potency of the progovernment party, and the fact that the political system increasingly resembled democracy—with its emphasis on competition and the posing of political alternatives—all combined to produce a situation in which continued support of the military government was an increasingly risky option for rational politicians. In other words, with the transition to full democracy imminent, the strategic calculus facing PDS politicians involved a choice between defecting from the government party or renewing support for the authoritarian *sistema*, with very little in between. The "payoffs" for each strategic choice would be highly rewarding or highly disastrous, depending on the outcome.[18] The critical juncture that finally forced PDS politicians to choose was sparked by controversy over who would succeed General João Figueiredo as president.

The military had again changed the constitutional procedures for electing a president. The election would be still be indirect, as had been the case since 1964, but now the election would be conducted in the expanded Electoral College, which included senators, deputies, governors, and state delegates. The Electoral College, scheduled to meet in January 1985, was designed to have a PDS majority: the party held 356 of the 686 seats (52 percent), thereby virtually guaranteeing that the next president would come from the ranks of the PDS. However, two unforeseen events spoiled the plan

17. Prior to 1984, the only substantial defections from ARENA/PDS had occurred in 1980–82, during the formation of the center-right Partido Popular. The PP was formed in part by the *grupo independente* of ARENA, which wished to speed the transition to democracy. The true extent of ARENA defections to the PP nationwide is unknown, but can be partly inferred from Fleischer's data on party realignment in the National Congress (Wesson and Fleischer 1983: 109). During the PP's brief existence, the party's congressional delegation consisted of about 40 percent ex-ARENA members and 60 percent ex-MDB members, almost all of whom were absorbed into the PMDB in February 1982. The PP drew twenty-six deputies and seven senators from ARENA, but at the time these were only small percentages of ARENA's total delegation to Congress (11 percent of the ARENA deputies and 17 percent of the ARENA senators elected in 1978, respectively).

18. Adam Przeworski brilliantly described the strategic calculi of politicians in his essay "Some Problems in the Study of the Transition to Democracy" (Przeworski 1986). Elsewhere, I attempted to apply Przeworski's analysis to events in Brazil in 1984–85 (Power 1987). See also Collier and Norden (1992).

for a smooth succession—and for the first time ever, provoked major schisms within the government party.[19]

The first event was the *Diretas Já* ("Direct Elections Now") campaign of January–April 1984. On April 25 of that year, the Chamber of Deputies was scheduled to vote on a constitutional amendment, proposed by PMDB member Dante de Oliveira, which would have restored direct presidential elections for the fall of 1984. Although few believed the amendment could muster the necessary two-thirds vote of a chamber where the PDS still controlled nearly half the seats, the opposition parties went ahead with a series of energetic public rallies in support of direct elections. Due to the astonishing success of the rallies and the overwhelming support of public opinion for *Diretas Já*, a number of prominent PDS politicians—including the vice president of the Republic, Aureliano Chaves, the first civilian to hold that post in many years—took the bold step of endorsing the direct elections movement. When the Dante de Oliveira Amendment finally came up for a vote on April 25, it fell short of the two-thirds majority by a mere 22 votes. The 298 votes in favor included those of fifty-five PDS deputies who ignored immense pressure from the military (Skidmore 1988: 244). While the *Diretas Já* movement had failed to achieve its stated objective, it succeeded in dividing the PDS (Mainwaring 1986b).

The second event that sundered the PDS was the nomination of its presidential candidate for January 1985. With the Dante de Oliveira episode showing clear cracks in the progovernment alliance, it was clear that the PDS could only win in the Electoral College if it ran a candidate capable of unifying all factions in the party. This did not happen. Instead, the nomination was captured in June 1984 by the most divisive of all possible candidates, former governor Paulo Maluf of São Paulo, a wealthy, abrasive conservative and declared opponent of direct elections. Upon Maluf's nomination, the president of the PDS, Senator José Sarney of Maranhão, resigned in protest. Soon after, a newly formed wing of the party calling itself the Frente Liberal—led by powerful figures such as Vice President Chaves and Senators Marco Maciel (Pernambuco) and Jorge Bornhausen (Santa Catarina)—also decided to abandon the PDS. The Liberal Front (later formalized as a party, the Partido da Frente Liberal or PFL) then opened negotiations with the opposition presidential candidate, Minas Gerais governor Tancredo Neves of the PMDB, a centrist. With an eye to the math of the Elec-

---

19. The events of 1984 are related in two engaging journalistic accounts: Dimenstein et al. (1985), and "A historia secreta da sucessão," *Veja*, January 16, 1985.

toral College, Tancredo quickly sealed a "democratic alliance" between the PMDB and PFL, and took José Sarney as his vice presidential running mate. The Aliança Democrática then had the votes to win, and thereafter only military intervention could avert the certain defeat of the PDS in the presidential election.

In the final months of 1984, Tancredo Neves negotiated behind the scenes to pacify the armed forces and ensure that they would permit his inauguration. Meanwhile, Paulo Maluf's PDS candidacy went nowhere as the Aliança Democrática benefited from a bandwagon effect. When the votes were counted in the Electoral College on January 15, 1985, the PDS ticket received only 180 votes to the 480 won by Tancredo of the PMDB and Sarney of the PFL.[20] The party that had supported authoritarian military rule since 1964, ARENA/PDS, had lost a presidential election for the first time in its history. As 1985 began and Tancredo's inauguration approached, the PDS was also drastically reduced in size, as the PFL drew away many of its members. In fact, in the first year of the New Republic the PDS shrank to less than a third of its size in 1983 (Table 3.5).

Twenty-one years of military rule ended on March 15, 1985, but as is well known, the occasion was marred by the illness and subsequent death of president-elect Tancredo Neves. His running mate, José Sarney, was sworn in as president instead. The irony of this was that only nine months earlier, Sarney had been the president of the promilitary PDS. So in a sense,

Table 3.5 Party realignment in Congress, 1983–1986 (number of seats)

Party	January 1983	January 1985	July 1986
PDS	280	204	81
PMDB	222	225	246
PFL	—	73	149
PDT	24	24	26
PTB	14	14	13
PT	8	8	6
New Parties[a]	—	—	27
TOTALS	548	548	548

SOURCE: Kinzo (1989, table 1).

[a] Reflects realignment after Constitutional Amendment no. 25 of May 1985, which removed restrictions on the creation of parties and legalized the two Communist parties.

20. Technically, Sarney was a member of the PMDB by this time, because the electoral law forced him to join the PMDB to run on the same ticket as Tancredo. Politically, however, he was the representative of the PFL in the Democratic Alliance.

the old PDS *did* win the presidency of Brazil yet again, and the historic opposition to authoritarian rule could not savor Tancredo's victory.

Sarney's unforeseen accession to power was perhaps the most obvious indicator of the immense continuity between the 1964–85 military regime and the New Republic, but it was hardly the only one. The negotiations that built the Democratic Alliance had led Tancredo Neves to include several former PDS luminaries in his cabinet, including Marco Maciel, Aureliano Chaves, and Olavo Setúbal, a former PDS mayor of São Paulo. Sarney governed with Tancredo's cabinet for several months, but then began replacing the original members with old allies, many of whom were fellow veterans of the ARENA/PDS party structure.[21] Also, the PFL attracted so many new "converts" from the PDS that the "Democratic Alliance" was hardly worthy of the name. In a sense, this was entirely predictable. In previous regime transitions in 1946 and 1964, Brazilian politicians, true to the clientelistic style of politics practiced in the country, had tended to gravitate to the new party in power, whatever its identity. In the mid-1980s, politicians flocked to *both* parties of government—the PMDB was growing rapidly as well (Table 3.5). The fact that the executive branch was still largely in the hands of ARENA/PDS veterans, combined with the uncontrolled *adesão* (literally "adhesion" or joining, but figuratively "bandwaggoning") of many of these former supporters of military rule, meant that the New Republic and the Democratic Alliance had ambiguous identities—in other words, it was difficult to determine who in the new governing alliance really belonged to the democratic camp (O'Donnell 1992).

The muddled politics of the transition does not mean that the early New Republic was not a form—albeit an incipient one—of political democracy. Though the president had not been directly elected, he oversaw the resurrection of many democratic institutions in Brazil. The armed forces, while still powerful, were at least not directly administering the country's affairs. Political censorship was abolished, and the president refrained from using most of the arbitrary powers granted him by the authoritarian Constitution of 1967 (though a thorough, democratic constitutional revision would have to await the Constituent Assembly of 1987–88). Working together in mid-1985, Sarney and the Congress abolished all restrictions on the formation of political parties and legalized the outlawed Marxist parties. All elections

21. In early 1986, a cabinet shakeup gave fifteen ministries to the PMDB and only five to the PFL. However, these PFL ministries (mines and energy, communications, education, foreign relations, education, and presidential chief of staff) controlled budgets that were two and one-half times as large as the PMDB's ministries (Smith 1987: 227–28).

were made direct once again, and municipal elections for state capitals and "national security" cities were held extraordinarily in November 1985. By the end of 1985 only Sarney himself and a third of the Senate had not been elected by the people in free and fair elections. The events of 1985, if not defining Brazil as having a completely democratic regime, at least identified Sarney's as a democratic government (Mainwaring 1986b).

The Brazilian Right at the Onset of Democratic Rule

Having reviewed the circumstances that led to the division of the ARENA/ PDS cohort in 1984–85, it is important to place these events in the context of recent historical trends within the Brazilian political right.

First, the division of PDS in 1984 says much about its internal cohesiveness and about the relationship of conservative politicians to the armed forces. The 1984–85 presidential succession was unlike any other conducted under authoritarianism in that the outgoing president (in this case, General João Figueiredo) did not impose his own choice of a successor. Had he done so, his party would most likely have remained in power until 1991. Instead, Figueiredo's neutrality instead turned the succession into a power struggle among conservative civilian politicians, who quickly became factionalized, thereby fatally wounding the party's chances in the Electoral College. This outcome underscored the "artificiality" of the PDS, a party created by the military regime in order to aggregate and institutionalize its support within the conservative sectors of the political class. When Figueiredo chose to take the lid off the servile PDS, he exposed old political rivalries within the party and revealed new ones that had developed over twenty years of "cohabitation" within the authoritarian coalition.

Second, the circumstances of the military's withdrawal, while apparently dealing a fatal blow to the PDS party, paradoxically were *favorable* to *some* sectors of the political class. The division of PDS and the founding of a splinter party, the PFL, gave former supporters of military rule an opportunity to break publicly with the increasingly unpopular authoritarian regime. The events of 1984 permitted the Liberal Front dissidents to renew their political viability through two successive infusions of democratic legitimacy: the first from their endorsement of direct elections (which was only partial—not all PFL founders supported this) and their opposition to Maluf, and the second from Tancredo Neves, a politician of oppositionist and democratic credentials who welcomed the PFL into his fold. These two events— the defection of Liberal Front dissidents from the PDS and Tancredo's invitation to an alliance—can be explained quite persuasively in terms of rationality: these actors all had in common the desire to be on the winning side in the presidential election. But the symbolic level of politics was not lost on the PDS defectors. The unusual circumstances of the regime transition allowed them to obfuscate their political past and to associate themselves with what the Brazil of 1984 viewed as desirable: civilian rule instead of military rule, democracy instead of authoritarianism. Moreover, the indirect nature of the presidential election and the splintering of one party into two allowed the PDS to escape the crushing verdict that might have been delivered in a popular vote.[22] Considering the declining legitimacy and the spiraling economic collapse of the military regime in the early 1980s, the outcome of the 1985 transition could hardly have been more favorable to the right.

One important result of the transition to democracy is that it may have stalled, or at least slowed, the long-term decline of the electoral right in Brazil. In the Second Republic (1946–64), conservative parties lost support over time. This process was interrupted by the 1964 coup and the subsequent creation of ARENA in 1966. After only two electoral cycles, however, the process began anew: ARENA/PDS followed the same downward trajectory as the PSD and UDN earlier (Soares 1984). Between 1966 and 1984 ARENA/PDS was always perceived as the conservative alternative in the party system, and after 1974 paid a heavy price for this; thus, we can presume that one wish of conservatives in the mid-1980s was to avoid being congregated in one large, identifiably conservative party. The result of this, as we shall see in the next chapter, was a massive dispersion of former *arenistas* into many other parties, most of them founded after 1985. This "right flight" seems to have been successful. In 1983, the PDS controlled 53.4 percent of the National Congress; in 1987, after the first legislative elections in the New Republic, *veterans* of ARENA/PDS, now in seven parties, occupied 39.2 percent of the seats—a significant decline, but still quite remarkable in light of the *desgaste* (erosion) of the military regime and the PDS's standing in opinion polls in 1984. The conservative diaspora, then, may have enhanced the electoral viability of individual rightist politicians, simply because they were—and are—no longer an easy target.

22. According to opinion polls taken in early 1984, Vice President Aureliano Chaves would have been a formidable candidate for the PDS in a direct presidential election. But these polls were taken early on, before the PMDB had defined its candidate. Had Paulo Maluf run in a direct election, he probably would have lost badly. In the end, both the PDS and PMDB nominated candidates who were much better suited to indirect elections than to a popular vote.

Conclusion

This chapter has reviewed the recent history of the Brazilian political right. The analysis revealed that in the postwar era, the right's once-secure hegemony has been challenged whenever the rules of political competition have been relaxed enough to permit real participation and contestation. The longer democracy existed in the Second Republic, the weaker became the civilian right. When in 1963–64 the right briefly lost its control over the national political agenda, its panic was short-lived as the armed forces stepped in to restore both "order" and the political dominance of conservative elites, especially at the state and local levels of government.

Under the "limited pluralism" of the authoritarian regime, especially after the 1974 elections, the electoral right's position began to erode once again as its senior partner—the military—increasingly tolerated opposition activity. Though the military was in a good position to control the pace of the political opening, the advent of real democratization in 1982 (with the election of state governors) and the prospect of a presidential election in 1985 combined to speed the process dramatically. Ultimately, the toleration of participation and contestation undid the authoritarian alliance of the military and the civilian right.

Just as the institutional architecture of the authoritarian regime pulled conservatives together, so the institutional environment of democracy began to tear the right apart. The logic of competition and of vote maximization was not lost on ex-ARENA/PDS politicians, who gleefully fled the artificially imposed "cohabitation" of ARENA/PDS for the greener pastures of a multiparty system in 1984–85. The "diaspora" of the former *arenistas* is the subject of the following chapter.

ARENA in the Afterlife 4
A Portrait of the Political Right in the New Republic

Introduction

Having traced the trajectory of the electoral right from the beginning of the Second Republic to the end of the 1964–85 military regime, we may now proceed to review the situation of the right in the New Republic. This chapter draws on survey research, biographical sources, and published demographic and electoral data in order to paint a portrait of the contemporary ARENA/PDS cohort: where it has been, where it is going, and whom it represents. This information is essential for understanding the right's engagement in the institutional arenas of Brazilian democracy, which is the subject of the two subsequent chapters.

Much of what follows is based on data about the Brazilian federal legislators who served in the first three legislative sessions under democracy. Because the 48th Legislature (1987–91) sat simultaneously in its first two years as a National Constituent Assembly, it became the most closely studied Brazilian legislature ever. In early 1990, I conducted a survey of its membership via written questionnaire. This survey was replicated in 1993 for the 49th Legislature (1991–95), and again in 1997 for the 50th Legislature (1995–99; see Appendix B). The three waves of survey research are supplemented by numerous other documentary and secondary sources. In painting a portrait of the postauthoritarian right, I focus on the regional and partisan identities of the ARENA/PDS veterans still in politics, on their occupational and recruitment backgrounds, and on their political ideologies.

As discussed in Chapter 2, the experiential approach used in this study defines the right as those politicians who supported the 1964–85 military regime: in other words, as veterans of the ARENA/PDS party structure. When using biographical sources and legislative documents, I searched for officially reported party affiliations in order to determine inclusion in the ARENA cohort (see Appendix A). When using my own survey data, I relied on the self-reported party affiliations of the respondents during the 1966–79 two-party system and the 1980–85 multiparty system. The general thrust of these criteria is to identify individuals who, by virtue of lending their name to the ARENA/PDS party, made a *public and institutional commitment* to the military regime. These politicians were the foot soldiers of the authoritarian power structure. Because they worked on behalf of a nondemocratic regime, it is imperative to see how they fare in a democratic one.

Who Survived the Transition?

In November 1986, elections were held for the entire Chamber of Deputies (487 seats) and two-thirds of the Federal Senate (49 seats), as well as for all state governors. After these contests, only a handful of officials remained who had been elected under the rules of the authoritarian regime: President Sarney, elected by the Electoral College, and one senator from each of twenty-three states, who had been elected directly (although under November Package restrictions) in 1982. The 1986 contests were important not only because they were the first major elections under democratic rule but also because they elected the body that would write Brazil's new constitution. When the new legislature convened on February 1, 1987, just under 40 percent of its membership met the criteria above as veterans of ARENA/ PDS.

Continuing the cohort analysis through the two subsequent legislatures, we see that the number of ARENA/PDS veterans naturally declined. This was to be expected given the aging of the politicians of the 1960s and 1970s and their gradual replacement by younger colleagues. In the 49th Legislature (1991–95) and the 50th Legislature, the share of ex-*arenistas* dropped to 30.7 percent and 24.5 percent, respectively. Still, however, it is impressive that ten years after military withdrawal, one out of every four Brazilian federal legislators elected in October 1994 had served the authoritarian regime. Further insight can be gained by comparing the ex-ARENA and never-ARENA cohorts with the aid of various grouping variables, including party, region, occupation, age, and political experience.

Table 4.1 ARENA's afterlife in the first three legislatures under democracy (ex-ARENA/PDS penetration of various groups in Congress, in percentage)[a]

Category	48th (1987–1991)	49th (1991–1995)	50th (1995–1999)
CONGRESS	38.4	30.7	24.5
Deputies	37.7	28.5	22.8
Senators	43.1	44.7	34.5
PMDB	20.9	20.5	12.4
PFL	77.1	67.9	60.0
PDS	86.5	NA	NA
PPR/PPB[b]	NA	50.0	31.3
PSDB	NA	14.3	14.9
PDC	28.6	NA	NA
PDT	19.2	13.0	13.2
PRN	NA	27.3	0.0
PTB	27.8	25.6	31.6
PT	0.0	0.0	0.0
PL	57.1	46.7	21.4
PCB/PPS	0.0	0.0	0.0
PC do B	0.0	0.0	0.0
PSB	0.0	0.0	0.0
North	37.1	23.6	14.8
Northeast	52.9	49.7	39.3
Center-West	41.1	23.2	18.9
Center-South	27.0	20.8	17.2
South	31.8	24.7	23.3
"Modern" Brazil[c]	27.4	21.2	18.3
"Traditional" Brazil	49.1	39.6	30.2
Total N ex-arenistas	214	188	146
Valid N Congress	558	612	597

NA = Not Applicable (the party in question did not exist at the time)

SOURCES: Coded by author from *Repertórios biográficos* published by Câmara dos Deputados, Senado Federal, and Assembléia Nacional Constituinte, 1987–1995.

[a] To insure comparability of data, equivalent sources were used for all three legislative sessions: the official biographical handbooks published quadrennially by Congress. Because of some missing biographies and the inclusion of alternate members (*suplentes*) serving in Congress, the totals do not correspond exactly to the number of legislative seats at the time. For the same reason, there are minor differences between the figures in this table and those reported elsewhere in this study, which are drawn from various sources.
[b] The figures for the PPR in the 49th Legislature include members elected on the PDS and PDC tickets in 1990. The PPR was created by the merger of these two parties in 1993. Similarly, the figures for the PPB in the 50th Legislature include members elected on the PPR and PP tickets in 1994. The PPB was formed by the merger of the PPR and PP in 1995.
[c] "Modern Brazil" is defined here as the three Southern states, the four Center-South states, and the Federal District. "Traditional Brazil" is defined as the remaining nineteen states in the North, Northeast, and Center-West.

The Partisan Diaspora

At the time of José Sarney's inauguration in March 1985, only two major conservative parties existed: the PDS and the new party formed by PDS dissidents, the PFL. A smaller right-of-center party was the PTB, founded in 1980. Some ARENA/PDS veterans belonged to the PMDB at the moment of the democratic transition (most of them having entered the party via its incorporation of the short-lived Partido Popular in 1982), but they were still few in number and were clearly subordinated to the party's center-left leadership, who had captained the opposition to military rule since the 1960s. But with the liberalization of party legislation in May 1985 and the electoral campaign of 1986, a handful of new conservative parties entered on the scene.

Ideologically, the most important of these new groups was the Partido Liberal, a small party based mostly in urban Rio de Janeiro and São Paulo. Influenced by the neoliberal economics being practiced in the United States and United Kingdom at this time (Nylen 1992), and appealing primarily to middle class voters, the PL elected 7 representatives to the Constituent Assembly. The PL's principal leaders, Afif Domingos, a former lieutenant of Paulo Maluf in São Paulo, and Álvaro Valle, a longtime *arenista* deputy from Rio de Janeiro, were two of the biggest vote-getters in the country in 1986. After Valle's failed run for mayor of Rio in 1988 and Afif's disappointing campaign for president in 1989, the PL never lived up to its early promise. Still, the party has consistently held 2–3 percent of the seats in the Chamber of Deputies.

Another new group called itself the Christian Democratic Party. Founded in 1985, it had no relationship to the pre-1964 PDC, and was more conservative than any of its namesakes throughout Latin America. The PDC drew support from large landowners, especially in the agricultural state of Goiás. There, the political machine of a right-wing former ARENA governor, Siqueira Campos, aligned the party with the separatist movement in the northern part of the state, which led to the creation of the state of Tocantins in 1988 (Siqueira became the new state's first governor). In 1993, the PDC merged with the PDS to form the new PPR, the Reformist Progressive Party (see below).

In the pivotal elections of 1986, ex-*arenistas* who sought a right-of-center party affiliation could choose between the two large, nationally organized ARENA offshoots (PFL and PDS), or among one of the three small, regionally limited conservative parties (PTB, PDC, and PL). Instead, many of them chose instead to join a party that until then had no conservative profile: the PMDB.[1] Their decision reflected the immense popularity of the PMDB in that year, which derived less from the former opposition party's democratic image than from the (temporary) success of the Plano Cruzado, the package of economic reforms originated by PMDB economists and instituted by President Sarney in February. After the biggest landslide victory ever seen in a fair election in Brazil, the PMDB controlled 305 of the 559 seats of the National Constituent Assembly (ANC)—and no less than 71 of these were occupied by former members of ARENA/PDS (the party affiliations of the ARENA/PDS cohort are presented in Tables 4.1 and 4.10). Looking back at the great electoral struggles between ARENA/PDS and MDB/PMDB under the military regime, it is ironic that better than one in five PMDB *constituintes* was actually a veteran of ARENA/PDS—or, to put this another way, that one out of every three ex-*arenistas* in the ANC got there thanks to the party ticket of the former enemy, the PMDB. This "infiltration" of these individuals into the PMDB gave the party a large conservative wing for the first time beginning in 1987, and the party's shift to the right was partially responsible for sharp internal divisions within the PMDB. In June 1988, the progressive wing of the party exited to form the Partido da Social Democracia Brasileira, or PSDB. By the end of the 1980s the PMDB had taken on many of the characteristics of the dominant parties in the Second Republic and in the authoritarian regime: its main strengths lay in small towns, the Northeast, and in its links to the presidency.

With its new presence in the dominant PMDB, after 1986 the ARENA/PDS cohort had a hand in the three largest parties of the legislature. Ex-*arenistas* made up 20.9 percent of the PMDB's delegation to the Constituent Assembly, 77.1 percent of the PFL's delegation, and 86.5 percent of the scaled-down PDS (see Table 4.1). These proportions led the author of an important study of recruitment to the ANC to comment that "the most surprising fact of this analysis is that largest delegation in this Constituent Assembly was not the PMDB of today, but rather—in 1979 terms—it was ARENA" (Fleischer 1988: 31).

While most visible in the major parties, in fact ex-*arenistas* were fairly well dispersed. In 1986 these rightists were successfully elected by no fewer than seven political parties. Besides the three mentioned above, ex-*arenistas*

1. At least at the collective level, in 1986 the PMDB was not identifiably conservative. However, the party did add a small conservative wing through its incorporation of the PP in 1982. The party always contained a number of politically conservative individuals, for example, Roberto Cardoso Alves, who became prominent in the New Republic.

arrived to the ANC in the PL, PTB, PDC, and even in Leonel Brizola's PDT. By November 1989—only thirty months after the ANC began its deliberations—the cohort was dispersed even more, into *twelve* parties (Table 4.2). The reasons for this ongoing diaspora are several. First, regional, personal, and ideological cleavages within parties were aggravated by the sensitive work of the ANC, leading legislators to express dissatisfaction with their parties and to form new ones. The PSDB was the most important new party born of the constitutional strife. Second, the first direct presidential election in twenty-nine years, held in two rounds in November and December 1989,

Table 4.2 Party affiliations of ex-ARENA/PDS legislators, February 1987 and November 1989[a]

Party[b]	Number of Ex-*arenistas*, February 1987	Percentage of Cohort	Number of Ex-*arenistas*, November 1989	Percentage of Cohort
PFL	100	45.7	79	36.1
PMDB	71	32.4	45	20.5
PDS	33	15.1	26	11.9
PTB	5	2.3	10	4.6
PDT	5	2.3	4	1.9
PL	4	1.8	8	3.7
PDC	1	0.5	7	3.2
PRN	—	—	7	3.2
PSDB	—	—	4	1.9
PSD	—	—	1	0.5
PLP	—	—	1	0.5
PRP	—	—	1	0.5
Data unavailable	—	—	22	10.0
Deceased	—	—	4	1.9
TOTALS	219	100.0	219	100.0

SOURCES: Compiled from ANC (1987); Rodrigues (1987); Semprel (1989); congressional attendance lists; and various newspaper sources.

[a] These data refer to the 219 veterans of ARENA/PDS who were sworn in to the Constituent Assembly on February 1, 1987. The data do not reflect subsequent changes in the composition of the Assembly due to legislators' leaves of absence and their substitution by *suplentes* (alternates). The actual size of the ex-ARENA/PDS cohort fluctuated slightly because of these substitutions. The twenty-two individuals for whom party data was unavailable in November 1989 were almost all *licenciados* (on leave), most of them serving as cabinet secretaries in the federal, state, and local governments.
[b] Of the last five parties in this column, all formed after mid-1988, only two are important: the Party of Brazilian Social Democracy (PSDB: see text), and the National Reconstruction Party (PRN), created as a vehicle for the presidential candidacy of Fernando Collor de Mello in 1989. (The new PSD has nothing to do with its Vargas-era namesake.)

led to additional party realignments.[2] Third, the permissiveness of rules governing the formation of parties (see Chapter 5), combined with certain congressional rules,[3] made the creation of new party labels a rational and viable option for all politicians, not only those on the right.

With the realignments during the 1987–91 legislature, the PTB and PL doubled their number of ex-*arenistas*. The PDC went from one ARENA veteran (Siqueira Campos) in 1987 to seven in 1989. Also in 1989, Fernando Collor de Mello created his National Reconstruction Party (Partido da Reconstrução Nacional, PRN) as a personalistic vehicle for his presidential bid. The new PRN also drew many ARENA veterans: in its first year, about one third of the party's congressional delegation had, like Collor himself, supported the former military regime. In the 1990 elections—held at the conclusion of Collor's tumultuous first year in office—the PRN performed respectably well, electing forty deputies and two senators. Approximately 25 percent of these individuals were veterans of ARENA. After Collor's impeachment and resignation in 1992, the PRN virtually disappeared from the political map in 1994, electing only one federal deputy.

After Collor's resignation, there was a minor re-agglutination of sorts of the ex-ARENA cohort beginning in 1993. The rapid demise of the PRN led some politicians into the PL and PTB and others back into older, larger parties such as the PFL and PDS. Two conservative microparties previously in Collor's orbit, the PTR and PST, merged to form a new Partido Popular (PP). The PP was based largely around two figures: ex-governor Álvaro Dias of Paraná, formerly of the PMDB, and incumbent governor Joaquim Roriz of the Federal District, a Collor crony and a throwback to the paternalistic populism of the 1950s. The short-lived PP (1993–95) is surely destined to be a minor footnote in the history of Brazilian party politics, but the circumstances of its creation speak volumes about the machinations of opportunistic conservatives. Dias and Roriz achieved two things: by creating a new "party" label, they rid themselves of undesirable connotations associated

2. This was true not only because new parties were created for presidential candidacies but also because politicians were induced to switch parties by the legal requirements for access to free television time. The more representatives a party had in Congress, the more free TV time for its presidential candidate.

3. In the Brazilian Congress, parties have a right to certain resources, such as office space, telephones, secretarial assistance, chauffeurs, and so on. Party leaders have the right to speak at times when ordinary members cannot. Until reforms in the early 1990s, a party with only one member in Congress could claim all these perks for its "leadership." At one point in 1990, there were six party leaders in Congress leading only themselves, yet enjoying these advantages.

with their prior affiliations, and by increasing the size of their "party" caucus in Congress, they were essentially able to trade legislative support for
high-level positions in the executive branch. Desperate for partisan support,
the weak new president, Itamar Franco, awarded the PP the Ministry of
Agriculture in mid-1993. The PP strategy worked, and it is typical of many
of the smaller parties discussed above.

Also in mid-1993, after protracted negotiations, the PDS and PDC concluded a merger that led to the creation of the Reformist Progressive Party
(Partido Progressista Reformador, PPR). The PPR was born as the third
largest party in Congress, rivaling the PFL in size. With the merger, the PDS
leadership (firmly in control of the new PPR) gained two advantages. First,
by increasing the size of their congressional delegation, they would maximize the amount of free television time allotted to their candidate in the
1994 presidential elections. Second, with the PDS label finally laid to rest
some fourteen years after its creation, members of the PPR were free of the
most obvious link to the military era. Two years later, the PPR also absorbed the PP, and changed its name once again, to the Brazilian Progressive
Party (Partido Progressista Brasileiro, PPB). The only constant in these shifting names has been a touch of irony: from "Social Democratic" to "Progressive," the PDS and its direct descendants have always chosen names that
imply a left-of-center orientation.

A review of this confusing partisan diaspora shows that within the ex-
ARENA "family," only the PFL and the much smaller PTB and PL maintained consistent party labels through the first decade of the New Republic.
In the same period, the PRN, PDC, and PP all rose and fell. By reputation,
the closest thing to a direct successor of the old ARENA/PDS party structure
would be the new PPB, which as recently as 1993 called itself the PDS, and
which still contains most of the diehard PDS luminaries of the 1980s and
early 1990s. But on closer inspection, the PPB does not have a convincing
claim to the ARENA legacy. In 1987, 87 percent of the congressional delegation of the PDS, the third largest party in Congress, was comprised of
veteran supporters of military rule. By 1995, the now-renamed PPB was still
the third largest party in Congress, but only 31 percent of its delegation had
been in ARENA/PDS in the time of military rule. The absorption of satellite
parties, combined with the out-migration of leading politicians to the PFL
and PMDB, has drastically diminished the *arenista* quotient of the Brazilian
Progressive Party.

The data in Table 4.1 reveal the true heir of the old ARENA party: the
PFL. The PFL has consistently been the second largest party in the New

Republic, and it is astonishing that even ten years after military withdrawal, some 60 percent of the PFL congressional delegation had been active in promilitary politics. What explains this phenomenon? First, as a party, the PFL's survival skills are second to none. The party has supported each of the four postauthoritarian presidents from Sarney through Cardoso; arguably, the core leadership of the PFL—many of whom belonged to the UDN of the 1950s—has not been dislodged from power since 1964. Brazilians often joke that the PFL's motto is *Há governo? Sou a favor* ("There's a government? I support it!"). Second, one could make the converse argument that the PDS politicians who went into opposition beginning in 1985 were committing a form of political suicide (despite the occasional individual lured into a Cabinet post, by and large the PDS/PPR/PPB has either opposed the last four presidents or sat on the fence). This is a decidedly Darwinian interpretation of Brazilian political recruitment, in which progovernment clientelism serves as the mechanism of natural selection. Given two catch-all parties representing similar regions and social forces, it is likely that the politicians who remained in the state's orbit in 1985 (clustered in the PFL, and not in the PDS) would likely have higher reelection rates, and would work to maintain their access to state resources by keeping their national party squarely behind the president of the day. Without more data on individual rather than group trajectories, we are unable to say if this interpretation is correct. But if it were, we would expect the PDS/PPR/PPB, mostly in opposition after 1985, to be gradually emptied of its clientelists and reduced to a leaner, more ideological party. There is some evidence that this indeed is the case, given the loyalty to the PDS/PPR/PPB of such unreconstructed former *arenistas* as Delfim Netto, Roberto Campos, and the late Amaral Netto.

In any case, in terms of consistent access to political power, the PFL has been the greatest success story among the political parties of the New Republic, and it remains thoroughly dominated by veterans of the military regime. Arguably, neither Tancredo Neves in 1984 nor Fernando Henrique Cardoso in 1994, both principled opponents of military rule in the 1960s and 1970s, could have come to power without the PFL's support. In many ways, the role of the PFL in the New Republic is similar to that of the old PSD in the 1950s: it is a machine built to support governments. The same was true of the PFL's forerunner from 1966 to 1984, ARENA/PDS.

Regional Origins

The regional origins of the ARENA/PDS cohort follow patterns established long ago in Brazilian politics. As was true in the Second Republic and during the military regime, conservative politicians in the New Republic are still elected from the least developed regions, states, and municipalities. The desperately poor Northeast region, which was the stronghold of ARENA/PDS under authoritarian rule, remains a solid conservative base today (see Table 4.1).

The right's social base is seen more clearly if we collapse the five Brazilian regions into the "two Brazils" of social science fame. In Table 4.1, "Modern Brazil" consists of the three Southern states (Paraná, Santa Catarina, and Rio Grande do Sul) and the four heavily populated Center-South states (Rio, São Paulo, Minas Gerais, and Espírito Santo). The modern sector also includes the Federal District, which—while nominally in the Center-West—is clearly a wealthy island in a poor region: Brasília is 100 percent urbanized and has the highest per capita income of any federal unit. "Traditional Brazil" consists of the remaining states in the North, Northeast, and Center-West. In the Brazilian Congress, each of the "two Brazils" controls almost exactly half of the seats. But while former supporters of military rule won only 27 percent of the seats in "modern Brazil" in 1986, they were able to win 49 percent in the more backward regions. This pattern has continued throughout the New Republic.

The data in Table 4.1 show clearly that the former ARENA/PDS is still geographically concentrated. But what does it mean to be the "party of the Northeast" in the New Republic? It is useful to introduce some very recent social indicators to illustrate the disparity between the region where the right is strongest—the Northeast—and the region where it is normally the weakest, the Center-South. The data in Table 4.3 are drawn from the 1989 *Pesquisa Nacional por Amostra de Domicílios* (PNAD), an annual survey of households conducted by the Brazilian Census Bureau. The cross-regional comparisons are astonishing in their own right, independent of political analysis. But by juxtaposing electoral data with these figures, we can better appreciate the social environment—of utter misery—in which the Brazilian right has traditionally thrived.

In Chapter 3, I emphasized the disproportionality of political representation in Brazil, which is strikingly visible once again in Table 4.3. Because (1) the apportionment formula enhances the political importance of the less developed regions and (2) the electoral right has traditionally dominated these regions, this disproportionality magnifies the importance of the right in the political system. This observation is nothing new to students of Brazilian politics, who have long emphasized how this phenomenon benefited the right in both the Second Republic and the recent authoritarian regime

Table 4.3 Social indicators and the right in Northeast and Center-South Brazil, 1989

Indicator	Northeast Brazil	Center-South Brazil
Population	24,203,144	55,470,520
Urban (percentage)	57.3	85.9
Rural (percentage)	42.7	14.1
Employed persons earning less than 1 minimum wage[a] (percentage)	51.8	21.8
Persons earning between 10 and 20 minimum wages[b] (percentage)	1.2	4.2
Average monthly income[c]	NCz$304	NCz$753
Income distribution (percentage)		
10 percent poorest	0.6	0.7
10 percent richest	43.2	37.6
1 percent richest	20.4	16.7
Gini coefficient of income inequality	0.659	0.634
Illiteracy rate (percentage)	39.3	11.9
Persons with <1 year of formal education (percentage)	35.0	12.0
Persons with >8 years of studies (percentage)	15.5	29.2
Noncontributors to social security (percentage)	70.7	36.1
Families with 3–4 members (percentage)	36.1	44.3
with >7 members (percentage)	16.7	6.6
Homes with piped water	51.3	85.9
w/ electric lighting	68.7	95.2
w/ radio	68.8	90.2
w/ television	46.5	85.0
Share of national population (percentage)	16.8	38.4
Share of congressional seats (percentage)	31.8	32.4
Elected representatives drawn from ARENA/PDS cohort (percentage)	52.9	27.0

SOURCE: 1989 PNAD, reported in the *Jornal do Brasil,* November 15, 1990.

[a] In 1989 the minimum wage floated in a range of approximately $35–$50 per month.
[b] This is a commonly used, though imperfect, definition of middle class in Brazil.
[c] For a number of reasons I have not attempted to arrive at a dollar equivalent. The absolute values of these figures are less important than their values relative to each other.

(Soares 1973; Lamounier 1989). However, few have remarked on how this disproportionality has actually been *aggravated* in recent years (see Fig. 4.1).

A recent trend in Brazilian politics has been toward the creation of new states. Without exception, the new states created since the late 1970s (Mato Grosso do Sul in 1978, Tocantins in 1988, Amapá and Roraima in 1990) are located in the North and Center-West regions, and are backward areas with traditional, conservative politics.[4] Rodrigues (1995: 83) points out that the former federal territories plus Tocantins account for 1.3 percent of the Brazilian electorate but elect 8 percent of the Chamber of Deputies and 18.5 percent of the Senate. In their early years these states have packed the National Congress, especially the upper house, with additional right-wing politicians who have a history of supporting authoritarian rule. It is important to point out that the historical trend toward a decline of the electoral

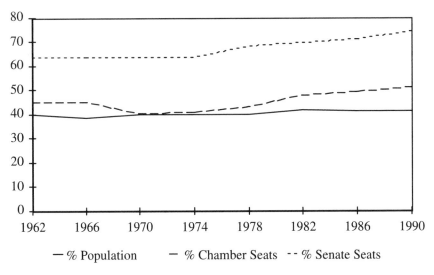

— % Population   — % Chamber Seats   - - % Senate Seats

Fig. 4.1
Overrepresentation of less-developed regions in the National Congress, 1962–1990 (North, Northeast, and Center-West)
SOURCE: Calculated by author from published congressional and census data.

4. This trend is partially offset by the granting of political representation to the Federal District (Brasília) in 1986. Because Brasília is 100 percent urbanized, has relatively high levels of education and income, and is home to large numbers of state employees, its electorate has been hospitable to progressive parties. Interestingly, in 1986 the Federal District was the *only* state or territory (of twenty-six) not to elect an ARENA/PDS veteran to Congress.

right—if confirmed in the politics of the New Republic—will be mitigated by these changes in the federal structure, which are so consistently favorable to conservative forces.

Occupational Backgrounds

Any discussion of the surviving ex-ARENA cohort should logically address their occupational and economic backgrounds. Professional and economic formation of professional politicians often prove instructive as to their class interests, policy orientations, and paths to political power. However, the available occupational data on Brazilian federal legislators are notoriously unreliable. This is partly the result of the Brazilian practice of reporting as one's "profession" whatever one studied at the university level: the holder of an undergraduate degree in economics is officially described as an *economista*, in journalism as a *jornalista*, and so on, even if the person has never worked a single day in these jobs (as an example, Fernando Collor's congressional biography from the early 1980s places him in both of these occupations). A second, more serious problem is that most Brazilian politicians—who tend to overlap considerably with the economic elite—are typically involved in two or more economic activities simultaneously. The practice of reporting multiple professions makes it difficult to discern which is actually the dominant activity. Finally, official data never describe political life as an occupation, but unofficial surveys will turn up many individuals who are quite content to describe themselves as professional *políticos*.

My 1990 survey included a question on occupation, reproduced verbatim from a Brazilian survey with the kind permission of Maria D'Alva Gil Kinzo (see Appendix B). The question asked the respondent's to name only one occupation, the "principal" one in recent years. There were 26 stimulated responses and one open-ended category for "other" occupations. Some 52 of the 246 respondents (21 percent) wrote in their own response, with "politician," "federal deputy," and so on, being the most popular by far. The other categories were collapsed into broad economic sectors and are reported in Table 4.4.

The data should be treated with considerable caution, due to the conflation of categories, the relatively small sample size, and the caveats listed above. Moreover, the interpretation of what constitutes a *funcionário público* (a government employee) is open to question. For what they are worth, the data illustrate broad similarities in the occupational profiles of the ex-ARENA and ex-opposition cohorts as of 1990; in only two of the seven categories were there statistically different patterns of employment.

Table 4.4 Occupational background of the ARENA/PDS cohort, 1990 survey

Occupation	ARENA/PDS Veterans Percentage (N)		Opposition Veterans Percentage (N)	
Owns agricultural enterprise	14.2	(15)	13.4	(17)
Owns retail enterprise	2.8	(3)	3.9	(5)
Owns industrial enterprise	9.4	(10)	4.7	(6)
Professional	31.1	(33)	45.7	(58)*
Government employee	19.8	(21)	10.2	(13)*
"Politician," etc. (not stimulated)	11.3	(12)	7.9	(10)
Others, miscellaneous	11.3	(12)	14.2	(18)
TOTALS	100.0	(106)	100.0	(127)

*Difference of means significant at .05. KEY: For question wording, see Appendix B. "Owns agricultural enterprise" combines the responses *"fazendeiro, grande proprietário," "fazendeiro, médio proprietário,"* and *"fazendeiro, pequeno proprietário."* Retail and industrial enterprises encompass equivalent categories of *comerciante* and *industrial*. Professionals include doctors, lawyers, educators, engineers, accountants, pharmacists, etc. "Government employee" is either federal or state-level public service without reference to career specialization. "Politician" denotes spontaneous responses such as *deputado* and *senador* in the open-ended option of the question; all other spontaneous responses were placed in the residual category.

Notably, both cohorts boast economic elites: 27 percent and 22 percent, respectively, say that managing their own firms in the agricultural, retail, or industrial sectors is their primary economic activity (this almost certainly underrepresents the actual degree of ownership or partial control of firms). One significant difference between the cohorts was that members of the professional classes (lawyers, professors, doctors, engineers, and so on) were considerably less likely to have belonged to ARENA/PDS during military rule. This is consistent with expectation, given that the liberal professions are key elements of urban civil society in Brazil, and that the corporative associations representing these sectors played an important role in delegitimating the military government in the late 1970s and early 1980s. It is reasonable to assume that many (though of course not all) politicians drawn from the professions continue today to represent constituencies of the urban middle class. The second statistically significant difference between the cohorts is that ex-authoritarians were nearly twice as likely (19.8 percent versus 10.2 percent) to be *funcionários públicos* than were former oppositionists. This contrast is best explained as a legacy of the near-total control of the national- and state-level executive branches by ARENA/PDS between 1966 and 1982.

Further insight can be gained by breaking down the occupational data by region. In comparing "Modern Brazil" to "Traditional Brazil," an interesting difference emerges. In the less developed areas of Brazil, some 33.8 percent of ex-*arenistas* were liberal professionals, compared to 38.9 percent of opposition veterans—not a significant difference. But in "modern" Brazil, the equivalent figures were 28.2 percent and 51.4 percent, respectively, and the difference is statistically significant ($p<.05$). The relationship between the liberal professions and the opposition cohort is sharpest in the prosperous South, where only two of eleven ex-authoritarians were drawn from the professions, compared to fifteen of the twenty-seven federal legislators who never belonged to ARENA/PDS. The Southern results are again significant at the 95 percent confidence level. These findings suggest that the relationship between the professions and the authoritarian-era cleavage is mediated by the intervening variable of level of development: the organizational capacity and political impact of the professional classes is magnified in the more urban and developed regions of Brazil, where resistance to military rule was strongest. The relative strength of professionals in the opposition cohort is the legacy of the "resurrection of civil society" in the late 1970s (O'Donnell and Schmitter 1986), in which journalists, lawyers, and intellectuals all played major roles.

In the final analysis, however, we should emphasize that the occupational data regarding Brazilian politicians continue to have many limitations. Apart from some of the expected findings concerning the role of the professional classes, the similarities between the cohorts appear to outweigh the differences—or so the imperfect data imply. It remains difficult to advance any definitive conclusions about occupational backgrounds and economic activities, due to some of the methodological difficulties described above.

Age, Experience, and Recruitment

In the first three legislatures under democracy, the mean age of the Brazilian Congress (sampled in the first year of each quadrennial session) has been remarkably stable at about 49 years. However, as Table 4.5 illustrates, the parliamentary delegations of the ARENA/PDS and ex-opposition cohorts have been aging at different speeds. The difference of mean ages of our two cohorts was already statistically significant at the 90 percent confidence level in 1987, when the average age of ARENA veterans stood at 50.5, or about 1.7 years higher than that of opposition veterans. In 1991, the mean age of ex-*arenistas* was 53.3, or about 1.8 years higher than ex-opposition-

Table 4.5 Aging of the ARENA/PDS cohort (in first year of legislative session)

Category	48th Legislature (1987–1991) Mean Age (N)	49th Legislature (1991–1995) Mean Age (N)	50th Legislature (1995–1999) Mean Age (N)
ARENA/PDS veterans	50.5 (214)	53.3 (188)	55.5 (147)
Opposition veterans	48.8 (210)	51.5 (160)	52.2 (105)
All members of Congress	48.7 (558)	49.5 (612)	49.7 (597)

NOTE: Statistical significance for difference of means between ages of veteran cohorts: in 1990, $p = .07$; in 1993, $p = .07$; in 1997, $p = .01$.

SOURCE: See notes to Table 4.1.

ists. By 1995, the average age of ex-authoritarians was up to 55.5 years, some 3.3 years higher than opposition veterans, and the difference of means was now significant at the .01 level. Although it is difficult to draw conclusions based on aggregate data, the results suggest that there may be less turnover among the ex-ARENA group (producing a more stable cohort that ages more uniformly) and more turnover among the ex-opposition group (producing a more dynamic cohort that can replenish itself with younger individuals, thus aging more slowly on an aggregate basis).

Data from the 1997 survey demonstrate also the greater levels of national political experience among the ARENA/PDS veterans. In mid-1997, the typical ex-authoritarian then in office had spent 11.1 years in the National Congress, and this experience was equal to about 20 percent of his or her life to that date. By comparison, the equivalent figures for opposition veterans were 6.9 years and 13.4 percent, respectively. The differences of means for both variables—years of national legislative experience and percentage of life spent in Congress—were statistically significant at the .001 level.

Political experience must be measured qualitatively as well as quantitatively. In Brazil, as in most Third World democracies, there is a tremendous imbalance of power between the executive and legislative branches. The precarious existence that many individuals lead in developing countries lends itself easily to what Brazilians call *imediatismo político*, or the perceived need for problems to be solved yesterday. The politicians who can most clearly make an impact on people's daily lives—whether it be a public works project, an offer of employment, or the granting of a favor—are those who occupy executive offices. Politicians know this, and so do even the most "parochial" voters: few average Brazilians can describe the functions of legislators, yet virtually all know that executives—governors and mayors in particular—have the ability to make a difference in their lives. Add to this a legacy of arbitrary rule and Congressional emasculation (see Chapter 6), and it is not difficult to see why the executive-legislative imbalance is both real and perceived.

Brazilian politicians consistently demonstrate their awareness of these "rules of the game." Perhaps the best indicator of this is how federal legislators vote with their feet every four years when municipal elections are held. In the 1988, 1992, and 1996 electoral cycles, each time more than one hundred federal legislators tried to leave Congress for a *prefeitura* (mayoralty) in their home state, often with little regard to the size or objective importance of the municipality.[5] The goal, as politicians repeatedly told me in interviews, is to win executive office and have control over a budget, no matter how small: political power in Brazil is the ability to *nomear e demitir* (hire and fire). In sharp contrast to the United States, in Brazil it is quite common to see federal senators running for mayor.

How intense is the attraction to the executive branch? In 1993, exactly half of the federal legislators surveyed agreed that it was better to hold executive than legislative office. (It is worth nothing that all respondents were legislative incumbents, and that their agreement with this statement was a tacit admission of job dissatisfaction). Not surprisingly, prior experience in the executive branch was a positive and statistically significant predictor of agreement: 56 percent of those who had served as mayor, governor, state-level cabinet officer, and so on, agreed that the executive branch was preferable, compared to 43 percent of those whose political careers were entirely in legislative life. Controlling for the authoritarian-era cleavage showed this relationship to hold only among opposition veterans; ex-*arenistas*, by contrast, preferred executive office no matter what their own career path had been. This suggested that the preferences of ex-authoritarians for executive office were uniquely intense; such a pro-executive bias has theoretical significance, as we shall see in Chapter 6. However, the 1997 survey, undertaken shortly after the passage of a watershed constitutional amendment permitting executives (notably President Fernando Henrique Cardoso) to seek immediate reelection for the first time in Brazilian history, produced radically different results. In 1997, preference for the executive branch rose to 72.8 percent among all politicians ($N = 158$), and the figure was hardly

5. For a wide-ranging study of careerism and electoral incentives under the post-1985 democracy, with special attention to this phenomenon of legislative out-migration toward mayoralties, see Samuels (1998).

any different among those with prior executive experience (73.8 percent) or ARENA experience (75.0 percent). These results suggest that the reelection amendment has made the pro-executive proclivities of Brazilian politicians more intense than ever before, and after 1997 it was no longer possible to detect the hypothesized exaggeration of this tendency on the political right.

The 1990, 1993, and 1997 surveys showed that the ex-*arenistas* have been largely successful in realizing their executive ambitions. Recall that between 1966 and 1982, the rules of the authoritarian regime mandated that virtually all important executive offices apart from the presidency (ministries, governorships, state cabinet posts, and mayoralties of the 205 most economically important cities) were de facto reserved for the ARENA/PDS party. Table 4.6 illustrates the legacy of these recruitment patterns in the first decade of democracy, focusing on respondents' experience in eight major political offices in Brazil. The expected pattern is that ARENA veterans should have more executive experience, and that opposition veterans should have more legislative experience. In 1990, this pattern was confirmed for seven of the eight positions listed on the survey, with the only exception being the office of senator (and this in fact is understandable, given that in 1990 there were still "bionic" or unelected ex-ARENA senators serving in Congress). In 1993 and 1997 the expected pattern held for five of the eight offices in each survey year. Ex-authoritarians generally have more experience in the executive branch than do other politicians, though this advantage will likely weaken over time.

It is important to note that there are vast differences in the political power and prestige of the eight offices listed in Table 4.6. Governors and ministers dwarf the other positions, largely because of the enormous potential for these office-holders to dispense patronage and cultivate political clienteles. ARENA/PDS "owned" these positions under military rule—but even in the post-1985 democracy, ex-authoritarians have continued to enjoy excellent opportunities to capture governorships (because of the large number of less developed states where their electoral bases are strong) and ministries (because of the strong ex-ARENA presence in the Sarney, Collor, and even Cardoso cabinets). Glancing at Table 4.6, one notes that ex-*arenistas* have generally been from two to three times more likely than opposition veterans to have had gubernatorial or ministerial credentials. These figures draw attention to the *qualitative* aspect of prior political experience. While it is difficult to assign quantitative weights to these positions, it is undeniable that in the context of Brazilian politics, *uma passagem pelo Executivo* (a "stint" in the executive branch) is normally "worth more" in terms of

Table 4.6 Self-reported political experience of the ARENA/PDS cohort, 1990–1997 (prior offices held by survey respondents, percentage)

Public Office	1990			1993			1997		
	ARENA/PDS Veterans	Opposition Veterans	Chi-square Sig. (p)	ARENA/PDS Veterans	Opposition Veterans	Chi-square Sig. (p)	ARENA/PDS Veterans	Opposition Veterans	Chi-square Sig. (p)
LEGISLATIVE OFFICE									
City councillor	19.4	35.1	.01	25.4	22.0	NS	23.6	18.7	NS
State deputy	40.8	44.1	NS	49.2	39.0	NS	43.6	40.0	NS
Federal deputy	84.3	91.0	NS	93.7	96.0	NS	87.3	92.0	NS
Senator	14.7	11.7	NS	17.5	18.0	NS	20.0	13.3	NS
EXECUTIVE OFFICE									
Mayor or vice-mayor	26.2	18.9	NS	30.2	19.0	.10	25.5	21.3	NS
State secretary (cabinet officer)	42.7	28.8	.05	34.9	37.0	NS	49.1	26.7	.01
Governor or vice-governor	13.6	5.4	.05	14.3	7.0	NS	14.5	8.0	NS
Minister (federal cabinet)	7.8	3.6	NS	12.7	3.0	.01	9.1	6.7	NS
N	103	111	214	63	100	163	55	75	130

NS = Not Significant

political power than even considerable time spent in legislative life. With this reservoir of executive experience, it is safe to conclude that the contemporary ARENA/PDS veterans possess influence beyond their numbers.

A notable feature of Brazilian political recruitment is the impressive degree to which the political elite manages to reproduce itself. When asked if they had any relatives who had served in one of the key political offices (listed in Table 4.6) over the past fifty years, in 1990 exactly 50 percent of all pre-1985 veterans responded affirmatively. In 1993, this percentage declined to 38.6 percent, but in 1997 it had climbed back to 49.1 percent. In all three surveys, the ex-authoritarian cohort was more clearly drawn from the traditional political elite: the percentage of ARENA veterans claiming politically successful relatives went from 57.1 percent to 51.1 percent to 59.0 percent, while among other opposition veterans the equivalent figures were 46.0 percent, 33.0 percent, and 43.8 percent (Table 4.7). While it is premature to draw definitive conclusions, the data do support the impressions of many observers that the New Republic is having a democratizing effect on national political recruitment: the incorporation of legislators from nontraditional backgrounds such as trade unionists, ecologists, Protestant fundamentalists, and members of women's and social movements have made the membership of the Brazilian Congress more diverse than ever before. The data also suggest that the ARENA/PDS cohort, with its firmer grounding in the traditional political elite, is presently immune to these diversifying trends—but the aging and diminution of the authoritarian cohort portend that the overall democratization of Brazilian political recruitment will accelerate as the ARENA/PDS veterans disappear.

Ideology and the Postauthoritarian Right: The *Direita Envergonhada*

When we turn to the question of political ideology we touch on one of the most interesting aspects of the ARENA/PDS veterans and of the Brazilian

Table 4.7 Family political tradition

Q. "Has any relative of yours held one of the offices above [see Table 4.6] in the past 50 years?" (percent and number responding yes)

Survey Year	ARENA/PDS Veterans Percentage (N)	Opposition Veterans Percentage (N)	All Veterans Percentage (N)	Chi-square Sig. (p)
1990	57.1 (70)	46.0 (124)	50.0 (194)	NS
1993	51.1 (45)	33.0 (100)	38.6 (145)	.05
1997	59.0 (39)	43.8 (73)	49.1 (112)	NS

NS = Not Significant

political system in general. Much of my discussion here could be summarized in the following sentence, which states a rule well known to all players in the game of Brazilian politics. The right does not admit that it is the right. The right has a bad name in Brazil. This was true long before 1985 or even 1964, according to elite interviewees. Throughout Brazilian history, conservatism has been linked to opposition to social change and the redistribution of income in a country that desperately needs both. In the twentieth century, the rise of socialism, and later and more important, of populism, constituted major challenges to conservatism and those who dared to defend it. In the past fifty years, conservatism has been linked both to fascism, whose spectacular defeat in World War II was a factor in Vargas' downfall, and to post-1964 military authoritarianism, which suspended elections and civil liberties and engaged in gross violations of basic human rights. ("We were associated with the *gorilas da Revolução*," a former ARENA politician complained to me.) Twenty-one years of military dictatorship, in which rightist civilian politicians were visibly complicit, eroded the appeal of conservative political ideologies, as did the economic crisis of the early 1980s. By the time of the democratic transition in 1985, few politicians were willing to defend the record of military government, and fewer still would publicly declare themselves to be on the right.

In a nutshell, the right was widely perceived as antidemocratic. It is important to recall that PDS opposition to the *Diretas Já* movement and the Dante de Oliveira Amendment in 1984 reinforced this impression. In the 1986 election campaign it was widely believed that voters would seek revenge on the PDS deputies who had torpedoed the proposal for direct presidential elections. There is evidence that such revenge actually took place: on April 25, 1984, PDS deputies voted 76 percent against the Dante de Oliveira Amendment and 24 percent for it. But of the fifty-three deputies who voted that day and managed to be reelected to Congress in 1986, the proportions are inverted: 68 percent supported direct elections, and only 30 percent were opposed. As one student of Brazilian conservatism wrote in the aftermath of the 1986 elections, "In the Brazil of the democratic transition, for politicians who depend on winning votes, a rational cost-benefit analysis suggests that it is not very advisable to confess to being on the right" (Pierucci 1987: 38).

Pierucci refers to the phenomenon known in the New Republic as the *direita envergonhada* (literally, the "abashed right"), meaning political conservatives who do not wish to identify themselves as such (M. Souza 1989). This phenomenon was detailed empirically in Leôncio Martins Rodrigues' excellent book on the membership of the Constituent Assembly (Rodrigues 1987). When Rodrigues asked 428 federal deputies to classify themselves ideologically on a five-point scale, he found that not a single deputy would accept the label "radical right," and that only 6 percent called themselves moderate or center-right. The rest of the deputies claimed to be of the center (37 percent), center-left (52 percent), and radical left (5 percent) (Rodrigues 1987: 97). Another survey conducted by the newspaper *Folha de São Paulo*, which used almost the same categories as Rodrigues, obtained the same results: again, only 6 percent of the ANC members would classify themselves as right of center. These findings led Rodrigues to comment wryly that "judging by the political self-definition of the deputies, Brazil is a country without a right" (ibid., 99).

There is ample empirical evidence of the existence of the *direita envergonhada*, and impressionistic evidence abounds as well. In observing elections in the early years of the New Republic, it was clear that (with a few notable exceptions) most right-of-center politicians went out of their way to avoid labeling themselves conservatives and to contest journalistic accounts that did so. Though I am unaware of any systematic documentation of this, observation of political marketing strategies also indicates that it is quite common for candidates of conservative parties to omit their party label from their campaign literature and advertising. This generalization might be skewed by my greater familiarity with the large urban centers, where conservative parties tend to do poorly in elections. In 1987, a voter in Brasília tried to explain the *direita envergonhada* to me by remarking of the candidates: "If they don't say what party they are, they're usually PFL."

Ideological self-classifications—a favorite question of survey research—should be interpreted with caution in cross-national analyses, because elite political culture, discourse, and nomenclature vary tremendously across national contexts. However, left-right self-placement does have the virtue of documenting some peculiarities of Brazilian elite culture, of which the *direita envergonhada* is clearly such an important facet. As far as labels go, both left and right tend to be shunned by politicians, though left is still far more desirable than anything right of center. In contemporary Brazilian political society, the designation *centro* is widely understood as a euphemism for conservatism. The *direita envergonhada* commonly seeks refuge in this "center," meaning that only a handful of individuals constitute the *direita assumida* (the openly right wing).

Reflecting this "right flight," the number of unabashed conservatives of political importance in the New Republic is extremely small. Some prominent names are those of Roberto Campos, the former planning minister for Castello Branco and the high priest of free-market economics in Brazil; the late Roberto Cardoso Alves, a close Sarney ally who ironically was stripped of his political rights by the military regime; Ronaldo Caiado, scion of a wealthy landowning family and former president of the Rural Democratic Union, the anti-agrarian reform lobby; Jarbas Passarinho, a retired colonel who was a minister in three military governments and in Collor's administration; Jair Bolsonaro, a hardline spokesman for military prerogatives, and the unofficial voice of enlisted men and their families; and the late Amaral Netto, a self-proclaimed "Shiite of the Right" whose one-note samba was the restoration of the death penalty.[6] Once again, this is a partial list of well-known politicians who are or were *openly* right-wing. Because of the near extinction of this species, in the New Republic it became commonplace for progressive politicians to issue backhanded compliments to the *direita assumida*, paying them grudging respect and praising them for their rare honesty in public life.

In the cafeteria of Brazilian politics, no one wants to sit at the table reserved for the right. But there never seem to be enough seats at the most popular table, that of the ubiquitous "center-left." These impressions about the undesirability of rightist images and the desirability of progressive images are borne out in data from the 1990 survey. When asked to place their party on an ten-point ideological scale, members consistently placed their own party to the left of where non-members else placed it. This was true *for all of the thirteen parties* in this survey of more than two hundred legislators. (This was true even for a party like the ultraradical, Albanian-line PC do B, whose two respondents apparently wanted to be viewed as even more Stalinist than the rest of the Congress thought them to be.) No better evidence exists of the biases at work among the political class in Brazil, which evidently views moderate leftism as the safest, most vote-maximizing political station, and rejects an image of conservatism as a political albatross to be avoided at all costs.

6. The eccentric Enéas Carneiro of PRONA (Party for the Rebuilding of National Order), a presidential candidate in 1989 and the surprising third-place finisher in 1994, is commonly described by the media as being of the far right. This is understandable, given that his rhetoric is replete with fascist-sounding calls for the imposition of a clearly authoritarian form of "order." However, his discourse also contains significant elements of nationalism, populism, personalism, as well as a peculiar strain of unabashedly elitist positivism. Given his outlandish cult of personality and his tendency toward paranoia and conspiracy-mongering, I would not classify Enéas as a "rightist," but would rather keep him in the special niche he has so ingeniously carved out for himself.

The discrepancy between the desired and actual images of the contemporary Brazilian right is examined in Table 4.8, which presents some indicators of political ideology among the Constituent Assembly (ANC) membership. Two indicators report left-right placement by the legislators themselves (Rodrigues' survey and my own), and two others are independent assessments. The first is by a team of journalists from the prestigious *Folha de São Paulo*, which used a reputational approach to classify politicians; the second is drawn from a well-known study of ANC voting records on critical social and labor reforms compiled by DIAP, a lobby of major labor unions. For a number of reasons, these data must be used cautiously, and the measurements they yield are not strictly comparable to one another.[7] But they are interesting in that they present more evidence of the

Table 4.8 Left-right classifications of the ANC membership, 48th Legislature, 1987–1991

Survey	ARENA/PDS Veterans (A)	Opposition Veterans (B)	Mean Score For All Legislators (C)	Deviation of Ex-ARENA/PDS From Mean (as Percentage of Mean) [(A-C)/C]
SELF-CLASSIFICATIONS				
Rodrigues 1987 (deputies only)[a]	3.23	3.76	3.56	9.3 rightward
Author's survey, 1990[b]	5.21	3.69	4.42	17.9 rightward
INDEPENDENT CLASSIFICATIONS				
Folha de S. Paulo, 1987[c]	2.12	3.43	2.93	27.6 rightward
DIAP, 1988[d]	3.04	6.18	4.98	39.0 rightward

[a] On a 5-point scale where 1 equals "radical right," 2 equals "center-right," 3 equals "center," 4 equals "center-left," and 5 equals "radical left" (Rodrigues 1987).
[b] On a 10-point scale where 1 equals "left," 5 equals "center," and 10 equals "right" (see Appendix B).
[c] On a 5-point scale where 1 equals "right," 2 equals "center-right," 3 equals "center," 4 equals "center-left," and 5 equals "left" (*Folha de São Paulo*, January 19, 1987).
[d] On a scale of 0 (least favorable) to 10 (most favorable) used by DIAP (*Departamento Intersindical de Assessoria Parlamentar*) to "grade" legislators' ANC voting records on issues of interest to workers (DIAP 1988).

7. The *Folha* journalists, like most political journalists, are of course not bias-free. Likewise, the votes selected for analysis by DIAP reflect the interests of that organization, which is admirably nonpartisan but whose agenda overlaps with that of the left. The indicators produced by the *Folha* and DIAP are also markedly different in that one attempts to measure attitudes and the other behavior.

direita envergonhada: the independent classifications place the ARENA/ PDS veterans far to the right of where they would like to place themselves. For example, the Rodrigues (1987) survey and the *Folha* classification, which used similar intervals (see notes to Table 4.8), yielded wildly different mean scores for the ex-*arenistas*: 3.23 and 2.12, respectively. For both of these scales the "center" position is 3. Therefore, Rodrigues' data showed that in 1987, the typical ARENA/PDS veteran considered himself/herself to occupy a political position that was actually *left* of center. In light of this *direita envergonhada*—this "right flight" in which ex-*arenistas* seek legitimacy by claiming a political space in the center or even to the left of it—it is probably safe to say that the democratic transition has rendered the *centro* a meaningless concept in Brazilian politics.

A study by Kinzo (1989) of the political parties in the ANC also addressed the issue of ideology. Kinzo studied roll-call voting behavior to compile composite partisan indexes of nationalism, support for the Sarney government, "democraticness," and conservatism. The conservatism index incorporated votes on such issues as agrarian reform, labor legislation reform, and property rights (Kinzo 1989: 117–18). She found the PFL to be the most conservative party, slightly ahead of the PDS, and followed by the PL, PDC, and PTB. Not surprisingly, there is considerable overlap between a party's ranking on Kinzo's scale and its share of the ex-*arenistas* serving in the ANC. The three most conservative parties (PFL, PDS, and PL) are also the parties with the greatest proportion of former supporters of the military regime (Table 4.10).

These data are presented here to demonstrate that despite the uncon-

Table 4.9 Left-right classifications of the 49th Legislature, 1991–1995

Survey	ARENA/PDS Veterans (A)	Opposition Veterans (B)	Mean Score For All Legislators (C)	Deviation of Ex-ARENA/PDS From Mean (as Percentage of Mean) [(A-C)/C]
SELF-CLASSIFICATIONS				
Author's survey, 1993[a]	5.33	3.90	4.49	18.7 rightward
DIAP 1993[b]	2.88	1.98	2.28	26.3 rightward

[a] On a 10-point scale where 1 equals "left," 5 equals "center," and 10 equals "right" (see Appendix B).
[b] On a 5-point scale where 1 equals "left," 2 equals "center-left," 3 equals "center," 4 equals "center-right," and 5 equals "right" (DIAP 1993).

Table 4.10 Conservatism and ARENA/PDS successor parties in the ANC, 1987–1988

Party[a]	Number of Constituintes in February 1987 (A)	Number of Former Members of ARENA/PDS (B)	Percentage Ex-*arenista* Membership (B/A)	Ranking in Percentage of Ex-*arenista* Membership	Ranking in Kinzo's Conservatism Index, 1987–88
PDS	37	33	89.2	1	2
PFL	134	100	74.6	2	1
PL	7	4	57.1	3	3
PTB	19	5	26.3	4	5
PMDB	305	71	23.3	5	6
PDT	26	5	19.2	6	7
PDC	6	1	16.7	7	4
PT	16	—	—	—	—
PCB/PC do B	6	—	—	—	—
PSB	1	—	—	—	—
Others	2	—	—	—	—
TOTALS	559	219	39.2	—	—

Sources: Kinzo (1989) and sources listed in Table 4.2.

[a] Parties are ranked according to the percentage of former ARENA/PDS politicians in their delegations to the National Constituent Assembly on February 1, 1987. Data correspond to Table 4.2 but not exactly to Table 4.1 (see notes to Table 4.1). The PTB and PDC parties have no relationship to their namesakes in the Second Republic.

ventional approach to the Brazilian right used in this study—an approach that does not rely on an a priori definition of the right based on ideological nor sociological factors, but instead is experiential, being based on the past commitment to a nondemocratic regime by a cohort of politicians—there is in fact considerable overlap between my operational definition and a more traditional definition based on political conservatism. While in the following chapters I will focus on these politicians' commitment to democratic institutions rather than on their allegiance to conservative ideology, it is well to recall that, obfuscation aside, these politicians cluster around one pole of the political spectrum. Despite its members' frequent protestations to the contrary, the ARENA/PDS cohort is of the right.

Conclusions

In the Brazil of the 1990s, an examination of the backgrounds of political elites, in this case federal legislators, shows the old ARENA/PDS party to be alive and well. Although the veterans of ARENA/PDS are dispersed into a number of different political parties, they continue to impart to Brazilian politics much of the flavor of the old authoritarian coalition. They are elites, both socially and politically; they represent the least developed areas of Brazil, drawing their electoral strength from regions where the levels of political information are low and the indicators of social misery are high; and they are politically conservative, though they engage in frequent ideological obfuscation.

Throughout this study I have remarked on the conservative nature of the Brazilian process of democratization. The fact that so many former *arenistas* were successfully propelled into the New Republic is one of the most significant legacies of the 1964–85 military regime. Their presence in democratic institutions has been established in this chapter; it is to their attitudes and behavior that we shall now turn, in the two subsequent chapters.

The Right in the Party System   5

Politicians Against Institutions

Introduction

The political party system in postauthoritarian Brazil offers an excellent case study with which to explore the interplay of democratization, political continuities, and institutional design. The reason for this is the notorious historical weakness of Brazilian parties, which is commonly cited as a handicap of Brazilian political development (Lamounier and Meneguello 1986; Mainwaring 1995, 1999).

The extraordinary fragility of political parties was familiar to both practitioners and students of Brazilian politics long before the advent of democracy in 1985. However, in the New Republic, calls for the building of stronger and more representative parties have been steadily mounting. The widespread perception has been that for democracy to succeed in Brazil, the country needs to make up some institutional ground. Certain contrasts are illuminating. Party underdevelopment is striking in light of the level of Brazil's socioeconomic development (Mainwaring 1992–93: 677), which until the 1980s was the envy of Latin America and the entire Third World. The weakness of parties also presents a sharp contrast to the growing organizational density of Brazilian civil society. Independent political mobilization has exploded over the past fifteen years, leading to a rich fabric of social movements, trade unions, grassroots religious communities, and NGOs, yet political parties continue to lag behind.

Political parties have proved so ephemeral in Brazil that their study is increasingly restricted to those with good retention of dates, abbreviations, and numbers. As Lamounier and Meneguello (1986) have stressed, even party *systems* have been short-lived—there have been three distinct party configurations since 1979. Furthermore, electoral rules, which to a great extent determine the number and cohesion of parties in the political system, have also changed frequently and remain notoriously arcane (in Brazilian practice, rarely are any two elective offices filled or governed by the same set of rules). Quite clearly, these discontinuities pose serious obstacles to the sustainability of democracy—or, for that matter, of any stable regime—in Brazil. They also present challenges to systematic political analysis. However, because the intent of this study is to trace the behavior of a certain cohort of politicians over time, it is necessary to confront the institutional setting of Brazilian representation. The party and electoral systems comprise the environment in which politicians work, interact, and compete with one another, as well as the context in which they relate to citizens and voters. Under conditions of democracy, it is simply impossible to study politicians in isolation of the formal institutional environment in which they are embedded.

This chapter examines the attitudes and behavior of ARENA/PDS veterans vis-à-vis the party and electoral systems in the New Republic. The primary emphasis is on the potential for institutionalization of parties; but since parties cannot be discussed without some reference to the legal-institutional framework governing elections, the party and electoral systems are taken together and understood as constituting the "representation regime" (Schmitter 1992). The analytical perspective employed here emphasizes the importance of political parties to the consolidation of democracy. Parties exist in almost all modern political systems, and exercise a bewildering panoply of functions within them. But under democracy there are several aspects of parties that assume special importance: the structuring of electoral choices, the performance of the representative function, and the promotion of political accountability. In these ways, parties can provide the linkages between elites and masses, or between the state and civil society, which are so critical to citizen assessment of the political order and therefore to democratic legitimacy. It is from this institution-building perspective that the performance of professional politicians is appraised. In 1985 it fell to the entire Brazilian political class to build a coherent system of competition and representation that would significantly advance the process of democratic consolidation. Nearly fifteen years later, most observers would concur that a crucial window for potential institution building was poorly exploited; democracy continues, but a vigorous and consolidated party system has yet to be realized.

This chapter also examines the relationship between authoritarian legacies and the failed institutionalization of parties in the early years of the New Republic. Although the ARENA/PDS cohort was not solely responsible for antiparty outcomes, its presence was a permissive cause for weak party institutionalization, and its weaker commitment to institution building colored early debates on party system reform and helped solidify the antiparty environment of the post-1985 democracy. The orientation of ARENA veterans against early reform efforts might well have been predicted before democracy even began, given their peculiar institutional trajectory under military tutelage in the 1960s and 1970s. However, by the early 1990s, institutional deadlock and economic crisis led to an attitudinal sea change within the entire political class, and the evolution of orientations toward strong parties was most pronounced within the ARENA/PDS cohort. Although attitudinal change holds out some promise for the reshaping of party life, meaningful reforms have been difficult to achieve—a result both of political process factors and of the pre-existing institutional malaise itself.

After a brief review of the historical legacy of party weakness in Brazil, this chapter examines party life under authoritarian rule between 1964 and 1985. The experience of ARENA and MDB—the two parties created by the military government—is essential to the analysis. ARENA's internal structure, its relations with the armed forces, and its performance in elections all helped to shape the attitudes and behavior of individual rightist politicians toward the party and electoral systems under the subsequent democratic regime. The next subject is the critical juncture presented by the National Constituent Assembly of 1987–88. The constitutional convention held out the opportunity for significant party and electoral reform, an opportunity that was largely squandered, due in part to the actions of the right. Subsequent sections discuss the right in the party system in the post-ANC period, reviewing the results of the survey questionnaires and of interviews with present and former ARENA/PDS politicians. A concluding section distills this material and offers some reflections on the interrelationships among the right, parties, and political democracy in contemporary Brazil.

The Legacy of Party Weakness in Brazil

In recent years, students of Brazilian politics have produced an impressive literature on parties.[1] An exhaustive overview of the scholarly literature is

---

1. For general works, see Souza (1976) and Lamounier and Meneguello (1986). On the 1946–64 regime, see Benevides (1981), Hippolito (1985), Soares (1973), Lima Júnior (1983), and Lavareda (1991). On the authoritarian period of 1964–85, see Cardoso and Lamounier (1978), Jenks (1979), Kinzo (1988), and Lamounier (1989). For works on the New Republic,

not necessary, yet it is important to review some of the major perspectives that have been brought to bear in the study of Brazilian parties. Generalizing broadly, one could say that explanations of Brazilian party weakness have revolved around one or more of the following factors: the state, federalism, clientelism, authoritarianism/military intervention, and the electoral system. In reviewing these perspectives, it is clear that many of them overlap or are strongly complementary.

The Role of the State. In a pioneering study, Maria do Campo Campello de Souza (1976) drew on earlier social science contributions that stressed the enormous role of the state in Brazilian political development.[2] Souza viewed the state, principally in its post-Vargas corporatist form, as intimately intertwined with the creation and sustenance of modern political parties. In reviewing the preexisting literature on Brazilian parties, Souza noted that most analyses had emphasized the clientelistic nature of these institutions, but had done so only in a "normative" way that failed to grasp the organic link between the state and parties. One of her innovations was to cast clientelism not as a defect of political culture or a reflection of class domination, but as a distinctly *political* phenomenon related to the institutional viability of parties. In Souza's words: "[W]e cease to see view 'clientelism' as a specific characteristic of Brazilian politics, or even as a 'stage' of development, and understand it instead as a mode of control over political resources and of their utilization by political organizations (in this case, parties) which seek, in this way, to generate power for themselves and to consolidate themselves as institutions" (1976: 35). The second of her innovations was to point to the differential development of parties and the state apparatus—in other words, to stress the importance of the "timing" of the crystallization of state and societal institutions. In Brazil, Souza argued, "the existence of a centralized state structure *before* the advent of a party system constitutes, in and of itself, an obstacle to institutionalization [of parties] and a stimulus to clientelistic politics" (36). Souza's analysis remains convincing: her emphasis on the close relationship between the state and parties has influenced much subsequent work on party organization in Brazil.

Federalism. In his 1948 dissertation on the subject of *coronelismo*, Victor Nunes Leal (1977) presented the first systematic study of relations among the three levels of government in Brazil—federal, state, and *munici-*

---

see Lamounier (1990, 1991), Kinzo (1993), Lima Júnior (1990, 1993), Nicolau (1995), and Mainwaring (1999).

2. The seminal work in this area is by Raymundo Faoro (1958).

pio—and their effects on parties and competition. Leal's point of departure was the Old Republic (1889–1930) and its famous "politics of the governors." In this period, "national" politics, in the sense of the post-Vargas era, did not exist in Brazil. Gubernatorial powers were at their peak, and the municipalities of the interior were so weakened that no rural political boss could come to power who did not "conform politically to the ruling groups in the state" (Leal 1977: 132). Because all factions in any given municipality were continually struggling for the favors of the state government, the governor could easily pick his preferred lieutenant in each rural area. At the same time, the out-of-favor local faction would continue to try to gain the good will of the state elites. "The position of the local leader in opposition is so uncomfortable that, as a general rule, he only remains in opposition when he is unable to attach himself to the government" (ibid., 19). Thus resulted the "exaggeratedly pro-government character of state and federal representation" in Brazil (131).

Leal's analysis of *coronelismo* drew heavily on two factors: the traditional social structure of the Brazilian interior and the unequal relationships among the three levels of government. Leal made much of the fact that in the Old Republic, formal representative democracy was "superimposed" upon this "inadequate" structure.[3] Political democracy and *coronelismo* combined with federalism led to a proliferation of weak, nonprogrammatic parties oriented only toward the necessities of local politics. Many students of Brazilian politics would argue that these phenomena are still visible today. Leal's observation is particularly suggestive: "Anyone who observed the multiplicity of alliances made in the last state and municipal elections could not fail to conclude that our parties are little more than labels or pegs on which to hang the legal and technical exigencies of the electoral process" (1977: 132). This was as true of the 1998 elections as it was of the 1946 contests, and this continuity has led more recent analysts (Lamounier and Meneguello 1986; Mainwaring 1999) to cite the ongoing importance of federalism to the fragmentation and fragility of Brazilian political parties.

Clientelism. Political scientists, sociologists, and anthropologists have long stressed the importance of patron-client relationships in Brazilian social and political life.[4] These networks were intertwined with oligarchic fac-

3. Cammack (1982) disputed the importance of this point, arguing that the minimal levels of political participation in the Old Republic tend to to deflate Leal's claims about the macropolitical relevance of *coronelismo*.
4. Among the many works, see Flynn (1974), Hutchinson (1966), Cintra (1979), Da-Matta (1991), Leal (1977), Mainwaring (1991a), Weyland (1996a), and Nunes and Geddes (1987).

tionalism and *coronelismo* in the Old Republic, and with the local protoparties of the day. But clientelism was also present at the creation of modern Brazilian parties upon the demise of the Estado Novo in 1945. Vargas's twin creations, the PSD and the PTB, were conscious efforts to preserve the extensive patronage networks that he had constructed over the course of his fifteen-year dictatorship. Generalizing broadly, the PSD was given to local oligarchs to sustain a rural clientele, and the PTB overlapped with the corporatist union structure that organized urban workers. The PSD and the PTB were innovations in that they were the first national political parties in Brazil; however, the resilience of patronage politics meant that the Vargas parties were still not able to crowd out rival clientelistic machines in the most important states, such as Adhemar de Barros's PSP in São Paulo and Artur Bernardes's PR in Minas Gerais. The main party of the anti-Vargas oligarchy, the UDN, was less identified with clientelism than its principal competitors, though the subsequent trajectory of its leaders would seem to indicate that this was due less to a rejection of traditional political practices than to the party's infrequent access to state power.[5] The post-1945 parties were integrated with little difficulty into the preexisting environment of personalism and patronage, and these phenomena in turn fragmented the parties and gradually increased their number. Hence, Souza's observation that early analyses of Brazilian parties focused heavily on the pervasiveness of clientelism.

Recently the clientelist perspective on Brazilian parties has seen a resurgence in popularity.[6] Like Souza before them, Lamounier and Meneguello (1986) attempt a more sophisticated analysis of clientelism based on rational behavior by individual politicians. They argue that two factors discussed earlier—the powerful role of the state in Brazil and the federal organization of the country—have historically combined in a way that makes politicians value their access to state resources more than their allegiance to political organizations or parties.

The federal structure and the financial preponderance of the central power force professional politicians to consider above all their role as *procuradores* for their respective states and municipalities. . . . The

5. Hippolito (1981) characterized the contradiction between the UDN's antipatronage rhetoric and its clientelistic orientation in practice as one of the many "ambiguities of Brazilian liberalism." Her view is supported by Nunes and Geddes (1987).
6. See Jenks (1979, chap. 1) for a discussion of clientelism as an analytical perspective for the study of parties under authoritarian rule.

weight of the federal government in the economy, and the enlargement of its strategic role as a result of development projects and industrialization, produce the same effect . . . [and] the dominance of the executive branch over the legislative branch, at all levels of government, pulverizes the [party] system even more and stimulates political individualism. (Lamounier and Meneguello 1986: 59–60)[7]

These observations were made about the party system of the 1946–64 democratic regime, but in recent years their relevance has been increasing rather than decreasing. Indeed, several recent works have documented a secular trend toward the intensification of clientelistic political practices. Both Cammack (1982) and Diniz (1982) have demonstrated the persistence of clientelism and machine politics among both the government and opposition parties under the authoritarian regime of 1964–85. Hagopian (1996) argued that the growth of "state capitalism" under authoritarianism permitted elites to develop the kind of patronage networks that allowed them to survive, in many cases unscathed, the transition to democratic rule. Mainwaring has continued this story into the politics of the New Republic, arguing that clientelism has become more pervasive (and more destructive of political and economic stability) than ever before in the history of Brazil. The decade of the 1980s saw three developments—the interventionist Brazilian state at its zenith, a newly competitive political system, and an unprecedented explosion in the number of clients (potential voters)—that combined in a way that exacerbated older traditions such as patronage politics and the patrimonial state (Mainwaring 1999: chap. 6). This could not fail to affect the party system. Some parties, notably the PFL and the smaller right-of-center parties that supported both the Sarney and Collor governments, practiced clientelism so intensely that they appeared capable of little else.

In some countries—for example, the United States, Italy, and Chile—patronage has proven to be an effective party-building resource.[8] Yet in contemporary Brazil, clientelism is usually seen as destructive of parties. Why is Brazilian clientelism so qualitatively different? The answer lies in two related phenomena: the incentives to political individualism provided by the country's unique electoral system (see below), and the resulting weakness of party authority over politicians. Personalism, localism, and the laissez-faire attitudes that often prevail in party politics tend to make patronage

---

7. The important issue of the power asymmetry between the executive and legislative branches is discussed in the following chapter.
8. On Chile, see especially Arturo Valenzuela (1977).

politics largely an individual affair; the benefits of clientelism accrue to individual politicians, and are lost to the party as a whole. The incentives to clientelism in the New Republic have been so powerful that the traditionally fragile parties have been weakened even further (Mainwaring 1999).

Authoritarianism and Democracy. Brazil's swings between variants of authoritarian and democratic rule have clearly obstructed the institutionalization of parties. This is perhaps such an obvious point that few analysts have chosen to dwell on it. But it is necessary to recall that all regime transformations in Brazil over the past half century have also entailed a fundamental restructuring of the party system. Lamounier and Meneguello have insisted on this point: there have been seven distinct party systems since Brazilian independence in 1822 and four since 1945. This would reveal an average "life span" for Brazilian party systems of around twenty-five years, but one that has declined to only about thirteen years since the end of the Estado Novo. The authors assert that "the shifts from one [party] system to another were always mediated by the coercive intervention of the central power, old or new. There can be no doubt that these interventions are one of the causes (although they may also be a consequence) of party instability" (1986: 20–21). Note that an emphasis on swings from authoritarianism to democracy does not necessarily explain the weakness of any *single* party system (although there are strong theoretical reasons why it could), but rather highlights the discontinuities between and among Brazilian party systems.

The Electoral System. No discussion of Brazilian party weakness could be complete without reference to the country's highly unusual electoral system. As mentioned earlier, in Brazil nearly every elective office is governed by a different set of selection procedures, incorporating elements from both the majoritarian and proportional traditions of representation. A complete overview of the electoral system is not possible here, but there are at least two elements of the existing code that exercise devastatingly corrosive effects on political parties.[9] The first is the system of preference voting used in the electoral contests governed by proportional representation (PR), which are those for the federal and state legislatures. Under the unusual Brazilian variant of preference voting, parties have no control and voters exercise absolute authority over the intraparty ranking of candidates. In other words, there is no "party list" of candidates in the PR contests but

---

9. There are many other elements of the electoral system that have pernicious effects on parties, but which will not be discussed here. For a complete review, see Mainwaring (1991b).

rather an "open list" in which voters choose their preferred candidate by name.[10] The ultimate effect of this system is to encourage fierce struggles not only among different parties but also among the PR candidates from within the same party. This internal competition is clearly destructive of party cohesiveness (Ames 1995a).

A second feature of the Brazilian electoral system inhibiting party development is the weak loyalty of politicians to their parties, as measured by the frequency with which they change party labels. While under the 1946–64 democratic regime individuals were clearly more important than their party labels, the practice of party-switching was temporarily curtailed by authoritarian-era legislation. With the advent of the New Republic in 1985, rules governing party loyalty were immediately relaxed, and the game of musical chairs began once again, quickly reaching unprecedented levels. Approximately one in three members of Congress changed parties during each of the first three legislative sessions under democracy (1987–99). The absence of any rules discouraging this practice makes it difficult for parties to have any control over their members, or for voters to expect a reasonably structured choice at election time. This is only one example of an electoral code that maximizes the autonomy of individual politicians at the expense of parties. There are many others.

To raise these factors in the study of Brazilian parties is to emphasize the "political consequences of electoral laws" (Rae 1967). However, Mainwaring (1991b) is correct in pointing out that electoral laws must not be conceived of solely as independent variables—the laws themselves are the results of strategic choices by politicians. In Brazil, politicians have consistently opted for what Lamounier and Meneguello (1986) term "permissive" electoral legislation that is inimical to party-building. In the late 1980s, when the Brazilian political class became "self-governing" for the first time in a quarter century, the ARENA/PDS cohort exhibited this tendency more clearly than other factions of the political class.

The Static Nature of Brazilian Party Underdevelopment. The powerful role of the state, the fragmenting effects of federalism, the strongly individualistic strain of clientelism, the permissive nature of electoral laws, and the

10. The term "open list" is somewhat misleading, because voters see no list at all. Brazilian ballots do not present the names of candidates for PR elections. It is the responsibility of the voter to know the name or number of his or her preferred candidate and write it on the ballot. Because parties are permitted to present more candidates than the number of seats available, the number of candidates in PR elections is staggering, and the entire "list" of candidate names is usually known only to officials of the electoral justice.

tendency to swings between authoritarianism and democracy have combined to stifle the development of strong and programmatic national political parties in Brazil.[11] The fact that Brazilian parties have failed to overcome
these obstacles in modern times has led many observers, politicians and
scholars alike, to aver that Brazilian political culture is hostile to political
parties (M. Souza 1976: 30; Lamounier and Meneguello 1986: 10). While I
prefer not to speculate in the language of culture, I agree that the long-
standing traditions of antiparty thought and action have shaped the expectations and attitudes of contemporary Brazilian elites—and masses as
well—vis-à-vis the institutionalization of political parties. In other words,
as Lamounier and Meneguello (1986: 25) have pointed out, Brazilian party
underdevelopment can accurately be described as static or *inertial*. In their
excellent synthesis of the reasons for Brazilian party weakness, some of
which were discussed above, the authors conclude that

> [t]his group of debilitating factors has become *inertial* in light of the
> very memory of party instability, and principally because of the "ratio-
> nal" preference of politicians for party and electoral legislation which
> is permissive—in other words, compatible with their permanent quest
> for access to public resources. (Lamounier and Meneguello, 1986: 25,
> italics in original)

In one important sense, however, the current Brazilian party system
may not be static: the current party system of the New Republic has a strong
claim to be the weakest and most fragmented ever. The increase in party-
switching has already been mentioned. The number of parties represented
in the National Congress increased from five in 1983 to eleven in 1987 to
nineteen in 1991. Volatility in legislative elections averaged higher than 40
percent in the 1980s (Mainwaring 1998: 527), a rate extraordinarily high
even for Latin America (Coppedge 1995). Electoral volatility is also visible
in the extraordinary vote differentials between executive and legislative contests. The two parties that together won nearly 80 percent of the vote in the
legislative elections of 1986 (PMDB and PFL), were able to win only 6 per-

11. When generalizing about the weakness of Brazilian parties, it is important to point
out that these generalizations do not extend to the small ideological parties of the left. These
include the Brazilian Communist Party (PCB, 1922–91), the Communist Party of Brazil (PC
do B, 1961–), and the larger and more influential Workers' Party (PT, 1980–). The Democratic Labor Party (PDT, 1980–) and the Party of Brazilian Social Democracy (PSDB, 1988–)
are also more programmatic and cohesive than most parties. Still, the generalizations about
party weakness in Brazil apply well to almost all of the two dozen or so parties of political
significance in the Second Republic and the New Republic.

cent of the vote in a presidential election held in 1989; similarly, the 1994 presidential election was fought between two candidates whose parties had each won about 7 percent of the vote in the 1990 elections for the Chamber of Deputies. Party weakness is also visible in terms of organizational characteristics. Looking at a basic indicator like chronological age, the oldest of the major parties (MDB/PMDB) dates only from 1966. In the New Republic, most parties have national committees that exist only on paper. They are usually totally devoid of resources, have little or nothing to do with the financing of campaigns, and sometimes do not even maintain a headquarters in Brasília. It is little wonder that in estimating the degree of institutionalization of twelve Latin American party systems, Mainwaring and Scully (1995: 17) placed Brazil near the bottom, along with Bolivia, Ecuador, and Peru—all of which are markedly less developed in socioeconomic terms.

The further decay of an already weak party system bodes ill for the consolidation of Brazilian democracy. But before examining the party question in the New Republic, it is necessary to review the immediate antecedents of the constitutional debate by looking at the party configuration of the authoritarian period of 1964–85.

Party Life under Authoritarian Rule: The Experience of ARENA/PDS

The two-party system that existed in Brazil between 1966 and 1979 was "artificial"—that is, it resulted not from the voluntary choices of politicians but rather from forced imposition by the military hierarchy. Despite its illegitimate birth, there are several important reasons why the two-party system is worthy of study. First of all, by the standards of Brazilian party politics, this system had a relatively long life. After thirteen years and four election cycles, the two-party system had endured for nearly as long as the freely constituted party system of the 1946–64 democratic republic, and thus left a clear generational imprint on the political system. Second, upon existing class, regional, and ideological cleavages in Brazilian politics, the 1966–79 system superimposed a new cleavage: authoritarian versus democratic. To the extent that a politician's choice of ARENA or MDB reflected his or her values—rather than pragmatism, expediency, or particularistic ties, which also came into play—the politician was ordering his or her preferences for one of two political regime types. In 1965–66, a majority of the political class opted for authoritarian rule.[12] These past preferences of

___

12. I base this observation on the partisan preferences of the federal legislators and governors, then in office, who had been elected democratically in 1962. In the wake of the Second Institutional Act (AI-2) of October 1965, some 64 percent of federal legislators and 100 per-

political elites matter. The two-party system set the stage for the transition to democracy, and the historic rivalry between ARENA and MDB was the main axis of Brazilian politics through 1985. Finally, the extinct two-party system is also crucial when the unit of analysis is individual politicians. The 1966–79 two-party system was a formative experience for many. Much of the Brazilian political class was socialized or resocialized to the institutional realities of party life under authoritarianism. Without a clear understanding of the interrelationships among parties, rules, and politicians under military rule, it is impossible to understand politicians' attitudes and behavior vis-à-vis parties in the New Republic.

The competition between ARENA/PDS and MDB/PMDB dominated the politics of military rule for two decades. Generalizing broadly, between 1966 and 1984 there was a secular trend away from solid ARENA hegemony toward a more competitive system. But such a generalization glosses over the intense interplay between government and opposition, in which momentum and initiative shifted from side to side, leading to a political opening that a number of scholars have characterized as a dialectical process (Bresser Pereira 1984; Alves 1985; Smith 1987; Diniz 1990). This interplay was cyclical in that every time the opposition MDB made a significant electoral advance, the military hierarchy would change the rules of the game to maintain ARENA/PDS hegemony. The alterations in rules were known as *casuísmos*. As discussed in Chapter 3, some of the best-known examples of *casuísmos* were Castello Branco's Third Institutional Act (AI-3, February 1966), Geisel's "April Package" (April 1977), and Figueiredo's "November Package" (November 1981). The macropolitical causes and consequences of these government initiatives—which were invariably justified with democratic rhetoric, though they skewed competition to favor ARENA—have been well covered elsewhere.[13] It is not necessary here to review these issues or the outcomes of electoral contests under authoritarianism; instead, what is necessary is to understand the aspects of party life under authoritarian rule that impacted on the way politicians—that is, former ARENA/PDS politicians—understand parties and competition today.[14] These can be reduced to two somewhat overlapping categories: the internal organization of

---

cent of the state governors joined ARENA (Jenks 1979: 106–26). These figures exclude the *cassados*, those who were stripped of their political rights.

13. For details on *casuísmos*, see Fleischer (1984); for more general treatments, see Lamounier (1984) Alves (1985), and Skidmore (1988).

14. For obvious reasons, I focus on the trajectory of ARENA/PDS politicians under military rule. For a study of the MDB, see Kinzo (1988).

ARENA/PDS as a party, and the rules intended to maintain individual and collective allegiance to the military government.

The ARENA party structure. In its heyday from the mid-1960s to the late 1970s, the ARENA/PDS party was notable for its combination of external strength with internal weakness (Jenks 1979). The military's desire to retain some kind of party system after the coup of 1964 resulted in the hasty construction of a progovernment coalition. Given that the state governors wanted to retain the favor of the federal government, all those surviving the initial purges fell in line behind Castello Branco and joined ARENA; and given the powerful incentives of state-level politicians to retain the favor of the state governors, it was not difficult to set up the party in the states and *municípios*. In many states, the local and state-level directorates of the old UDN and PSD parties were simply absorbed into the new ARENA party structure. Despite the rapidity of this process, the party's sponsors and organizers could not guarantee much cohesiveness within the government coalition. There were at least three reasons why individual politicians, even while joining ARENA, had cause for antipathy toward their own new party:

1. The creation of ARENA was carried out in large part against the wishes of professional politicians. In 1964 and 1965 the politicians who had supported the military coup were organized in the National Congress as the *Bloco Parlamentar da Revolução* (BPR), a supra-party voting bloc. Such blocs are a revealing feature of Brazilian legislative politics.[15] The advantage of the BPR was that it allowed politicians in various parties (the UDN, sectors of the PSD, and smaller conservative parties) to support the Castello Branco government while maintaining their own party structures and electoral bases intact. Castello Branco's adoption of a two-party system in late 1965 gave rise to ARENA, and progovernment politicians could no longer have it both ways. Thus, the creation of ARENA was *not* voluntary. The fact that the great majority of Brazilian politicians

15. Traditionally, politicians prefer *blocos* to more formalized party or factional organization in the legislature, because *blocos* allow individual legislators to draw a clear line between national and state-level politics. Inside the informal blocs, legislators can support or oppose the federal government without altering their party affiliation in their home state, which is where real political competition takes place. Also, there are powerful incentives for party or factional leaders to act within *blocos*: they can move their parties or *grupos políticos* in and out of the *blocos* as they please, altering the balance of power for the other players. They may reap great benefits from this power capability. Finally, *blocos* allow these individuals to retain the perks and privileges that come with party leadership in Congress.

joined the party did not mean that they were satisfied with this option; it simply reflects the realities of Brazilian politics.

2. The formalization of a single progovernment party and the abolition of previously existing parties implied that the military hierarchy was insensitive to local and state party conflicts. ARENA made for strange bedfellows: in many states, rival political factions and machines found themselves eyeball to eyeball within the new party structure. For example, in the state of São Paulo, the political machines of three powerful rival bosses—Jânio Quadros, Carvalho Pinto, and Adhemar de Barros—all vied for control of the state apparatus (Jenks 1979: 110).[16] The complaints of state party bosses about this perceived insensitivity led to the military's adoption of a balloting mechanism that permitted intraparty competition—the *sublegenda*, to be described below. But it was apparent from ARENA's very beginning that the party would be an uneasy federation of state-level forces, with very little intraparty solidarity.

3. A final organizational feature of ARENA, much to the dislike of politicians, was its utter lack of autonomy. Most basic decisions on policy were made by the presidency and the military hierarchy, and communicated to the governors and to the ARENA leadership in Congress. The leadership of the party had little real power, and consisted mainly of notables who were chosen to be reliable interlocutors between the armed forces and the party rank and file. Though during the *abertura* period party leaders began to distance themselves somewhat from the government, they maintained ARENA in the authoritarian coalition right through the end of the military regime in 1985; hence, the oft-repeated observation that under authoritarianism, ARENA was the party *of* the government, but not the party *in* government. Over time, this was an increasingly uncomfortable position for the party: ARENA politicians were forced to defend government policies over which they had little control. Without overlooking the fact that politicians also benefited greatly from col-

16. Interestingly, Adhemar was *cassado* by the military regime in 1966, and then led his political group into the opposition MDB. A short time later, however, the former governor led his group back into the ranks of ARENA. His son attributes this to his father's instincts for political survival: the only way to put *adhemaristas* in positions of influence was to join ARENA, which controlled all access to state power. This episode illustrates both the continuing importance of patronage politics under authoritarianism and the heterogeneous nature of ARENA, which was described by the younger Barros as a *"saco de caranguejos"* (a sack of crabs). Interview with Adhemar de Barros Filho, Brasília, October 17, 1990.

laboration with the armed forces, it is clear that by the early 1980s, the declining legitimacy of the military regime had painted them into a tight corner (Kinzo 1993: 36–39). Just as ARENA politicians had profited from the regime's successes in the early 1970s, so they suffered from its unpopularity in the early 1980s—but the party itself had little to do with either phenomenon.

In examining the origins and trajectory of ARENA, it is apparent that some of the problems that made ARENA weak—for example, its "artificial" birth, and the difficult issue of state-level intraparty competition—should logically apply also to MDB, the opposition party. Is there any compelling reason to believe that MDB was significantly different from ARENA? It is clear that MDB would not have emerged had not AI-2 required the creation of a single opposition party. Moreover, MDB was a very heterogeneous coalition, incorporating elements as diverse as PSD oligarchs, PTB populists, and Moscow-line Communists. But it is also true that the nature of interparty competition and the absence of certain political constraints allowed MDB to develop in a very different direction from ARENA. Jenks puts it succinctly: "MDB developed more internal autonomy and democracy because it was not attached to the regime" (1979: 124). MDB was not subjected to the same constraints as ARENA, which suffered the debilitating experience of supporting a government in which had little influence—but upon which its survival depended. MDB's longtime status as an opposition party dictated an internal logic of détente and solidarity among its members. This was quite different from the logic of ARENA party life, which attempted the difficult regulation of individual and factional access to power and state resources.

These observations draw our attention to the relationship of unequal exchange between the military government and ARENA. It was always clear that ARENA would be the junior partner in the authoritarian coalition. Nevertheless, the military *needed* ARENA for three things. The first was to act as an "independent" party supporting the government, thus demonstrating the military's support within the political class and contributing to the democratic facade of the regime. The second was to serve as a vehicle for popular support. The third was to be a dependable ally, so that the military could be assured of ratification of its agenda in the Congress (another key part of the democratic facade) and enactment of its policies and programs in the states. In other words, the military's strategy depended entirely on ARENA's being a *cohesive* party—if the government party did not stick together, there would be little use in maintaining it. Thus, the military government formulated rules and institutions that were aimed at keeping ARENA together.

Rules affecting party cohesiveness and loyalty. As described above, in 1965 ARENA politicians perceived that the military government was not sufficiently sensitive to the home-state rivalries of its supporters. Therefore, the party's civilian founders pressured President Castello Branco to adopt the so-called *sublegenda* balloting mechanism (Jenks 1979: 110–12). In elections for mayor and for senator, parties could run up to three candidates for the same position. Each would run on a separate *sublegenda* representing a different faction or tendency. The most voted-for candidate within the most voted-for party (adding together all its *sublegendas*) would win. This innovation was a way to accommodate various groups within ARENA: politicians were permitted to join the party at the national level while maintaining their rivalries at the state level (Hagopian 1996: 188–92).[17] It is important to stress that the idea for the *sublegenda* originated not within the military hierarchy but in the organizing commission of ARENA itself. The *sublegenda* was an example of politicians' designing an electoral system to suit their own needs, to secure for themselves the best of both worlds.

ARENA was certainly held together by the *sublegenda* mechanism. But the most important "glue" guaranteeing party unity did not result from an ARENA suggestion: rather, it was imposed on the party by the military. I am referring here to the so-called Law of Party Fidelity, contained in the First Constitutional Amendment of 1969. The rule was imposed in the wake of the government's embarrassing Congressional defeat in the Márcio Moreira Alves affair of December 1968, the event that prompted the draconian Fifth Institutional Act (AI-5; see Chapter 6). The Law of Party Fidelity actually incorporated two different but related rules. An elected representative would lose his or her mandate if he or she (1) voted against the orders of the party leadership, or otherwise violated the directives of the party, or (2) left the party on whose ticket he or she was elected.[18] As is obvious from its stipulations, and from its introduction in the aftermath of AI-5, this law was not directed at the opposition MDB, *but rather at ARENA itself.* This

17. As such it was an effective solution for oligarchic states like Ceará, long dominated by three rival clans (of colonels Cals, Bezerra, and Távora) that all wished to join ARENA. Interview with César Cals Neto, Brasília, November 6, 1990.
18. Constitution of 1967, First Amendment (October 17, 1969), article 152, sole paragraph. The changes effected in the Constitution of 1967 were so extensive that the First Amendment is also known as the Constitution of 1969.

point is crucial, I believe, for understanding some of the present-day attitudes of ARENA/PDS veterans vis-à-vis certain forms of party institutionalization.

A comparison between two institutions governing party life, the *sublegenda* mechanism and the rule of party fidelity, is highly instructive. The institution that politicians chose of their own free will—the *sublegenda*—is one that decentralizes power, maximizes the freedom of individual politicians, and permits the "cohabitation" of strange bedfellows. The institution imposed on ARENA from without—party fidelity—is one that centralizes authority, minimizes the latitude of individuals, and promotes a strong, cohesive party organization. In other words, the Law of Party Fidelity and its attendant prohibition on party-switching were exactly the kind of institutional innovations that many would recommend today in order to reverse Brazil's long tradition of weak, undisciplined parties.[19]

The irony here is that reforms likely to strengthen parties and promote accountability under democracy were actually imposed by an authoritarian regime. More important, the fact that party-strengthening measures were directed against ARENA as a form of authoritarian control could only lead to antipathy toward the new rules, and perhaps toward the concept of party organization itself. Over the course of the authoritarian regime, this antipathy grew as ARENA suffered at the hands of the military and of the MDB, a process that finally led to the first defections from the party (the exit of the so-called Grupo Independente)[20] in 1980. Beginning in 1974, while ARENA politicians in Congress, the state assemblies, and the municipal chambers were forcibly compelled to continue ratifying the military's policies and programs, the MDB enjoyed major electoral advances. By themselves, ARENA politicians could do little to stem the opposition tide. All measures taken against the MDB by the authoritarian government (*casuísmos*, and so on) emanated from presidential strategists and not from ARENA, yet ARENA

19. I do not wish to go so far as to say that party fidelity is necessary in the Brazilian party system or for party consolidation in general: it most certainly is not. But whether one agrees with it or not, the Law of Party Fidelity put its finger on the major structural defects of modern Brazilian parties: lack of party control over elected representatives and the prevalence of party switching. As Mainwaring (1991b) has argued, politicians designed these defects, and many benefit from them. Thus, it is perhaps not surprising that in Brazil party fidelity has only existed under authoritarian rule.

20. The *Grupo Independente* was a liberal faction of ARENA/PDS that supported an early return to direct elections for executive offices. Led by former Minas Gerais governor Magalhães Pinto, this group joined PMDB moderates, led by Tancredo Neves (another former *mineiro* governor), in the formation of the short-lived Partido Popular (PP). The PP was absorbed by the PMDB in early 1982.

continued to be burned. This conflict came to a head in 1984, when forces linked to PDS presidential candidate Paulo Maluf moved to head off the rebellion of the Liberal Front, a dissident faction of the party. Maluf tried to use the Law of Party Fidelity to force all PDS delegates to the Electoral College to vote for him in the indirect presidential election rather than for the PMDB's Tancredo Neves, with whom the Liberal Front defectors had earlier sealed an alliance. In the end, Maluf's argument was rejected by the Supreme Electoral Court (which ruled that party fidelity did not apply to the Electoral College), but the episode was not forgotten by the Liberal Front delegates. It is likely that the Electoral College controversy delegitimated the institutions of party fidelity even further in the eyes of many ARENA/PDS politicians.

Cohesion via coercion. The purpose of these observations about ARENA party life has been to draw attention to what might be called the "paradox of compulsory institutionalization." On the one hand, we have the traditional mistrust by Brazilian politicians of rules and institutions limiting their personal freedom in party and electoral politics (Souza 1976; Lamounier and Meneguello 1986; Mainwaring 1991b). On the other hand, between 1969 and 1985 Brazilian parties, both in the two-party system and in the expanded system following the 1979 party reforms, were subjected to a set of rules that—had they been adopted voluntarily—would likely have corrected many of the perceived deficiencies of the parties. But these rules were *not* voluntary, they were mandatory—and one of the first actions of the Brazilian Congress after the return of democracy in 1985 was to abolish party fidelity and permit politicians once again to change parties at will. The paradox is that the introduction of party-strengthening rules by an *authoritarian* regime has made them less likely to be adopted in a *democratic* regime that might have profited from them. "Cohesion via coercion" was the dismal legacy of party life under authoritarian rule.

The Right and the Question of Party Reform in the National Constituent Assembly, 1987–1988

Under military rule between 1964 and 1985, the key institutions of Brazil's "representation regime"—the party system and the national legislature— were simultaneously redesigned and emasculated. One of the major goals of the antiauthoritarian coalition, led by the MDB/PMDB, was to hold a constitutional convention after the expected transition to democratic rule.

Many reformers believed that a new constitution would abolish the institutional framework of military rule—the so-called authoritarian debris—and permit the construction of more democratic political structures. The National Constituent Assembly (Assembléia Nacional Constituinte, or ANC) was finally realized between February 1987 and September 1988, and Brazil's current constitution (its eighth since independence) was promulgated on October 5, 1988. The experience of the ANC, in which 559 democratically elected legislators worked for twenty months to hammer out the final constitutional draft, is an excellent source of data; the ANC could accurately be described as a "laboratory" for democratic institutionalization. There are few better ways to study politicians' orientations toward representative institutions than to watch them *design* these same institutions. For this reason, this and the following chapter examine relevant roll-call voting data from the ANC data file.[21]

Before proceeding, it is necessary to note that the number of roll-call votes relating to the party system was relatively sparse in the ANC, at least when compared to the following chapter, which concerns the legislature. There are two plausible explanations for the paucity of roll-call votes on party system design. First, some of the rules and regulations governing parties and elections in Brazil fall under *lei ordinária* (federal statutes) and are not included in the constitutional text. This may surprise some readers familiar with what *is* considered constitutional material in Brazil; the ANC debated everything from faith healing to the legality of erecting fences on beachfront property. But in the case of parties and elections, Congress passes normal legislation that is continually revised and published in a dense tome known as *Legislação Eleitoral e Partidária*. The legislation serves as a set of guidelines for the Supreme Electoral Court (Tribunal Superior Eleitoral, or TSE). The TSE is the body responsible for interpreting legislation, converting the laws into *instruções* for local election boards, and then actu-

---

21. This data file was acquired from PRODASEN, the Brazilian Senate's modern computing center, in late 1990. It contains the entire set of 1021 roll-call votes in the ANC between January and September 1988. The votes indicate the legislators' positions on amendments presented to the evolving constitutional text (yes, no, abstain, or absent). Barry Ames and I worked together to read the *Diário da Assembléia Nacional Constituinte* (the equivalent of the *Congressional Record*) and create a codebook that reveals the substantive content of each vote. We reduced the size of the file by throwing out votes that were not contested, that is, in which the losing side did not win a least fifty votes. This left us with about 550 roll-calls. A number of the votes are discussed in this and the following chapter. All crosstabulations referenced in the text are significant at the .05 level or better.

ally holding the elections and counting the votes. The Constitution itself has little to do with such outcomes; its text is far more vague than that of *Legislação Eleitoral e Partidária.*[22]

A second reason for the scarcity of material on parties in the ANC is that some sectors of the convention resisted extended debate on the issue. This became clear early on in the second year of the Assembly, when one deputy introduced an amendment that would require parties to hold primary elections. The Workers' Party (PT) immediately resisted this. The PT, which controlled only 2.9 percent of the seats in the ANC, consistently opposed any explicit constitutional references to parties, such as their internal organization or their functioning in Congress (*funcionamento parlamentar*). The party was concerned that constitutional mention of such issues could establish a dangerous precedent, perhaps someday leading to German-style "thresholds" for parliamentary representation by small parties or other rules that might inhibit the PT's growth and autonomy (*Diário da Assembléia Nacional Constituinte*, March 4, 1988; hereafter abbreviated as *DANC*). The PT was typically straightforward in taking a position on this issue, but it is likely that many other sectors of the ANC were wary of a strong constitutional treatment of party representation—preferring instead to leave such questions to ordinary law, the making of which is less transparent than the very public forging of a constitution.

Despite these limitations on the data, there were at least three roll-call votes in the ANC that dealt with important issues of party and electoral reform and that reveal interesting attitudes on the part of the ARENA/PDS cohort. On the issue of party and factional organization in the legislature, the right was responsible for a change in Brazilian legislative tradition. The proposed language by the conservative coalition in the Assembly (the Centrão or "Big Center") gave formal recognition to the informal groups known as *blocos parlamentares* (supraparty blocs), of which the Centrão itself is perhaps the most outstanding recent example. *Blocos* have a long tradition in the Brazilian Congress, but never before had they been officially recognized. The Centrão's proposal gave *blocos* proportional representation on the Mesas (directing boards of the two legislative chambers) and in congressional committees, thus elevating them to the status of political par-

---

22. For example, on the subject of the "open list" variant of proportional representation discussed earlier in the chapter, the Constitution says only that federal deputies are to be elected according to "the proportional system" (Constitution of 1988, Article 45). Thus, any variant of PR would be legal according to the constitution; the actual details of the "open list" system are to be found in ordinary law.

ties. At the conclusion of the ANC, one deputy presented an amendment that would have denied this formal representation to parliamentary blocs. While supported by 72.5 percent of the legislators present, the amendment failed to pass because it fell 9 votes short of the necessary absolute majority of 280 *constituintes*. Some 45.2 percent of ex-authoritarians opposed the amendment, compared to only 12.2 percent of opposition veterans (Vote 886; Table 5.1). ARENA veterans were more than three times more likely than other members to maintain a legislative rule that is an incentive to continued party fragmentation. In the National Congress, according to the Constitution of 1988 (article 58), *blocos parlamentares* now stand equal in importance to political parties.[23]

A second roll-call vote is illustrative of the desire of politicians—in this case, the ex-authoritarians—to create or preserve electoral systems that benefit them directly. The amendment in question concerned the method by which Brazil would elect its future presidents. Traditionally, Brazil has had national direct election of the president, unlike the U.S. system of indirect election via the Electoral College. In March 1988, the ANC considered an amendment that would have instituted the so-called *voto federativo*, a method for presidential election modeled after the U.S. Electoral College. It is important to recall here that U.S. states' representation in the Electoral College is based on the size of their congressional delegations, which introduces a minor element of disproportionality into the election because each state has two senators. Thus, the less populous states are overrepresented. A Brazilian equivalent of the Electoral College would distort the principle of "one person-one vote" far more, because unlike the United States, in Brazil *both* houses of Congress use a representational formula that is not proportional to population. There is a minimum number of federal deputies per state (8) as well as a maximum (60 until 1994, and 70 thereafter). The minimum representation favors many underpopulated states. The maximum is in effect a limitation on the power of São Paulo, which in a truly proportional system would have nearly twice as many deputies as it is al-

23. Supraparty coalitions may seem a positive solution for a minority president, such as Fernando Collor de Mello (1990–92), whose National Reconstruction Party (PRN) held less than 10 percent of the seats in Congress. But the impact of blocs is sometimes negative for several reasons: they encourage an excessive number of parties in Congress, they induce clientelistic exchanges for government resources or cabinet positions between the president and leaders of electorally insignificant parties, and they are inherently unstable. Under both Sarney and Collor, the composition of the *bloco governista* changed frequently. Collor actually faced the spectacle of his own *bloco* and a rival *bloquinho* simultaneously competing for positions in his government.

Table 5.1 ANC roll-call votes on electoral and party system issues

Vote Number and Date	Content	ARENA/PDS Veterans Voting for Anti-institutional Position Percentage (N)	Opposition Veterans Voting for Anti-institutional Position Percentage (N)	Sig. (Chi-square)
No. 161, March 4, 1988	Amendment proposed the possibility of recall elections for office-holders elected in single-member districts (defeated)	85.5 (141)	46.2 (79)	<.001
No. 316, March 23, 1988	Amendment to remove direct elections for president and substitute a system modeled on the U.S. Electoral College. Would have effectively disenfranchised voters in the more populous, developed states, where the right is weak (defeated)	69.7 (129)	35.5 (59)	<.001
No. 886, August 27, 1988	Amendment to prevent the representation of "parliamentary blocs"—in addition to parties—on the Mesas (Directing Boards) and in congressional committees, which is an incentive to continued party fragmentation in the legislature (defeated)	45.2 (57)	12.2 (18)	<.001

SOURCE: PRODASEN (Centro de Processamento de Dados do Senado Federal)

lowed. Currently, São Paulo, with about 22 percent of the national population, has only 12.3 percent of the seats in Congress. Overall, the backward regions of the North and Northeast, which possess a combined 31 percent of the national population, are given 208 seats in the Chamber of Deputies, while the developed South and Southeast—having 45 percent of the population—are given only 189 seats (Carneiro 1990). The less developed, less populated states are exactly where the ARENA/PDS cohort has traditionally been strong: of the 219 ex-*arenistas* elected to the ANC, some 47 percent hailed from the Northeast, the poorest region of Brazil. These conservative politicians voted heavily for an amendment that would have deprived voters in the developed South and Southeast of an important role in presidential elections, and would have extended to the executive branch the dominance that the right has long exercised in the legislature (Vote 316). Although the amendment establishing the *voto federativo* was supported by 50.8 percent of the legislators present, it failed to win an absolute majority, and in the end the Constitution of 1988 preserved the tradition of direct popular election of the president.[24]

A third roll-call vote concerned an amendment again inspired by U.S. electoral legislation. A number of U.S. states have instituted procedures whereby voters can remove an elected official who is not performing satisfactorily: the so-called recall election. Recall elections are based on the principle that a popular mandate can be revoked by the people themselves, and thus constitute a powerful instrument of democratic accountability. In the ANC, a PMDB deputy from Bahia, Domingos Leonelli, proposed to introduce the recall election to Brazil, where the notorious lack of accountability of elected officials is perhaps the leading popular complaint against the political system (Moisés 1994). Leonelli's proposal would have made the holders of majoritarian offices (governors, senators, and mayors) subject to recall. The Assembly overwhelmingly opposed the idea (Vote 161), but what is interesting is the contrast between the ARENA/PDS cohort and the opposition veterans. While the former oppositionists gave 53.8 percent support to recall elections, the ex-authoritarians *opposed* the idea by a ratio of about six to one. This idea of recall elections is an excellent embodiment of

---

24. Ironically, the efforts of the right to place a lock on the presidency proved unnecessary in the subsequent presidential contest. The 1989 election was won by Fernando Collor de Mello, a longtime member of ARENA/PDS who hailed from the northeastern state of Alagoas, one of the smallest and poorest states in the Brazilian federation. The attempt to institute an indirect election system that would favor the ARENA/PDS cohort echoes the *casuísmos* of the 1964–85 military regime.

the normative notion of democratic "quality" discussed in Chapter 2. Quality democracy is accountable democracy, and one of the most accountability-enhancing institutions available in democratic politics is that of the recall election—an idea massively opposed by ex-*arenistas*.

These roll-call votes focus on only three aspects of the Brazilian party and electoral systems: weak accountability, party fragmentation in legislative politics, and the legacy of *casuísmos* (the institution of rules designed to favor the ARENA/PDS cohort). The roll-calls are noteworthy not because the votes of ex-*arenistas* were critical to the outcome—in fact, in these three cases they appear *not* to be decisive—but because of the attitudinal patterns they reveal. In each case, the ex-authoritarians disproportionately supported the position associated with weaker, less accountable forms of competition and representation. From an exploratory angle, the data suggest that antiparty attitudes are not distributed evenly across the Brazilian political class but rather clustered within the ARENA/PDS right.

The Right and Party Life: Legacies of Authoritarian Rule

The experience of Brazilian politicians under military rule generates interesting expectations about emerging cleavages in the postauthoritarian political class. The trajectory of ARENA/PDS members leads us to hypothesize that members of this cohort will resist institutional rules designed to produce strong, effective parties. Their socialization in 1964–85 was to a front party made up of civilian clients of the military executive, with few serious responsibilities. In contrast, politicians who resisted military rule were obligated to *utilize* the "artificial" democratic institutions of 1964–85: parties, elections, and parliament. The socialization of the cohort of politicians promoted institution-building attitudes and strategies, whereas the experience of *arenistas* discouraged such initiatives. Thus, we can expect politicians without any connection to the promilitary ARENA/PDS party structure to evince attitudes more favorable to party development in the New Republic. These hypotheses were tested by various questions in the 1990, 1993, and 1997 surveys of Congress.

A good starting point for this discussion is to examine the most basic indicator of individual commitment to parties. Do Brazilian federal legislators feel that their political party had an important role in getting them elected to Congress? It is clear from Table 5.2 that the overwhelming majority of Brazilian elected officials do *not* believe that they owe their mandate to their party. The data confirm that a reliance on personal rather than party organization is a general feature of Brazilian electoral politics. Here, consistent with expectations, we find this effect to be more pronounced among veterans of the authoritarian regime. The cleavage is statistically significant and remained stable across all three surveys.

To probe this question more deeply, legislators were given a list of alternative factors that might have influenced their election victory and were asked to use a 1-to-10 scale to assign a relative weight to each (Table 5.3). Two of the factors were institutional or organizational in nature, while the rest depended on the candidate's individual resources, personality, family name, and so on.

Table 5.3 traces eight electoral-success factors through three waves of surveys. Three of these variables ("declarations and promises," "possibilities for success," and "decline of competitors") have no a priori theoretical expectations relating to the authoritarian-era cleavage. However, for the other five variables, we should expect the right to place comparatively weaker emphasis on (1) party organization and (2) grassroots support, and comparatively greater emphasis on (3) support from economic elites, (4) benefits from familial ties, and (5) personalism, for which "charisma" is a crude proxy. Five variables across three surveys produces fifteen T-tests that have theoretical implications. We note that in fourteen cases, the differences of means have the expected polarity, and in twelve of these cases the T-tests are statistically significant. In all three surveys, ex-ARENA/PDS respondents assigned the factors relating to institutionally-based mobilization—"party organization" and "grassroots support"—a lower weight than did opposition veterans. Ex-authoritarians generally viewed candidate-centered politics or established clientele networks (especially "family name/historic loyalties") as better explanatory variables for their own electoral success.

The ex-authoritarians' lack of reliance on party organization draws our attention to the subjective distance between individual politicians and their parties. One way to gauge this distance is to subject the respondent to hypothetical cross-pressures emanating from party loyalties and local-regional loyalties. These cross-pressures are more than hypothetical: they erupt frequently in legislative life. In 1997 only, politicians were asked: "When there is a conflict between the necessities of your region and the positions of your party, do you vote most often with the party, in accordance with the needs of your region, or do you divide your votes evenly?"[25] Overall, only 32

25. I am grateful to Scott Mainwaring for permission to reproduce this survey question, which he first used in 1988. The overall frequency distribution of responses among Brazilian federal legislators was almost identical in 1988 and 1997.

Table 5.2 Perception of party role in election victory

Q. "Some legislators are elected because of their party label—in other words, because of the party's organizational strength or because of its image in public opinion. Others are elected due to their individual capacity for organization or to their personal performance (*atuação*) in politics. In your case, which was more important?"

	1990			1993			1997		
Response	ARENA/ PDS Veterans Percentage (N)	Opposition Veterans Percentage (N)	All Veterans Percentage (N)	ARENA/ PDS Veterans Percentage (N)	Opposition Veterans Percentage (N)	All Veterans Percentage (N)	ARENA/ PDS Veterans Percentage (N)	Opposition Veterans Percentage (N)	All Veterans Percentage (N)
Your party	10.6 (11)	24.8 (26)	17.3 (38)	7.9 (5)	29.4 (30)	19.5 (36)	7.5 (4)	30.3 (23)	17.5 (28)
Your personal efforts	88.5 (92)	74.3 (78)	81.8 (180)	85.7 (54)	57.8 (59)	70.3 (130)	88.7 (47)	64.5 (49)	78.1 (125)
"Both" (invalid)	1.0 (1)	1.0 (1)	0.9 (2)	6.3 (4)	12.7 (13)	9.7 (18)	3.8 (2)	5.3 (4)	4.4 (7)
TOTALS	100.0 (104)	100.0 (105)	100.0 (220)	100.0 (63)	100.0 (102)	100.0 (184)	100.0 (53)	100.0 (76)	100.0 (160)

Significance levels (chi-square):
1990 data: p. < .05
1993 data: p. < .001
1997 data: p. < .01

Table 5.3 Perceived factors in election victory

Q. "Why do you believe the voters voted for you in the last election? Using a scale that goes from 1 (least important) to 10 (most important), please indicate the relative weight of the following factors."

Factor	1990			1993			1997		
	Mean Score ARENA/PDS Veterans (A)	Mean Score Opposition Veterans (B)	Difference of Means (A-B)	Mean Score ARENA/PDS Veterans (C)	Mean Score Opposition Veterans (D)	Difference of Means (C-D)	Mean Score ARENA/PDS Veterans (E)	Mean Score Opposition Veterans (F)	Difference of Means (E-F)
ORGANIZATIONAL VARIABLES									
The organization of your party	4.79	6.17	-1.38***	4.98	6.05	-1.07**	4.10	6.32	-2.22***
Grassroots support	5.98	7.03	-1.05***	6.60	7.37	-0.77*	6.23	7.42	-1.21**
NON-ORGANIZATIONAL VARIABLES									
Your declarations and promises	7.32	7.11	0.21	6.73	5.55	1.18**	6.60	6.54	0.06
The support of economic interests	2.26	1.99	0.27	2.65	2.01	0.64*	2.82	1.85	0.97
Your possibilities for success	7.23	6.90	0.33	6.61	6.52	0.09	6.40	6.65	-0.25
The decline (*desgaste*) of other competitors or parties	4.47	4.55	-0.08	4.76	4.79	-0.03	4.16	4.31	-0.15
Family name/historic loyalties	6.10	5.21	0.89*	6.91	5.47	1.44***	6.62	5.48	1.14**
Your personal charisma	7.59	7.04	0.54*	7.19	6.51	0.68*	6.98	7.28	-0.30

NOTE: In 1990, N responding ranged from a low of 206 to a high of 233 on the various items; in 1993, the range of N was 145 to 162; and in 1997, 137 to 148.
Significance levels: *p<.10, **p<.05, ***p<.01

percent of all veterans said that they voted with their party, compared to 54.7 percent who voted for local interests and 13.3 percent who split their votes. But the localistic vocation was far stronger among ex-*arenistas* (66.7 percent) than among ex-oppositionists (45.9 percent). Put another way, the ratio of parochials to partisans is more than twice as high within the ARENA/PDS cohort as it is among opposition veterans (Table 5.4). Once again, the evidence suggests a more individualistic, anti-party impulse at work among the ex-authoritarians.

Two additional questions explored elite views of the relationship between politicians and their parties. The first concerned a classic dilemma of parliamentary representation: should a member of the legislature vote the party line, or should he or she vote according to his or her personal beliefs? The second question concerned the institution of party fidelity, which existed under authoritarian rule but was immediately abolished in 1985.

In the 1987–91 legislature, the question of whether a politician should answer to party leaders or to personal beliefs was perplexing to the Brazilian political class: the respondents were fairly evenly divided (Table 5.5). The two groups, ex-*arenistas* and the former opposition to military rule, mirrored one another, splitting by roughly 55/45 margins on opposite sides of the issue. From 1990 to 1993, however, overall support for party authority among veteran politicians rose from 51.6 percent to 63.3 percent, dropping somewhat to 57.4 percent in 1997. In all three survey waves, ex-authoritarians were significantly less likely to support the idea of the party whip, and more likely to defend the individualistic prerogatives of elected legislators.

The question on party fidelity revealed that in the early aftermath of the authoritarian regime (in the 1987–91 legislature), veterans of the promili-

Table 5.4 Partisan and parochial cross-pressures, 1997

Q. "When there is a conflict between the necessities of your region and the positions of your party, do you vote most often with the party, in accordance with the needs of your region, or do you divide your votes evenly?"

Response	ARENA/PDS Veterans Percentage (N)	Opposition Veterans Percentage (N)	All Veterans Percentage (N)
Votes Party Line	24.1 (13)	37.8 (28)	32.0 (41)
Votes Local Interests	66.7 (36)	45.9 (34)	54.7 (70)
Splits Votes	9.3 (5)	16.2 (12)	13.3 (17)
TOTALS	100.0 (54)	100.0 (74)	100.0 (128)

NOTE: Chi-square significance: $p<.10$

Table 5.5 Party line versus personal beliefs in legislative voting

Q. "Do you believe that generally in legislative activity a legislator should vote as the party indicates, or according to what he/she believes?"

Response	1990 ARENA/PDS Veterans Percentage (N)	1990 Opposition Veterans Percentage (N)	1990 All Veterans Percentage (N)	1993 ARENA/PDS Veterans Percentage (N)	1993 Opposition Veterans Percentage (N)	1993 All Veterans Percentage (N)	1997 ARENA/PDS Veterans Percentage (N)	1997 Opposition Veterans Percentage (N)	1997 All Veterans Percentage (N)
As the party indicates	44.7 (46)	57.8 (67)	51.6 (113)	54.2 (32)	68.7 (68)	63.3 (100)	45.1 (23)	66.2 (47)	57.4 (70)
According to personal beliefs	55.3 (57)	42.2 (49)	48.4 (106)	45.8 (27)	31.3 (31)	36.7 (58)	54.9 (28)	33.8 (24)	42.6 (52)
TOTALS	100.0 (113)	100.0 (116)	100.0 (219)	100.0 (59)	100.0 (99)	100.0 (158)	100.0 (51)	100.0 (71)	100.0 (122)

Significance levels (chi-square):
1990 data: $p<.10$
1993 data: $p<.10$
1997 data: $p<.05$

Table 5.6 Orientation toward concept of party fidelity

Q. "Do you believe that parties should close off debate on issues and use the institution of party fidelity?" [Original: "*O Sr. acha correto o partido fechar questão e usar o recurso da fidelidade partidária?*"]

Response	1990			1993			1997		
	ARENA/PDS Veterans Percentage (N)	Opposition Veterans Percentage (N)	All Veterans Percentage (N)	ARENA/PDS Veterans Percentage (N)	Opposition Veterans Percentage (N)	All Veterans Percentage (N)	ARENA/PDS Veterans Percentage (N)	Opposition Veterans Percentage (N)	Congress Percentage (N)
Yes	45.7 (48)	63.9 (78)	55.5 (126)	76.3 (45)	79.0 (79)	78.0 (124)	63.5 (33)	72.5 (53)	68.8 (86)
No	54.3 (57)	36.1 (44)	44.5 (101)	23.7 (14)	21.0 (21)	22.0 (35)	36.5 (19)	27.4 (20)	31.2 (39)
TOTALS	100.0 (105)	100.0 (122)	100.0 (227)	100.0 (59)	100.0 (100)	100.0 (159)	100.0 (52)	100.0 (73)	100.0 (125)

Significance levels (chi-square):
1990 data: $p<.01$
1993 data: NS
1997 data: NS

tary party evinced the hypothesized antipathy toward disciplined parties.[26] I interpret this as a logical outcome of these politicians' negative experience with the party fidelity rule under the military regime: the rule was directed at ARENA/PDS to maintain cohesion within the authoritarian coalition. Personal interviews conducted in 1987 and 1990 with seventeen former members of ARENA first suggested this hypothesis—many had not forgotten the authoritarian experience, and party fidelity remained an unpopular idea because of this. But the second survey showed this attitude receding impressively among ARENA/PDS veterans elected to the 1991–95 legislature. Support for party fidelity increased dramatically among Brazilian elites: by 22.5 percentage among all veteran politicians, and by 31.6 points among ex-authoritarians (Table 5.6). By 1993, a pro-authoritarian trajectory was no longer predictive of an individual legislator's orientation toward disciplined parliamentary parties. The same held true in 1997, when overall support for party fidelity dropped by 9.2 percentage points overall, but was still more than 13 percent higher than it was in the first survey in 1990. In all three surveys the cross-tabulations show the expected pattern—that opposition veterans should be more tolerant of party fidelity than veterans of ARENA—but only in the first survey is the relationship statistically significant.

To provide an additional handle on this issue, a third, closely related question was asked. Respondents were queried about a potential punishment for legislators who do not vote with their party. In 1990, only 42.9 percent of ex-*arenistas* agreed that "a political party should expel a legislator who votes against the instructions of the party," while 63.4 percent of the former opposition to military rule was in agreement with this statement (Table 5.7). In 1993, support for sanctions against party mavericks rose to 61 percent among ex-authoritarians and to 71.7 percent among the opposition group. The difference was no longer statistically significant ($p = .16$). In the third survey wave in 1997, overall support for sanctions fell by 9.5 percentage points from the 1993 results, but was still 10 points higher than in 1990. The 1997 cross-tabulation for the two cohorts narrowly missed statistical significance at the 90 percent confidence level ($p = .12$).

Taking these three survey questions together, some interesting results emerge. First, comparing our two cohorts, there is a strong and apparently

26. Again, this analysis should not be taken to mean that I believe party fidelity is "necessary" for either party representation or effective democracy. I do believe that asking a politician for an opinion on party fidelity is an acceptable way of gauging some aspects of his or her attitude toward party authority in general.

Table 5.7 Attitudes toward hypothetical sanctions against antiparty actions by politicians

Statement: "A political party should expel a legislator who votes against the instructions (*determinações*) of the party." (Percent in agreement, with total respondents in parentheses)[a]

Survey Year	ARENA/PDS Veterans Percentage (N)	Opposition Veterans Percentage (N)	All Veterans Percentage (N)	Chi-square Sig. (p)
1990	42.9 (105)	63.4 (123)	53.9 (228)	.01
1993	61.0 (59)	71.7 (99)	67.7 (158)	NS
1997	55.6 (54)	68.9 (74)	63.3 (128)	NS

NS = Not Significant

[a] Possible responses were *concorda, plenamente; concorda, em termos; discorda, em termos; discorda, plenamente*. Agreement combines the first two of these.

stable difference in the purely attitudinal or philosophical component—that is, the abstract notion—of political individualism. Ex-authoritarians are much more likely to believe that personal views rather than party strictures should govern legislative behavior, and this relationship held across all three surveys. Second, turning from abstract orientations to concrete institutions, there is an increasing recognition across the board of the utility of party fidelity rules. In the first survey, ex-authoritarians were significantly less likely to approve of party fidelity, but their views changed sharply toward convergence with ex-oppositionists, such that there were no significant differences between the two cohorts in 1993 and 1997. Third, politicians are more likely to support the concept of party fidelity than they are to approve of its actual enforcement via a real-world tool—expulsion from the party. Again, the two cohorts were divided in 1990 (with the ex-*arenistas* taking the hypothesized antiparty position) but converged in 1993 and 1997.

Note that in all three questions related to party fidelity, the "slope" of the responses across the three surveys was remarkably similar—there was a sharp increase in pro-party attitudes from 1990 to 1993 and then a moderate decline in 1997, but the 1997 results still registered significant improvement over the 1990 baseline. This suggests that there were some key differences between legislators elected in 1986 and 1990, or something unique about the 1990–93 period—or both—that caused political learning to occur. The hyperinflation and "ungovernability" of this period, the advent of a virtually no-party populist president in 1990 (Fernando Collor), Collor's impeachment in 1992, a national plebiscite on parliamentary rule in early 1993 (which generated a national debate on how to strengthen parties), as well as the apparently steady advance of the disciplined, well-organized leftist parties (especially the PT), are all prime suspects for the unmistakable shift in pro-party attitudes. This political learning effect was clearly more intense among ex-authoritarians than among the former opposition to military rule.

The final party-related item drawn from the questionnaire attempted to measure potential party cohesion by probing for participation in the formal partisan structures. Legislators were asked how frequently they had met with their party's national executive committee over the preceding twelve months. Both in 1990 and 1993, ex-ARENA/PDS members were roughly twice as likely as ex-opposition members to report meeting "rarely or never" with their party leaders, and the cross-tabulations were statistically significant (Table 5.8). In 1997, the contrast between the two cohorts disappeared. The percentage of ex-authoritarians meeting "frequently" or "once in a while" with their party leaders rose steadily from 60.2 percent in 1990 to 80.6 percent in 1993 to 87.3 percent in 1993, when it actually surpassed the figure for opposition veterans.[27]

To provide a more comprehensive overview of politicians' orientations toward strong parties, I created a composite index of support for party institutionalization. This index was based on responses to four questions discussed above: those concerning party fidelity, party line versus personal beliefs in legislative voting, sanctions against antiparty voting by legislators, and frequency of meeting with party leadership. To these I added a question about a critical proposed reform to electoral legislation: whether the respondent would support changing the current system of open-list PR to a party list.[28] In each case the antiparty position was scored as a 0 and the pro-party position as a 1, generating a range of 0 to 5 for the composite index. To allow for easier visual interpretation, the data were multiplied and converted to a 0–100 range, creating a variable called PROPARTY. On the PROPARTY index, a score approaching 100 indicates support for party institutionalization in the organizational sense, implying that the interests of the party organization should take precedence over the interests of the individual legislator. A score approaching 0 implies preference for individualism over organization, that is, for weaker, looser parties.

27. The change in 1997 probably results from the presence of many ex-authoritarians (especially PFL members) in Fernando Henrique Cardoso's support coalition, a coalition that was heavily managed by the presidential palace with a view toward passing a large number of constitutional amendments in a short period of time. The intense legislative orchestration in 1995 and 1996 encouraged frequent caucus meetings.

28. On open-list PR in Brazil, see Mainwaring (1991b) and Ames (1995).

Table 5.8 Reported meetings with party leadership

Q. "Please tell me how often you have done the following activities over the past twelve months: frequently, once in a while, or never . . . meet with the National Executive Committee of your party."

Response	1990 ARENA/ PDS Veterans Percentage (N)	1990 Opposition Veterans Percentage (N)	1990 All Veterans Percentage (N)	1993 ARENA/ PDS Veterans Percentage (N)	1993 Opposition Veterans Percentage (N)	1993 All Veterans Percentage (N)	1997 ARENA/ PDS Veterans Percentage (N)	1997 Opposition Veterans Percentage (N)	1997 Congress Percentage (N)
Frequently/once in a while	69.2 (74)	84.4 (103)	77.3 (177)	80.6 (50)	91.2 (93)	87.2 (143)	87.3 (48)	82.4 (61)	84.5 (109)
Rarely/never	30.8 (33)	15.6 (19)	22.7 (52)	19.4 (12)	8.8 (9)	12.8 (21)	12.7 (7)	17.6 (13)	15.5 (20)
TOTALS	100.0 (107)	100.0 (122)	100.0 (229)	100.0 (62)	100.0 (102)	100.0 (164)	100.0 (55)	100.0 (74)	100.0 (129)

Significance levels (chi-square):
1990 data: $p<.01$
1993 data: $p<.05$
1997 data: NS

In 1990, the mean score for PROPARTY among all veterans was 53.4, a value in the middle of the range. However, among ex-authoritarians the mean value was 45.0 ($N = 108$), while among opposition veterans the mean climbed to 60.5 ($N = 128$). The difference of means was significant at the .001 level. In the 1993 survey, the mean PROPARTY score for all veterans rose to 63.9. The ARENA/PDS cohort scored 60.8 ($N = 63$), and the opposition group 68.7 ($N = 103$). The difference of means was significant at the relaxed .10 level. In 1997, the mean for all veterans on PRO-PARTY was 62.3, with ex-*arenistas* scoring 58.7 ($N = 55$) and ex-oppositionists scoring 65.0 ($N = 76$), and now the difference of means was no longer significant. Again we see the patterns discussed above: a sharp rise in pro-party attitudes from 1990 to 1993, and then a slight decline in 1997, but with a greater transformation within the ARENA cohort than within the opposition cohort.

The temporal and cohort-based variation in support for party institutionalization raises the question of whether support for party development is related to support for political democracy. Three survey questions gauged this support. One concerned respondents' opinions on the unusual constitutional role of the armed forces: the democratic constitution of 1988 still designates the army as the guarantor of internal law and order.[29] Respondents were also asked whether they believed that authoritarian regimes generated better economic results than democratic ones, and whether they believe that authoritarian regimes are better at maintaining social order. In each case the "democratic" position was scored as 1 and the "authoritarian" position was scored as 0. Responses to these three questions were coded and transformed similarly to the PROPARTY variable described above, creating a second variable called PRODEM.[30] A high score, approaching 100, indicates support for political democracy and rejection of authoritarian options. A low score on PRODEM, approaching 0, indicates belief in the "advantages" of authoritarianism and support for military tutelage. In essence, the PRODEM variable is the inverse of a hypothetical measure of authoritarian "nostalgia." The mean values for both variables by party and authoritarian-era cohort are reported in Table 5.9.

29. For analysis of continuity in the military's prerogatives during the early years of the New Republic, see Stepan (1988); changes in the military's mission under democracy are examined by Hunter (1997).

30. The values of the 0 to 1 responses to the three questions were summed, creating a scale of 0 to 3. The values were then multiplied by 33.333 and transformed into a 0 to 100 scale for ease of interpretation. Thus, the PRODEM variable has the same range as the PROPARTY variable discussed earlier.

Table 5.9 Support for political democracy and party institutionalization by current party and authoritarian-era cohort

		1990				1993				1997		
Group[a]	N	Percentage ARENA/PDS Veterans[b]	Mean PRO-DEM	Mean PRO-PARTY	N	Percentage ARENA/PDS Veterans	Mean PRO-DEM	Mean PRO-PARTY	N	Percentage ARENA/PDS Veterans	Mean PRO-DEM	Mean PRO-PARTY
LEFT-WING PARTIES												
PT	7	0.0	100.0	78.1	17	0.0	89.2	85.6	17	0.0	96.1	83.1
PDT	17	12.5	76.5	62.5	16	13.3	67.7	62.2	5	0.0	63.3	72.0
CENTER PARTIES												
PSDB	37	16.2	73.0	58.4	17	11.8	72.5	67.4	32	25.0	70.8	60.1
PMDB	77	28.6	58.4	50.0	38	15.8	62.3	68.1	33	12.1	76.3	65.2
RIGHT-WING PARTIES												
PDS	15	100.0	47.8	61.3	—	—	—	—	—	—	—	—
PDC	8	57.1	66.7	31.3	—	—	—	—	—	—	—	—
PPR/PPB[c]	—	—	—	—	27	84.6	38.3	67.4	19	68.4	59.6	58.9
PFL	45	97.8	51.1	48.5	28	71.4	47.6	54.0	40	67.5	52.5	53.0
PTB	8	50.0	45.8	54.4	7	28.6	38.1	42.1	5	20.0	53.3	54.0
PL	9	55.6	48.1	37.8	5	80.0	53.3	40.0	—	—	—	—
PRN	7	16.7	42.9	41.4	6	33.3	52.8	56.7	—	—	—	—

POST-AUTHORITARIAN
CLEAVAGE

ARENA/PDS veterans	108	100.0	53.7	45.0	63	100.0	49.5	60.8	55	100.0	61.2	58.7
Opposition veterans	128	0.0	68.6	60.5	103	0.0	66.7	68.7	76	0.0	78.5	65.0
All veterans	236	45.8	61.8	53.4	166	38.0	60.1	65.7	131	42.0	71.2	62.3

NOTES: Data for subpopulations are reported only if the party or grouping had an N of five or more in all three surveys. Data for entire sample include several additional respondents in very small parties or without party affiliation.

Correlations of PRODEM with PROPARTY (individual-level): in 1990, $N = 249$, $r = .14$, $p <.05$; in 1993, $N = 185$, $r = .28$, $p <.001$; in 1997, $N = 162$, $r = .13$, $p<.10$. T-tests for difference of means between ARENA/PDS veterans and opposition veterans: for 1990 PRODEM and PROPARTY, $p <.001$; for 1993 PRODEM, $p <.001$; for 1993 PROPARTY, $p <.10$; for 1997 PRODEM, $p <.001$; for 1997 PROPARTY, not significant.

[a] Major parties in the New Republic: PT = Workers' Party, radical left (founded 1980); PDT = Democratic Labor Party, left-populist (1980); PSDB = Party of Brazilian Social Democracy, center-left (1988); PMDB = Party of the Brazilian Democratic Movement, remnant of the opposition front to military rule, founded as the MDB in 1966; PDS = Democratic Social Party, promilitary front, founded as ARENA in 1966; PDC = Christian Democratic Party, conservative (1985); PPR = Renovating Progressive Party, conservative, one of two main successor parties to ARENA/PDS, founded by merger of PDS and PDC in 1993, later changed name to PPB (Brazilian Progressive Party) after absorbing small Popular Party (PP) in early 1995; PFL = Party of the Liberal Front, conservative, other main successor party to ARENA/PDS (1984); PTB = Brazilian Labor Party, conservative-populist (1979); PL, Liberal Party, conservative (1985); PRN = Party of National Renovation, conservative (1989). Not reported here are Brazilian Socialist Party (PSB), Communist Party of Brazil (PC do B), and the Brazilian Communist Party (PCB), which was renamed the Popular Socialist Party (PPS) in 1991.

[b] Percentage of ex-authoritarians in each party is calculated over the N of respondents from the party, and thus may not accurately represent the composition of the party as a whole. See Tables 3.1, 3.2, and 3.10 for alternative estimations.

[c] PPR created 1993 by merger of PDS and PDC; PPB created 1995 by merger of PPR with short-lived PP (Partido Popular).

Correlating the variables at the individual level for the entire sample provides weak confirmation of a positive association between support for democracy and for strong parties (see notes to Table 5.9). When means for PRODEM and PROPARTY are computed by parties, the positive relationship is easier to perceive. The correlation coefficients for partisan means of PRODEM and PROPARTY were .63 in 1990 ($N = 10$, $p = .05$), .71 in 1993 ($N = 9$, $p = .03$), and .87 in 1997 ($N = 7$, $p = .01$). Brazilian parties have distinct profiles in terms of their inclination toward party-strengthening reforms and in terms of their nostalgia for authoritarian rule, and there is a clear inverse relationship between these two orientations at the party level. Moreover, the greater the presence of ex-*arenistas* within a given party, the less likely is that party to favor party-building reforms. The correlation between the PROPARTY variable and the percentage of the party that is ex-ARENA was $-.33$ in 1990 ($N = 10$, $p = .35$), $-.52$ in 1993 ($N = 9$, $p = .15$), and $-.71$ in 1997 ($N = 7$, $p = .08$).

Overall, the findings of the three waves of survey research can be summarized by the following:

1. The first legislature elected under democracy evinced an observable cleavage regarding orientations toward strong parties. Although the Brazilian political class as a whole generally lived up to its reputation as individualistic and antiparty, the data showed that this orientation was significantly stronger among those politicians who were pro-authoritarian in 1964–85.

2. In the second legislature elected under democracy, the salience of this cleavage diminished somewhat. Ex-authoritarians were still more individualistic: they remained less likely to participate in their party organizations, and continued to believe that they owed their electoral mandates to themselves and not to their parties. They continued to be significantly more likely to say that personal beliefs rather than party rules should govern legislative voting. But on critical issues such as whether party fidelity should be adopted, and whether transgressors of party fidelity rules should be punished, ex-authoritarians' attitudes shifted in the direction of convergence with ex-oppositionists.

3. In the third legislature elected under democracy, the trend toward attitudinal convergence was confirmed. The one major exception was that ex-authoritarians continued to endorse an essentially individualistic concept of representation; on the question of party line

versus personal beliefs in legislative voting, there was still a significant difference between the two cohorts. Indeed, the ex-*arenistas* regressed to their 1990 levels of antiparty attitudes on this variable, and the cleavage here was greater than it initially had been in 1990. But moving from attitudes to concrete institutions, the panoply of possible party-strengthening reforms (measured via the PROPARTY composite index) turned up no statistically significant differences between ex-authoritarians and others. The data suggest that the ex-*arenistas* retain a latent and stable preference for political individualism, but at the same time have become more open to institutional reforms that might temper this very individualism.

4. From the 1987–91 legislature to the 1991–95 legislature, the political class as a whole demonstrated sharply greater support for strengthening parties. There was a slight drop-off in overall support for strong parties in the 1995–99 legislature, but this support still remained higher than the 1990 levels. The results suggest that most political learning—the revising of attitudes—occurred in the late 1980s and early 1990s.

5. The greatest overall change in the direction of party-building orientations was recorded by the ex-authoritarians, who departed from a lower baseline on this variable.

6. Although the data are not quite as strong nor the trends quite as stable as our hypotheses about authoritarian legacies might suggest, the overall results do lend significant support to the idea that the ARENA/PDS cohort entered democratic rule with attitudes unfavorable to the construction of a stronger, more representative political parties.

How the Right Sees Party Life

Survey research cannot reveal qualitative, informal, and personal aspects of how elites view their relationships to political parties. For this reason, the survey research reported above was complemented by a number of open-ended interviews with some thirty-five sitting members of the Brazilian Congress, conducted between May 1990 and June 1993. Of these politicians, twenty-three were members of ARENA/PDS during the military regime, and nearly all the rest had been active opposition figures. This is a small sample of unstructured personal interviews, with no pretense of statistical inference; rather, the intent here is merely to present some general observations which, taken alongside the other data sources presented in this chapter, can sketch a broader portrait of rightist involvement in the party system.

In personal conversations, Brazilian politicians across the political spectrum voiced considerable dissatisfaction with the state of parties and the party system. For some politicians, this posture carries contradictions. As Mainwaring has pointed out, Brazilian party representation is weak largely because of the formal rules chosen by politicians, yet this does not stop politicians from continuing to opt for the permissive party and electoral legislation responsible for the state of affairs they so loudly bemoan (Mainwaring 1991b). This observation should not be construed to mean that each politician is bent on sabotaging political institutions for personal gain, although clearly that is sometimes the case. Some elites do not understand the relationships between formal political rules and macropolitical outcomes, or do not conceive of constitutional design as an important element of democratization.[31] Since parties have not been as politically salient in Brazil as in the other more economically advanced Latin American countries, it is perhaps not reasonable to expect politicians to have as strong a grasp of institutional issues as their counterparts in countries like Uruguay or Venezuela.[32] In practice, the level of such information varies greatly among Brazilian political elites, and in interviews politicians discussed party life from a variety of angles.

Ex-authoritarians were queried about the post-1985 diaspora of their cohort. Until mid-1984, ARENA/PDS had navigated the period of political liberalization largely intact. This changed drastically with the founding of the PFL and the formation of the Democratic Alliance, when many longtime ARENA/PDS stalwarts quit the party. By the end of the decade, ex-*arenistas* were found in no less than *twelve* political parties with representation in

31. Having a comparative perspective on democratic institutions is a luxury usually reserved for political scientists. Probably politicians everywhere are ignorant of the great variety of institutional experiments in other countries (how many members of the U.S. Congress could explain how German parliamentary elections work?). But the transcripts of Brazil's 1987–88 constitutional debate indicate a very low level of information indeed. Two years later, I interviewed a federal deputy who—to my great amazement—was not at all familiar with the "open list" system of proportional representation used in Brazil (in other words, with how he got elected to Congress). Of course, there are many knowledgeable exceptions to this generalization.

32. In recent years, for example, Venezuelan elites have been involved in a heated debate about reforms in the party and electoral systems. Based on the account by Levine and Kornblith (1995), it appears that Venezuelan politicians are much better informed than Brazilian elites regarding alternative party and electoral models.

Congress. Why was it not possible for former authoritarian-era incumbents to remain united in one political party?

Easily the most common response given to this question revolved around local and state-level politics. This reaction recalls some of the problems encountered upon the creation of ARENA in 1965, when progovernment politicians perceived military elites to be insensitive to political rivalries within the states. Informants made reference to the "artificial" nature of the ARENA/PDS party, which existed solely to sustain the authoritarian coalition, and which was (as explained earlier in this chapter) held together by military will, by the logic of two-party competition, and by a number of institutions designed to alleviate or mask the persistence of intra-party rivalries, such as party fidelity and the *sublegenda* system. Several ARENA/PDS veterans who today are on the center-left explained how "cohesion via coercion" led them into a party whose ideology and practices they did not share. Deputy Adhemar de Barros Filho (PRP-São Paulo), although sharing his father's *trabalhismo*, followed the elder Adhemar into ARENA after the family spent the mid-1960s in the political wilderness without access to patronage (interview, Brasília, October 17, 1990). At the time of the 1964 coup, Sen. Antonio Mariz (PMDB-Paraíba) was in the old left-of-center PTB but was a client of the political machine of João Agripino, a traditional oligarch. Thus, Mariz was taken as a "prisoner" (his term) into the ARENA party structure (interview, Brasília, June 1, 1993). In the 1960s, Deputy Zaire Rezende (PMDB-Minas Gerais) was a city councilor in São Sebastião, São Paulo, who joined ARENA for "political convenience"—even though as "national security" port city, São Sebastião had no direct elections for mayor, and the city council was forced to tape-record its meetings and send the tape to the military command in nearby Caçapava (interview, Brasília, June 15, 1993). All three of these individuals displayed strong center-left or leftist credentials in their parliamentary action in the New Republic, thus illustrating how the old ARENA party made for strange bedfellows.

To many *arenistas*, it was always clear that when compulsory cohabitation was abolished and a multiparty system reestablished, that the ARENA/PDS cohort would splinter immediately. Indeed, this appeared so inevitable to some that they saw my line of questioning as rather curious: legislators from different political tendencies saw it as their duty to impress upon a foreign researcher the ongoing importance of state and local politics in Brazil.

One of the most active legislators in the first decade of democracy, former deputy Nelson Jobim (PMDB-Rio Grande do Sul), who opposed military rule, made a particularly strong case in this regard. "What goes on in national politics does not affect politics in the states," he said. Parties are organized at the local level. In the Congress, there is not one or PMDB or one PDS; there are several PMDBs and several delegations of the PDS, each representing state-level interests. In Jobim's visits to Rio Grande do Sul, the questions posed to him by his constituents concerned only local politics. Mayors and city councilors, in Jobim's view, do not care about what goes on in Brasília—for them "the world ends at the borders of the *município*." The only time "national" politics comes into play is when the election is the majoritarian election for president of the republic. According to Jobim, the electoral system encourages this inward-looking politics conducted at the state level. Unlike the majority of his colleagues, Jobim expressed frustration with this: "The federal deputy who thinks too much about *the nation* is done for."[33]

Former deputy Osmundo Rebouças (PMDB-Ceará), a Harvard-trained economist who served in PDS governments in his home state of Ceará, echoed Jobim's arguments. He characterized Brazilian politics as highly individualistic, a zero-sum game. Whatever resource a politician wins for his/her home state is taken away from another. "This is a 'state' Congress, not a national Congress. Individual politicians do not defend the Union—there are no votes in that. Individual politicians do not defend their party—there are no votes in that, either."[34] Veteran Paraná politician Affonso Camargo, a former "bionic" (unelected) senator for ARENA, agreed with both Jobim and Rebouças. "In Brazil, voting is 'municipalized.' " It is to this phenomenon that Camargo attributes the impressive political survival of former ARENA/PDS politicians like himself.[35]

33. Interview, Brasília, December 6, 1990. I found Jobim's last comment to be particularly interesting, because several months earlier, during the congressional election campaign, one of the most influential PFL senators had also argued to me the importance of paying attention to local politics. He said that excessive involvement in the federal legislature was a sure way to lose a reelection bid, and he gave an example of a talented federal deputy whom he predicted would lose in November because of his unwise dedication to the National Congress: Nelson Jobim. Despite his colleague's prediction, Jobim was reelected to the 1991–95 legislature. He did not run again in 1994, but in January 1995 was appointed minister of justice by President Fernando Henrique Cardoso. Later, Cardoso elevated Jobim to the Supreme Court.

34. Interview, Brasília, September 13, 1990.

35. Interview, Brasília, December 7, 1990. Camargo is a marvelous example of political survival instincts at work. After the 1964 coup he moved from the PDC to MDB, then to ARENA. He left ARENA to found the PP, and then helped merge the PP into the PMDB in 1981. In 1977 he was president of ARENA in Paraná, but by 1983 he was the national secre-

To the extent that politics is conducted locally and is influenced heavily by the ability of politicians to bring in outside resources, ideology is displaced from the political market. Interviewees agreed strongly that ideology plays only a small role in electoral politics, and practically none when it comes to ex-*arenista* politics. According to Senator Jorge Bornhausen (PFL-Santa Catarina), who has frequently held the presidency of his party, ideology had nothing to do with the division of the PDS and the creation of the PFL in 1984—instead, the disagreement was over the methods that Paulo Maluf was using to capture the PDS presidential that year (interview, Brasília, June 5, 1990). Ideology does not appear to interest the ex-authoritarian cohort at all. The majority of former ARENA/PDS politicians hail from poor states where politics is characterized by intra-oligarchical disputes and *assistencialismo* (competition for and distribution of government aid). Federal deputy Enoc Vieira (PFL-Maranhão) described politics in his state—one of the poorest in the country—as revolving around the relationships of individual politicians with the dominant Sarney machine. Vieira put it succinctly: "In *maranhense* elections, it is difficult to think of something that matters less than ideology."[36]

Although political elites concurred that ideology is a minor factor in state-level politics, it is clear that ideological affinities have at least temporarily unified the national right on recent occasions. For example, the conservative supraparty coalition known as the Centrão was created in the 1987–88 National Constituent Assembly as a reaction to early victories by progressive forces. The experience of the Centrão raised an interesting question put to ex-authoritarians: why could the Centrão not remain united after 1988, or be transformed into a large conservative political party? The answers given to this question were particularly revealing about the nature of conservative politics in Brazil. There was a broad consensus that the Centrão was born of necessity—as a response to the domination of the constitutional convention by the progressive wing of the PMDB—and as such was a temporary alliance. In this sense, the Centrão was seen much like the early ARENA, as a broad, conservative alliance that coalesced around a specific political project, yet which masked serious state-level, local, and personal rivalries. As soon as the project was realized (in the case of the Centrão, this meant when the internal bylaws of the ANC were changed to permit greater

tary general of the opposition PMDB! A PMDB senator during the ANC, Camargo left the party soon after to join the PTB, on whose ticket he ran for president in 1989. As if that were not enough, he was also transportation minister in both the Sarney and Collor governments.
36. Interview, Brasília, September 13, 1990.

flexibility in amending the constitutional draft) and the immediacy of political danger disappeared, the alliance fell apart. Some of the principal reasons cited for the demise of the Centrão were the divisive effects of federalism, (that is, the simmering local and regional rivalries within the bloc), the efforts of some influential members to identify the Centrão with the unpopular Sarney administration, and the fact that a handful of prominent members—such as now deceased federal deputies Roberto Cardoso Alves (PMDB-São Paulo) and Amaral Netto (PDS-Rio de Janeiro)—were strong ideological rightists who claimed to speak for the alliance as a whole, and were therefore seen as major liabilities. (The rise and fall of the Centrão is covered in greater detail in Chapter 7.) The more outspoken members (Amaral Netto often referred to himself as a "Shiite of the Right") were blamed for provoking the left and unions, which responded to the Centrão with an effective public relations campaign.[37]

Each of the aformentioned reasons for the Centrão's collapse points to a specific tenet or unwritten rule of Brazilian conservatism. First, regional tensions within the bloc indicate that conservative collective action at the national level must not threaten competitive factionalism at the state and local levels of politics. Second, the resistance of members to identification with the Sarney government is a classic manifestation of the individualism of Brazilian politics. The Centrão already endorsed most of the government's agenda in the ANC, yet members did not want to "officialize" this support, because the Sarney administration was overwhelmingly vilified at the time; they preferred instead to prop up the government as individuals. The lesson is that Brazilian conservatives wish to avoid, at all costs, any conflicts generated by the clash of *governismo* and *individualismo*. Third, the strong resentment by rank and file Centrão members of certain high-profile right-wingers in their alliance is simply a reflection of a rule well known to all players in Brazilian politics: conservatives do not wish to be identified as such. All three of these factors, in combination with party-fragmenting electoral rules discussed elsewhere, militate against either the resurrection of ARENA/PDS or the creation of a single, identifiably conservative political party in Brazil.

So far the discussion of the right's participation in party life has been restricted mostly to factors specific to the ARENA/PDS cohort. There are,

---

37. The PT-dominated labor federation, CUT (Central Única dos Trabalhadores), assailed the Centrão as "*traidores do povo*" (betrayers of the people). Posters were printed containing the photographs of prominent members of the Centrão, including their addresses and telephone numbers, and were distributed in a number of cities around the country.

of course, many macropolitical and institutional factors which are also at work here. These were specified quite clearly by then-Senator Roberto Campos (PDS-Mato Grosso), a longtime advisor to military governments, and the high priest of free-market economics in Brazil. When I asked Campos why the PDS divided after the presidential succession of 1984/1985, he responded with typical directness: "Is there *any* party that remained united? Not one." Campos pointed out that the Constitution of 1988 failed to institute the *voto distrital* (the single-member district plurality method of election to the lower house of Congress and the state assemblies), destroyed party fidelity, and did not establish a national minimum threshold for party representation in Congress. Thus, it was possible for a party to have only one member in the legislature (in the 1990s, there have typically been from twelve to fifteen parties represented in Congress). According to Campos, postauthoritarian Brazil moved "from a two-party system that was restrictive to a multiparty system that is chaotic."[38]

In light of Campos's observations, it is clear that the most persuasive answer to the question "Why is the Brazilian right not united in one party?" really has two parts. The first part refers to the regional, personal, and ideological forces that exercise disintegrating effects upon the national right. In the postauthoritarian era, the state of the Brazilian right is one of fragmentation. The second part of the answer is that no rules or institutional devices have been instituted that could reverse the diaspora of the ARENA/PDS cohort. In other words, ex-*arenistas* have migrated to other parties and created new ones simply because nothing prevents them from doing so. The fragmentation of the right is rational, both politically and institutionally.

Conclusions

Brazilian political parties are traditionally weak, and in the New Republic the deficiencies have so far been glaring. The 1990, 1993, and 1997 questionnaires probed a number of issues traditionally associated with the underdevelopment of Brazilian parties. These included rampant individualism on the part of politicians, lack of formal party organization, low accountability of elected representatives, and lack of party cohesion, as measured both by commitment to one party label and discipline/fidelity in legislative politics. The intent of the research was to uncover what if any effect the authoritarian experience of 1964–85 had on the institutional orientations

38. Interview, Brasília, December 4, 1990.

of civilian politicians. These politicians emerged in the late 1980s as the sole custodians and architects of Brazil's democratic political institutions.

In the first survey (1990), the overall responses of the Brazilian political class did not raise hopes for imminent reforms that could facilitate the institutionalization of parties. After the first wave of research, I viewed veterans of the 1964–85 military regime as profoundly antithetical to the development of strong, disciplined political parties, and to the construction of an institutional framework oriented toward greater accountability. This I took to be an important qualification of the findings of authors like Souza and Lamounier and Meneguello, who have often conceptualized Brazilian party underdevelopment largely—though not exclusively—in more general terms, at the systemic or macropolitical level. The 1990 findings suggested that generalizations about the innate individualism of the Brazilian political class, or its preference for lax, permissive rules governing competition, representation, and party organization, would have to be revised to reflect an emerging cleavage in postauthoritarian politics: the ARENA/PDS cohort appeared far more prone than other sectors to harbor attitudes inimical to party development.

However, replication of the survey instrument in 1993 and 1997 produced different results, leading me to revise my preliminary conclusions. Ex-authoritarians began to modify, albeit unevenly, their orientations toward strong parties. Reconciling these divergent results requires a theoretical account addressing two main issues. The first question is why authoritarian rule generated a more pronounced anti-institutional orientation on the part of ARENA/PDS members in the first years of democracy. The second is why the Brazilian political class later moved toward increasing consensus on the need to strengthen political parties, thus "smoothing over"—although note completely erasing—the authoritarian-era cleavage regarding party institutionalization. These theoretical issues are addressed at length in the concluding chapter. In the meantime, my initial findings on the relationship between ex-authoritarians and political institutions will be cross-checked by examining the behavior of the ARENA/PDS cohort in yet another arena of political representation: the national legislature.

The Right in Congress 6

Implications for Legislative Institutionalization

Introduction

In its remarkable attention to institutional matters, the Brazilian authoritarian regime of 1964–85 was unlike its counterparts in the Southern Cone countries. The Brazilian military destroyed the functionality of democratic institutions in its 1964 coup but intentionally preserved the exteriors of these structures as part of its strategy of legitimation. One outcome of this strategy was the peculiar trajectory of the Brazilian National Congress. In contrast to Chile, where the legislature was sealed tightly from the time of the coup in 1973 to the return of democracy in 1990, in Brazil legislative activity persisted—despite some brief interruptions—throughout the entire period of authoritarian rule. Congressional elections were held on schedule every four years, and the bicameral legislature continued to meet in its chambers in Brasília. Legislators made speeches, served on committees, hired staff, and continued the physical expansion of the Congressional complex in the new capital. Tellingly, the annual sessions were numbered according to the democratic Constitution of 1946, as if the vanquished competitive regime were still in place. The intent was to persuade the casual observer that the National Congress occupied an important political space in military Brazil.

In truth, the outward appearance of Congressional activity obscured the most radical changes in the institution since Getúlio Vargas closed it by force in 1937. Beginning in 1964 and culminating with the proclamation of the Fifth Institutional Act in 1968, the Brazilian Congress was summarily stripped of almost all of its powers and functions in the political system. Although the executive branch has always overshadowed the legislative branch in Brazilian politics, the leaders of the movement of 1964 so aggravated this imbalance that Congress was basically irrelevant to decisional outputs for the better part of the authoritarian regime. And though all incarnations of the Brazilian national legislature may appear feeble to U.S. or European observers, such a perspective obscures the exceptional nature of Congressional marginalization under military rule. The 1964–85 Congress was far weaker than it was either in its "golden age" of the 1946–64 regime (Astiz 1975) or in the regime inaugurated by the Constitution of 1988.[1]

At the same time the National Congress was emasculated and marginalized, it was thoroughly dominated by the political right. Table 6.1 illustrates the extent of conservative control of Congress under authoritarianism.

The combination of these two postauthoritarian legacies—the intentional weakening of Congress and its longtime domination by the ARENA/PDS cohort—bring us to a second case study of the right's relevance to the imperative of democratic institutionalization. Once again we will return to the set of Weberian hypotheses about politicians and parliamentarians socialized to weak institutions: that they may turn to antidemocratic practices in the absence of serious political responsibilities, that they will show weak loyalties to institutions, and that the institutions in question are likely to suffer long-term consequences as a result of these factors. A major challenge to the Brazilian political system in the late 1980s and early 1990s was that of privileging the National Congress in the process of democratization. The

Table 6.1 ARENA/PDS domination of Congress under military rule (percentage seats held after legislative elections)

Year	Percentage Seats in Senate	Percentage Seats in Chamber
1966	71.2	67.7
1970	89.4	71.9
1974	69.7	56.0
1978	62.7	55.0
1982	66.7	49.0

SOURCE: Lamounier 1989.

1. I am referring here to formal attributes. In both democratic regimes the Congress still failed to maximize the power available to it, either by enacting relevant constitutional provisions or by utilizing the formal powers already instituted by law.

question was how to revive an emasculated institution and incorporate it into political life in such a way that it could begin to fulfill its functions as a locus of popular representation and as a countervailing power to the executive branch. As the newly democratic regime got underway after 1985, the hope was raised that a democratically elected and fully functional Congress could do for the New Republic what, ironically, the generals had hoped it could do for military rule: generate legitimacy for the regime.

As Brazil turned its attention to legislative institutionalization in the second half of the 1980s, and especially during the National Constituent Assembly (ANC) of 1987–88, the ARENA/PDS cohort played an important role in the shaping of the new legislative institution and politics. This chapter examines the attitudes and behavior ex-authoritarians in this process. I begin with historical background, reviewing the changes that took place in the National Congress under bureaucratic-authoritarianism and how these posed serious challenges to legislative reformers in the period of democratization. I then turn to the story of how the ANC undertook the challenge of defining new roles and powers for a postauthoritarian Congress, and what role the political right played in the process of institutional and constitutional revision. I also introduce survey data detailing the ARENA/PDS cohort's perception of the national legislature and its participation in the institution. I conclude by assessing the performance of the National Congress and the legislative right since 1988, with special attention to the question of Congress as a potential agent of democratic legitimation.

The National Congress: Background and Recent Transformations

The Dismantling of Legislative Authority under Authoritarianism

The military movement that deposed President João Goulart in April 1964 wasted no time in striking against the elected Congress. Unlike their counterparts in neighboring countries, the Brazilian generals did not simply close the legislature and lock the doors for years. Rather, they chipped away at legislative power gradually via the so-called Institutional Acts. The term was a euphemism for executive decrees originating in the military hierarchy.

The First Institutional Act (AI-1) of April 9, 1964, transferred many legislative powers to the executive branch. Any bill drafted by the presidency, including amendments to the Constitution, had to be considered within thirty days of its submission to each house of Congress. The president gained the power to order a joint session of Congress for rapid consideration of executive proposals, also within thirty-days' time. Article 4 of AI-

1 determined that if Congress did not explicitly reject a bill during the specified time period, it automatically became law. This was the device known subsequently as the *decurso de prazo*; it was important because a simple ARENA/PDS filibuster would guarantee the passage of an executive bill (Alves 1985). Congress also lost the power to initiate financial or budgetary legislation. Although either house could amend the president's budget, legislators were prohibited from increasing public expenditures (Packenham 1971). Congress was stripped of the power to declare a state of siege (a fact self-evident in the events of the previous week). Finally, AI-1 temporarily lifted parliamentary immunity so that the military could remove undesirable persons from any legislative body in the country. This termination of mandate was known as *cassação*, and its indiscriminate use continued into the mid-1970s. In the 1960s alone, some 513 legislators at different levels of government were stripped of their political rights or lost their mandates, including some 157 members of the National Congress (Table 6.2).

The First Institutional Act established the basis for dictatorship by the military-dominated executive. Its authors were unusually frank in stating the authoritarian regime's view of Congress.

In order to demonstrate that we do not intend to radicalize the process of revolution, we have decided to maintain the Constitution of 1946. We have limited ourselves to amending it in the part that deals with the powers of the president of the republic. . . . In order to further reduce the powers that rightfully belong to this victorious revolution, we have also decided to maintain the national Congress—only establishing certain limitations on its power.

Table 6.2 Suspension of political rights (*cassação*) of Brazilian legislators, all levels of government, 1964–1970

	1964	1965	1966	1967	1968	1969	1970	Totals
Senator	2	—	—	—	—	5	—	7
Alternate Senator	1	—	—	—	—	1	—	2
Federal Deputy	55	—	5	—	12	78	—	150
Alternate Federal Deputy	12	—	1	1	—	11	—	25
State Deputy	36	—	29	1	—	151	13	—
Alternate State Deputy	26	—	8	—	—	17	—	51
City Council	10	—	1	—	—	23	11	45
Alternate City Council	—	—	—	—	—	2	1	3
TOTALS	142	—	44	2	12	288	15	513

SOURCE: Dos Santos, Monteiro, and Caillaux 1990: 248; data originally collected by Marcus Figueiredo (1977).

Thus, it should be clear that the Revolution does not intend to legitimate itself through Congress. On the contrary, it is Congress that is made legitimate by this institutional act, which could only result from the inherent and revolutionary exercise of constituent power. (AI-1, quoted in Alves 1985: 32)

On October 27, 1965, the Castello Branco government decreed the Second Institutional Act, which further consolidated executive power. Some provisions of AI-2 merely made permanent some prerogatives the presidency had already seized in AI-1: *cassação, decurso de prazo,* and exclusive powers in budgetary policy. But military rulers wanted more: in order to limit any future legislative interference or challenge to the emerging regime, AI-2 ended all Congressional competency in military matters. In a related move, the executive was granted the sole power to declare a state of siege. Article 30 of AI-2 was the origin of another infamous tool of authoritarian governance, the *decreto-lei* or decree law.[2] Finally, in the *coup de grace,* Article 31 gave the president the right to close the National Congress at his discretion. If Congress were suspended, the president was permitted to legislate in its place (Alves 1985: 63).

In late 1966, the military announced plans for a constitution that would replace the 1946 document. When it became apparent that Congress would have little or no role in the drafting process, federal legislators—including some prominent ARENA politicians—began to criticize Castello Branco publicly. The president responded on October 20 by decreeing six new *cassações* and closing Congress for one month. Later, the Fourth Institutional Act of December 1966 forced the legislature to return for an extraordinary session in which it dutifully ratified the military's political charter. The authoritarian Constitution of 1967 codified almost all of the preceding Institutional Acts and related decrees, thereby perpetuating for two decades the tremendous imbalance in the separation of powers. This perhaps was illus-

2. Article 58 of the Constitution of 1967 permitted the president, "in cases of urgency or relevant public interest," to issue decree-laws on matters of national security and public finances. This was later amended to include a third area, that of the creation of public employment and the determination of wage levels. According to Article 58, decree-laws would have take effect immediately upon their publication, and Congress would have sixty days to approve or reject the decree. No amendments were permitted to the legislation. If Congress did not take action within the specified period of sixty days, the decree was "approved" automatically via the *decurso de prazo.* Finally, even if Congress explicitly rejected a decree-law (which did not happen until 1983, and then occurred only twenty-one times until decree-laws were abolished by the Constitution of 1988), this would not undo the juridical effects the decree had during its existence: that is, the legislature was permitted only *ex nunc* nullification of the decree-law.

trated most dramatically by Congress's loss of *any* power to either initiate or amend legislation dealing with public spending (Skidmore 1988: 56).

With Congress effectively stripped of any decision-making capacity, by 1968 the institution had largely been reduced to a forum for public and political debate. Because the new Constitution had respected the republican tradition of parliamentary immunity, many MDB legislators, and even the occasional *arenista*, began to take to the floor of Congress to denounce the regime's excesses. It was precisely in the exercise of this prerogative that Congress made a final, fruitless defense of its institutional autonomy. In August and September 1968, Deputy Márcio Moreira Alves (MDB-Guanabara) made a series of powerful speeches calling for popular resistance to the authoritarian regime. Among the actions he recommended were that all Brazilians boycott the Independence Day festivities and that young women refuse to date soldiers. Though Alves's appeals were largely rhetorical and hardly realistic, military officers were nonetheless incensed and became determined to "get" the congressman. Military ministers announced their intention to try Alves in a military court for treason, but the Supreme Court ruled that his parliamentary immunity would have to be lifted first. In the final months of 1968, the armed forces pressured the legislature to strip Alves of his immunity. The showdown came on December 12 in a special joint meeting of Congress. In a spectacular defiance of the executive branch, the armed forces, and authoritarianism generally, the Congress voted 216 to 141 to reject the military's demand. Most significant, some 94 ARENA legislators abandoned the government to defend the principle of parliamentary immunity (Skidmore 1988: 81).

On the morning after the vote, the government issued the infamous Fifth Institutional Act, ushering in the most repressive period in modern Brazilian history. All civil liberties were suspended, and thousands of opposition figures were arrested in the weeks following AI-5.[3] Congress was closed by force for an indefinite period, as were several state legislatures. Although the Fifth Institutional Act repeated some of the measures taken in earlier decrees, but there was an essential difference in that AI-5 had no date of expiration. Every provision of the act would continue in force until the

3. The crackdown continued for months, well into 1969, via a series of decrees and supplementary acts. Thus, in Brazilian political parlance "AI-5" refers not only to the original act itself but to this extended process or historical period of repression. To focus only on the legislative repercussions of this process is admittedly a narrow view that does not treat the scarring impact of AI-5 on Brazilian society. The human side of this story is presented compellingly in the Archdiocese of São Paulo's Brasil Nunca Mais project (Dassin 1986).

presidency revoked it. Through AI-5 the executive branch regained the power to close the National Congress and other legislative bodies at the state and municipal levels, to declare a state of siege without Congressional consent, and to legislate by decree. Federal legislators subsequently became liable to prosecution on national security issues (Packenham 1971) Though its destruction of legislative authority was nearly total, AI-5's effect on the judiciary was perhaps worse: the executive gained the right to dismiss judges, and no citizen could appeal to the courts any decision taken under AI-5. Thus AI-5 became the durable cornerstone of the authoritarian regime—whenever opposition demands tested the limits of controlled liberalization in the 1970s, AI-5 was the perennial trump card in the hands of the presidency. The act remained in force until it was revoked by President Ernesto Geisel in late 1978, a decade later.

In 1969, the military government decreed the First Amendment to the Constitution of 1967, which in effect revoked the old charter and created the Constitution of 1969. The new Constitution incorporated most of the provisions of AI-5 and of the new National Security Law (Lei de Segurança Nacional, or LSN), which defined crimes against the state. In November 1971, the military revealed perhaps its most creative usurpation of legislative authority. The so-called Secret Decree Statute enabled the executive to issue decree-laws whose texts would simply not be made public. As Maria Helena Moreira Alves points out, "This provided a basis for the arrest of a person for infringement of a law the existence of which was completely unknown" (1985: 119). Although AI-5 was revoked in 1978, much of the other baggage of the national security state, including the Constitution of 1969 and the LSN, remained in effect for over three years beyond the transition to civilian rule in 1985.

Effects of Marginalization on Legislative Life

General Médici, and his successors in the presidency, Generals Geisel and Figueiredo, maintained the National Congress open in an attempt to generate a minimum of democratic legitimacy for a nondemocratic regime. Meanwhile, the regime continued its assault on legislative authority, adjusting the intensity of antilegislative discourse and actions as the situation required. Especially in the period between the forced recess of 1969 and the elections of 1982, military presidents could count on a docile Congress with strong ARENA/PDS majorities in both houses. This period could be termed the era of legislative marginalization. To understand the challenges to legislative revitalization after 1985, it is necessary to review some of the institutional changes resulting from the deliberate emasculation of Congress.

Loss of legislative powers. The legal and institutional framework created by the Institutional Acts and the authoritarian constitutions had the effect of transferring the lawmaking function to the executive branch. Abranches and Soares (1972) documented this trend over the first seven years of authoritarian rule. They noted that this process was characterized not only by a rapid increase in the number of legislative proposals submitted by the presidency, but also by Congress's abdication of its authority in the wake of AI-5. Soares and Abranches hypothesized that "after the executive branch's show of force in closing Congress, [the legislature] preferred to abstain from legislation and oversight, maintaining a vegetative existence so as not to risk a new showdown with the executive" (1972: 275). The effect of the Fifth Institutional Act can be illustrated by the fact that in 1968 (before AI-5) and again in 1970 (after the forced recess), Congress approved 98 percent of the executive's bills. However, the percentage of its *own* bills that Congress approved declined from 80 percent to only 11 percent over the same period (ibid.). The persistence of this trend in the new legislature elected in 1970 is shown in Table 6.3.

Abranches and Soares depicted the new balance of power between the executive and legislative branches as the outcome of five distinct transformations. First was the secular trend toward an increasingly activist presidency—to a certain extent, the increase in legislative proposals by presidents was already evident before the 1964 coup. Second was the rapid increase in the approval rate of executive-initiated bills after the presidency fell to the military. Third, the invention of the *decreto-lei* gave the presidency the power to legislate autonomously. Fourth, in 1967 Congress lost its role in budgetary matters. Finally, AI-5 represented a turning point in that the legislature henceforth would rarely approve its own bills, ratifying instead the external legislative agenda submitted by military presidents (ibid., 276).

Table 6.3 Bills considered in Chamber of Deputies, 7th Legislature (1971–1975), by origin

Bills Introduced	Number Introduced	Number Approved	Percentage Approved	Percentage Rejected[a]
By executive	348	347	99	—
By legislature	2,052	173	8	27

Source: Baaklini 1977: 250.

[a] Some bills were neither approved nor rejected.

A footnote to this process was the unsuccessful attempt by Congress in the mid-1960s to apprise itself of executive intentions. Figure 6.1 illustrates how the legislature tried to conform to its reduced legislative capacity by increasing its oversight activities. The number of requests for information from the executive rose from a pre-coup annual level of 1,332 requests in 1963 to a record 3,598 in 1967, the year before AI-5. After the authoritarian crackdown, the number of requests dropped to 8 in 1970 and rose only to 25 in 1971. As in the case of Márcio Moreira Alves and parliamentary immunity, the efforts at oversight would seem to indicate that some sectors of Congress were willing to resist marginalization to the extent that this was feasible.

Structural dependence on the executive. The failed attempt in the mid-1960s to expand legislative oversight is only symptom of a larger affliction. In the wake of AI-5, and throughout the era of legislative marginalization, there existed a chronic dependency by the Congress on the executive branch for the information and resources necessary to perform legislative duties. During this period, the national legislature became more inwardly focused, and much of its work consisted of efforts to cope with and attempt to correct the imbalance of power between the branches of government. The result was a series of legislative reforms addressing numerous issues, including leadership structures, the committee system, the bill flow, technology and

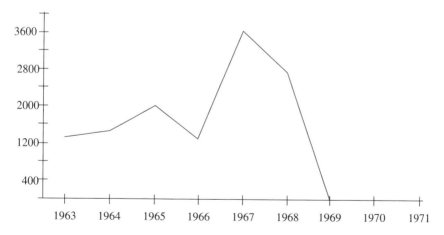

Fig. 6.1
Number of requests for information presented by Congress to the executive, 1963–1971
SOURCE: Abranches and Soares 1972: 277.

human resources, and image building. The bureaucratic infrastructure of Congress expanded greatly in the 1970s.

It is noteworthy that these technical, informational, and staffing reforms proved more important to the opposition MDB than to the progovernment ARENA/PDS party. In the 1971–75 legislature, MDB deputies reported that the Chamber's Legislative Directorate provided them with more than 75 percent of their information; however, ARENA deputies credited the Directorate with supplying only 25 percent of their information, with approximately 50 percent coming directly from the executive branch (Baaklini and Heaphey 1976: 36). These interesting findings confirm the close relationship between the clientelistic right and the military government, and foreshadow the low level of legislative participation by the right in subsequent years.

Changes in recruitment. As one might expect, the redefinition of the role of Congress in Brazilian politics after 1964 could not but affect the patterns of legislative recruitment. A decade after the coup, Astiz (1975) speculated that the National Congress was losing its importance as an agent of recruitment for the Brazilian political elite, but this argument was quickly disputed by Nunes (1978). In a study of patterns of political recruitment that compared the 1964–76 period with the democratic regime of 1946–64, Nunes found that while the Congress did indeed become less important for recruitment to ministerial posts, it remained a strong locus for political recruitment at the state level. At the federal level, some 60 percent of cabinet ministers between 1946–64 had prior legislative experience, compared to only 29 percent of their successors under the post-1964 authoritarian regime. This, of course, reflected the antipolitical and technocratic policymaking orientation of the military regime. But at the state level, the percentage of governors recruited from Congress stayed basically at the same level despite the change of regime (69 percent in the Second Republic and 64 percent under military government). It is important to recall that after 1965, the rules of the political game ensured that governors—for all intents and purposes—were appointed by the presidency, and that nearly all of these politicians belonged to ARENA/PDS. Contrary to its stated desires at the federal level, where the executive excoriated the traditional, locally oriented professional politician, within the states the military government extended an olive branch to this demonized figure. Nunes surmised that

[a]pparently, the central power sought networks and governors that were legitimate within the state-level political systems, thereby descend-

ing into the inner workings of the State Assemblies and local groups, and creating hitherto unknown patterns of power [made possible by] a peaceful political system free of direct intervention. (Nunes 1978: 59)

In Nunes' view, the survival of "political" governors recruited from the legislative branch, combined with the preservation of the National Congress, allowed for the "greasing" (azeitamento) of the convivium between the states and the federal government after 1964. However, a Congressional career was no longer so important for recruitment at the federal level. Also, the técnicos who increasingly dominated the Cabinet showed little interest in the Congress (Nunes 1978).[4]

An understanding of these changing patterns of political recruitment is essential to an understanding of the contemporary Brazilian political right. Most Brazilian politicians dream of occupying executive positions. While after 1964 the federal Cabinet became off limits to most professional politicians, the ARENA/PDS politicians at least had the hope of arriving to state executive office. Even if they did not get the nod from the federal government for this honor, they had the advantage (unlike their MDB colleagues) of having state governors who belonged to the same political party, and who in turn had the favor of the presidency. The ARENA/PDS state machines were reinforced at several levels, which allowed rightist politicians continued access to state resources, and thus to the tools necessary for the construction of durable political machines.[5] For the right, then, it was reasonable to assume that holding a seat in the National Congress would permit a politician to serve as a conduit between the federal government and the state governor. In light of the political realities of the military-authoritarian regime, even Congressional back-benchwarming stood out as a desirable option for most ARENA/PDS politicians. The MDB politicians, in contrast, had different reasons for serving in Congress (excepting, of course, those who played a similar clientelistic game). Often the emedebistas saw a

4. The classic case of a Cabinet-level técnico harboring a strong hostility toward the legislature was that of Roberto Campos, an economist and former ambassador to the United States. Ironically, as the military regime waned, Campos began a long career as a federal senator and deputy.

5. The strongest and most durable of these bases were in the Northeast, the least developed region of Brazil. This region has always been overrepresented in the National Congress, but the military regime aggravated the problem. With the deliberate manipulation of the electoral rules to favor ARENA/PDS, Congress underwent a process of nordestinização ("Northeasternization"), which could also be described as ruralization. After the coup of 1964, the number of legislators drawn from the agricultural sector increased sharply (Astiz 1975: table 5), and the percentage of members with college degrees dropped (Verner 1974: 622).

Congressional seat as a locus for real opposition activity, as a bully pulpit for condemning the authoritarian regime. In legislative activity, MDB members were far more active and participatory than the ARENA/PDS members (Soares 1979). In sum, MDB and ARENA politicians responded to different recruitment calculi, and behaved differently because of this. These socialization processes were important, and (as is discussed in a subsequent section) differences in the legislative behavior of the two cohorts are reflected even today.

Direct executive intervention in Congress. During the era of legislative marginalization, the executive intervened directly in Congress on numerous occasions. The policy of *cassações*—stripping legislators of their elective mandates and of their civil and political rights—was perhaps the most egregious method of intervention, but it was not the only one. Legislators who remained in office were subjected to more subtle forms of intimidation and manipulation. One goal of the military was to weaken the Congressional leadership system so severely that it would be difficult to achieve any kind of institutional cohesion or consolidation of the legislature. By ensuring a weak leadership system, it was easier for the armed forces to relegate the National Congress to the role of rubber stamp.

In a study of patterns of legislative leadership between 1970 and 1986, Baaklini (1989) found that in all three types of leadership—party leadership, committee leadership, and membership on the Mesa[6]—the military regime had succeeded in maintaining a high rate of turnover among leaders. In the case of party leadership, the military controlled ARENA/PDS independently of the Congress, and rotated the party's legislative leaders as it pleased. In the cases of committee chairmanship and membership on the Mesa, the military took care to institute rules prohibiting immediate reelection to the same position. Thus, no member was able to use a position of leadership to develop a power base within Congress, and the military saw to it that the institution would not emerge as a countervailing power to the presidency.

The military not only introduced massive instability into Congressional

---

6. Each chamber of Congress has a Mesa (governing board) of seven members. Each Mesa has a president (the president of the chamber), two vice-presidents, and four secretaries. The Mesa functions as a kind of board of directors in which each member has a functional responsibility, such as administration, salaries, staffing of the chamber, management of the physical plant and police, provision of housing, transportation, and medical services to the membership, and so on. Because members of the Mesa are in a position to dispense numerous favors to fellow members of Congress, election to the Mesa is highly valued.

leadership but also ensured that such leadership would not be representative. Once again, the Northeastern power base of ARENA/PDS was given a privileged position in the leadership structure. For example, in 1980 the developed South and Southeastern regions of Brazil—strongholds of the opposition MDB—together contained 60 percent of the population and 67 percent of the electorate. However, in the Senate between 1970 and 1986 these regions held only 24 percent (fourteen of fifty-eight) of the total positions on the Mesa. And of these fourteen Mesa seats ceded to the more developed regions, no fewer than ten were given to ARENA/PDS senators (Baaklini 1989: 52). It is safe to assume that the severe underrepresentation on the Mesa of MDB senators from these regions—who, by virtue of having been elected statewide in the most populous and developed areas, were always among the leading opposition figures nationally—was an effective ploy in maintaining the docility of the Federal Senate.

In sum, from the time of AI-5 through the early 1980s—the era of legislative marginalization in Brazil—successive military governments worked forcefully and cleverly to adapt the National Congress to the realities of an authoritarian regime. Changes were effected both internally, in the way Congress functioned and governed itself, and externally, in the legislature's macropolitical role. Emasculated in numerous ways and stripped of any real decision-making power, the Brazilian Congress arrived to the New Republic as an institution in need of drastic reconstruction.

The Right and the Question of Congressional Reform in the National Constituent Assembly, 1987–1988

Rebuilding Congress

Throughout its long struggle against dictatorship, the MDB had called for the election of a National Constituent Assembly with the power to completely rewrite Brazil's authoritarian constitution. It was expected all along that a major goal of the new constitution would be to strengthen the National Congress by correcting the egregious imbalance between the executive and legislative branches and privileging the institution as a locus of popular representation in the new democracy. In Brazil, as in other postauthoritarian regimes throughout the world, legislative consolidation was identified with democratic consolidation.

As the authoritarian regime drew to a close, Congress began to show some signs of life. However, these were due primarily to changes in its political composition (in the 1982 elections, ARENA/PDS failed for the first time in its history to win an absolute majority in the Chamber of Deputies) and to the revocation of AI-5 (in November 1978) than to any real increase in its institutional power. Change was slow in coming. As far as Congress was concerned, the ancién regime of executive-legislative relations continued well into the New Republic. Even President José Sarney (1985–90), in his first three and one-half years in power, still had recourse to such antidemocratic institutions as the *decreto-lei* and *decurso de prazo*. These and other legacies of military rule—what then-Senator Fernando Henrique Cardoso aptly termed the "authoritarian debris"—would have to be dismantled by the National Constituent Assembly in order for Congress to be revitalized. However, the political right in Congress did little to advance this goal, and even obstructed it in numerous ways. In the period of constitution making, the former defenders of authoritarianism were defenders of a strong presidency and a passive Congress, thus hindering the reforms necessary for democratic consolidation in Brazil. By examining the public record of the National Constituent Assembly (Assembléia Nacional Constituinte, or ANC) of 1987–88, we will see clear evidence of the right's ambivalence regarding legislative institutionalization.

Before proceeding, it is necessary to point out that the ANC *did* actually enhance the role of Congress in the Brazilian political system, at least on paper. The national legislature was assigned significant new powers by the Constitution of 1988.[7] The *decurso de prazo* was abolished, as was the hated *decreto-lei* (though its successor, the *medida provisória* or emergency measure, has been also been used as a weapon against Congress by the post-authoritarian presidents). Congress insulated itself from presidential power by making the veto override a *secret* vote, decided by a simple majority. Many administrative powers formerly attributed to the presidency shifted to the legislature. Powers of budgetary oversight were expanded considerably, and all development plans were required to pass through Congress (work may not begin on any public works project without prior legislative authorization). The Senate assumed the responsibility for determining the limits of indebtedness of the Union and the states. Congress gained a significant voice in foreign policy making, and a whole slew of presidential and judicial appointments were made subject to Congressional advice and consent, after the model of the United States Senate. Finally, in the new

---

7. This summary of advances in legislative powers is based on an evaluation of the constitutional text prepared by João Gilberto Lucas Coelho, which appears in Coelho and Oliveira (1989).

Constitution, no "exceptional acts"—such as a state of siege or federal intervention in the states—are permitted without explicit authorization from Congress.

Though the National Congress gained all these powers and many other formal attributes, the experience of democracy after 1988 has shown that the Congress did not avail itself consistently and fully of these new powers. Informed observers had predicted that this might occur. As former MDB deputy João Gilberto wrote in 1989,

> Finally, we have a Congress with powers and prerogatives. . . . [But] we should be alert to the fact that the problems with Congress were not just in the constitutional text, which was so restrictive of the legislature in the former regime. They were due just as much to Congress' being sluggish, careless, and difficult to mobilize. Congress rarely rejected decree-laws and allowed many bills to fall victim to the *decurso de prazo*. . . . A new organization, with a stronger role for committees and a better system of rules, is necessary and is being constructed so that the legislature can take its place as a branch of government. . . . However, all of this still depends on political will, which must express itself in day-to-day operations—in participating, in being present and making decisions. (Coelho 1989: 74)

To date, such political willpower has been slow in materializing: the Congress, while often using its newfound power in a negative sense to obstruct, slow, or amend externally introduced legislation has generally not succeeded in becoming a proactive force in Brazilian politics. Congress's disappointing performance since 1988 is due to many different factors, and not all of them can be related to the presence of the ex-authoritarian cohort. Nevertheless, the right is intimately intertwined with legislative weakness in Brazil. To state that the prolegislative forces in the Constituent Assembly prevailed on many issues in the constitutional text is misleading because they often did so in the face of indifference or obstruction on the part of the right. Also, it is partly because of the presence of a clientelistic and absenteeist right that Congress has not availed itself of the new powers available to it. This trend was already evident even in the work of the ANC, as we shall see below.

Roll-Call Voting in the ANC

Analysis of the ANC roll-call data file demonstrates that the ARENA/PDS cohort resisted the strengthening of Congress in a number of important areas.[8] While in several cases the right did not prevail, their contestation of key reforms is illustrative of their attitudes toward legislative revitalization.

Congressional powers and prerogatives. Throughout the first year of the ANC, the question of the proper system of government for Brazil— presidential or parliamentary—was hotly debated. The early momentum was with the "parliamentarist" forces, which included a semipresidential system in the first draft of the constitution in mid-1987.[9] Fearing that a switch to semipresidentialism would shorten his term, President José Sarney lashed out against the proposal. He found support in the armed forces, which saw in assembly government the risks of political instability and left-ist advances. Together, they resurrected the authoritarian-era alliance of the presidency, the military, and the ARENA/PDS legislative right, and suc-ceeded in forcing a return to a presidential constitution in March 1988.[10] Some 77.6 percent of the ARENA/PDS cohort voted to maintain pure presi-dentialism, compared to 43.1 percent among ex-oppositionists (Table 6.4). This was the only occasion in the twenty months of the ANC in which all

Table 6.4 Preference for the presidential system

Vote	ARENA/PDS Veterans Percentage (N)	Opposition Veterans Percentage (N)	All Veterans Percentage (N)
Yes	77.6 (163)	43.1 (87)	60.7 (250)
No	22.4 (47)	56.4 (114)	39.1 (161)
Abstain	—	0.5 (1)	0.2 (1)
TOTALS	100.0 (210)	100.0 (202)	100.0 (412)

DESCRIPTION OF VOTE 315: The Humberto Lucena Amendment removed parliamentarism from the constitutional draft and replaced it with the traditional presidential system. A yes vote is for presidentialism (*DANC,* March 23, 1988).

8. As in the previous chapter, all crosstabulations of roll-call votes discussed here were significant at the .05 level or better.

9. Brazilian sources commonly refer to this proposal as "parliamentary." In fact, the draft included a role for an elected president, and thus the proposed regime was properly semipresidential or "premier-presidential" (Shugart and Carey 1992). The important point here is that the proposal would have severely reduced the powers of future presidents (and by extension, those of the sitting president) and made future governments dependent upon assem-bly support. For an excellent and thorough discussion of the evolving drafts of the executive articles, see Martínez-Lara (1996: chap. 5).

10. It was later decided in the ANC that the question of system of government would be put to the electorate in the form of a plebiscite to be held five years later. In April 1993, despite strong support for parliamentarism among the Brazilian political class, Brazilian voters chose to maintain presidentialism by a wide margin.

559 members were present for a roll-call vote. In the New Republic, the right has consistently been the strongest supporter of presidential rule and strong presidential powers: later we will attempt to explain why this should be so.

The debate in the ANC then turned to the role of Congress in a traditional presidential system. One key issue was Congressional advice and consent in presidential appointments. A reform movement in the ANC aimed to democratize the Brazilian judiciary by allowing all three branches of government choose justices for the Supreme Court (Supreme Tribunal Federal, or STF), rather than the previous system based on the U.S. model of presidential nomination and Senate consent. Under the new proposal, four justices would be nominated by the president, four by the Chamber of Deputies, and three by the STF itself. The nominees would then face a public hearing, and then would need to win two-thirds approval from the senators. The Senate did not stand to lose any power by this change, and the overall role of Congress would have been enhanced in the nomination process. The ARENA/PDS cohort opposed this change overwhelmingly (only 20.7 percent of the right voted for this prolegislative reform, compared to 63.8 percent among the opposition veterans), even though the proposal did not threaten the right's built-in advantage in the upper house of Congress (Vote 354, April 6, 1988).[11]

A similar episode concerned the Federal Accounts Court (Tribunal de Contas da União, or TCU), an important element in federal administration in Brazil. While independent, the TCU is constitutionally required to assist Congress in the oversight of national accounts, property, and expenditures. This is a critical function in a country where public spending has often been riddled with "irregularities," and where officialdom sometimes confuses the public patrimony with its own (Weyland 1993; Fleischer 1994). The ANC central drafting committee had decided that two-thirds of the TCU ministers would be elected by the Congress, and the remaining third would be nominated by the president. An amendment was presented later which would have permitted Congress to choose *all* TCU ministers, via secret vote, in a clear effort to strengthen Congress's oversight function. Although the amendment was favored by 57 percent of the legislators present, it failed to

---

11. The right is drawn heavily from the lesser developed states of Brazil, which are far more numerous than the more modern states. With three senators per state, the less developed regions control about 70 percent of the seats in the upper chamber.

pass, due in part to opposition by the right, which opposed it by a margin of 53.3 percent to 43.9 percent (Vote 272, March 15, 1988).[12]

Because Congress was stripped of nearly all its budgetary powers under military rule, a leading goal of legislative reformers in the ANC was to restore to Congress the power of the purse. Federal budgeting is initiated annually by the president in a bill called the Law of Budgetary Directives (LDO). The LDO presents the spending targets and priorities of the federal government, although in practice Brazilian presidents have frequently deviated from these guidelines. In creating the LDO in 1988, the ANC attempted to correct this problem by forcing the presidency to be far more forthcoming on the specifics of federal spending: Congress is now permitted to examine details on outlays of capital, and the president is required to submit a bimonthly report on the ongoing implementation of the budget. The amendment that gave Congress these new powers was approved overwhelmingly (312 votes to 83) in April 1988. One would expect that professional legislators would automatically support such a clear interbranch transfer of budgetary powers. However, some 41.8 percent of the ARENA/PDS cohort chose to vote *against* such a fundamental restructuring of executive-legislative relations (Vote 471, April 20, 1988). One explanation for this might be that ARENA/PDS legislators were accustomed to a clientelistic

Table 6.5 Summary table of key ANC roll-call votes on legislative issues

Vote	Content (see text for full description)	Percentage of ARENA/PDS Veterans Supporting Pro-Legislative Position	Percentage of Opposition Veterans Supporting Pro-Legislative Position	Percentage of All Veterans Supporting Pro-Legislative Position	Sig. (chi-square)
354	STF nominating procedures	20.7	63.8	43.1	<.001
272	TCU nominating procedures	43.9	60.7	53.5	<.05
471	LDO budgetary authority	56.0	91.8	74.3	<.001
279	Quorum issue	17.3	70.3	43.4	<.001
290	Recess and session length	17.7	43.6	30.6	<.001
313	Popular introduction of enabling legislation	44.8	83.6	64.4	<.001

12. ANC rules stipulated that amendments to the draft would have to receive the votes of an absolute majority of the Assembly (280 votes). This amendment was favored by a clear majority of those voting but failed to muster the necessary 280 votes.

relationship with the executive branch, in which they dealt one-on-one with ministers seeking investments and public works for their home states and municipalities (Cammack 1982; Hagopian 1996). This kind of pork-barrel politics, which is highly individualistic, is favored by an environment in which the executive branch retains considerable discretion over the disbursement of funds. It should be expected that clientelistic politicians would resist increased transparency in the budgetary and spending processes (Krieger, Rodrigues, and Bonassa 1994).[13]

The foregoing observations find empirical support in Barry Ames's (1995b) study of the bases of voting in the Chamber of Deputies. One of Ames's dependent variables was the Congressional Power scale devised by Kinzo (1989), who combined nine key ANC roll-calls on legislative powers—including several discussed in the text above—into a composite indicator of support for the legislative branch. In studying the roll-call voting of 403 deputies during the ANC, Ames operationalized clientelistic orientations in terms of the frequency of deputies' audiences with ministers and of their success in securing intergovernmental transfers ("pork") to municipalities in their electoral strongholds. He then included these variables in multivariate models designed to predict support for Congressional Power. Clientelistic orientations were strong negative predictors of support for legislative institution-building. Interestingly, the single best predictor of Congressional Power was a dummy variable for prior membership in ARENA/PDS during the military regime, and the regression coefficient for this variable was negative as expected. In the ANC, Ames concluded, former members of ARENA were "pro-executive [and] anti-Congress" (Ames 1995b: 339).

Efficiency, workload, and image of the legislature. Traditionally, one of the most serious problems in the Brazilian National Congress has been its inefficiency, which is both widely perceived and empirically verifiable (Abranches and Soares 1972; Coelho 1989). This inefficiency is attributable in part to the chronic absenteeism of elected representatives, which tends to be

13. Interestingly, on the day after the new budgetary language was approved by the ANC, a second amendment was considered that was intended to streamline the budgeting process. The amendment would have required the Congress to approve the federal budget before adjourning the annual session; if Congress failed to do so, then the president would be able to implement the budget by decree. Some 94.4 percent of the opposition cohort favored this amendment, compared to only 48.5 percent of the former ARENA/PDS. This particular amendment died, but later a different version passed. The new Constitution mandates approval of the LDO before adjournment (Article 57, paragraph 2).

higher among rightists.[14] In the ANC the right was acutely aware of its own absenteeist tendencies and tried to avoid letting this play into the hands of progressive forces. If the right missed numerous sessions, the left could seize the initiative and dominate the legislative agenda—which is exactly what happened in the first months of the ANC. The right responded by consistently trying to raise the permanent quorum for decision making in the Congress. While the first draft of the new constitution allowed for normal congressional decisions to be taken by a simple majority of the members present, as long as the simple majority was equivalent to at least one-fifth of the total membership, the conservative coalition in the ANC (Centrão) changed this, requiring an absolute majority for all decisions. Later, partisans of the first draft fought back, and attempted to reduce the quorum level once more, arguing that in practice a higher quorum would mean continued inefficiency within the legislature. Their efforts were defeated by the ex-authoritarians, who voted 81.5 percent in favor of maintaining a higher quorum, compared to only 28.5 percent among ex-oppositionists (Vote 279, March 16, 1988). The quorum may seem a minor issue to some, but in reality the right's victory in the ANC has served to perpetuate congressional inefficiency under the Constitution of 1988. This has hurt the legislative agenda of the democratic presidents, but it has also damaged confidence in the National Congress and the political class in general, with worrisome implications for democratic legitimacy in Brazil.[15]

With an eye to the public image of the National Congress, one amendment attempted to increase the length of the annual legislative session. The

14. This is a common assertion in journalistic coverage of the Congress, and many legislators—not just conservatives—complain that the press unfairly criticizes them for poor attendance. However, both congressional staff members and academic Congress-watchers will testify that the political right has lower participation rates. In the ANC, the absenteeism rate for roll-call votes among ex-*arenistas* was 34 percent, compared to 23 percent among other legislators (calculated from Coelho and Oliveira, 1989). In the 1991–94 period, some twenty-nine legislators missed more than 50 percent of all sessions; nineteen of these were from conservative parties and six more from the conservative wing of the PMDB (*Folha de São Paulo*, September 18, 1994, special supplement entitled "Olho no Voto," A-26). In personal interviews, several leftist legislators privately expressed their satisfaction with the right's absenteeism, which occasionally permits the left to prevail in legislative battles that would be unwinnable otherwise.

15. To surmount the difficulties imposed by chronic absenteeism and the unrealistic quorum requirement, many bills are now passed by the "symbolic" vote of the party floor leaders. For example, the final budget bill of 1994, which was required to be approved by December 1993, was approved ten months later by a symbolic vote, after most of the funds in it had long since been spent. Beginning with his first election in November 1994, President Fernando Henrique Cardoso has frequently called on Congress to reduce the quorum.

constitutional draft had specified an annual recess of three months; the proposal shortened this to two. The amendment was rejected by the ANC by a margin of two to one. But once again the right showed itself to be the least favorable to increasing the legislative workload. While the opposition veterans voted against the amendment by a margin of 53.2 percent to 43.6 percent, the ex-*arenistas* opposed it by 79.7 percent to 17.7 percent (Vote 290, March 18, 1988).

Popular participation in the legislative process. Throughout the ANC the right was the sector most resistant to the idea of opening up the legislature to participation by ordinary Brazilians. In an early vote on whether to allow the people's initiative process within state legislatures (it was approved), the right was more than four times as likely as the opposition cohort to oppose the idea: 41.4 percent opposition from ex-*arenistas* versus 8.3 percent from opponents of military rule (Vote 210, March 8, 1988).

This issue returned later in the ANC when the assembly discussed the issue of "supplementary laws" (*leis complementares*), which is the Brazilian term for enabling legislation. These are specific acts of Congress that are required to activate the large number of non–self-executing articles or provisions of the 1988 Constitution. The first draft of the constitution had allowed *leis complementares* to be introduced in Congress by ordinary citizens. Later, in its alternative draft, the Centrão removed this provision. During the amendment phase, partisans of the first draft succeeded in restoring the original language permitting popular participation (Constitution of 1988, Article 61). Ex-authoritarians were deeply divided on this issue (44.8 percent support versus 49.4 percent opposition, with ten absentions), while ex-oppositionists supported the language by a margin of 83.6 percent (Vote 313, March 22, 1988). The reason for this lies in the practical importance of supplementary laws. By making it more difficult for Congress to consider supplementary laws, the Centrão had tried to ensure that many of the progressive advances of the new Constitution would never be converted into law. In this they would benefit from the normal lassitude of the Brazilian Congress, which would be aggravated by the higher quorum rules they had successfully advocated the week before. A study done in mid-1990, nearly two years after the promulgation of the new Constitution, showed Congress had still not passed enabling legislation for almost two hundred of its provisions (*Jornal do Brasil*, July 24, 1990). Even in late 1998, after the Constitution had celebrated its tenth anniversary, there will still major sections of the text that had never been enacted. One of these was highly relevant to the financial crisis consuming Brazil at the time: Article 192, which regulates the Central Bank and the entire national financial system (*Jornal do Brasil*, November 29, 1998).

Finally, as the voting phase of the ANC drew to a close there was heated debate over the issue of popular ratification of the new Constitution. In the first week of June 1988, three amendments were proposed, each with a different approach to securing a popular mandate for the new charter. One called for a simple referendum on the finished document, a solution which has been followed in other countries (Vote 618, June 1, 1988); a second called for popular amendments to and vetoes of specific provisions of the new Constitution (Vote 619, June 1, 1988); and a third proposed that if the Constitution were rejected by a majority in a plebiscite, then elections would have to be held within ninety days for an "exclusive Assembly," in other words, a constitution-making body different from the National Congress (Vote 620, June 2, 1988). All of these amendments were defeated easily by an Assembly weary after eighteen months of deliberations and fearful that the process would never be resolved. But in each case, ex-*arenistas* were two or three times more likely than ex-oppositionists to reject the idea of popular ratification.

This refusal is not necessarily an antidemocratic posture—after all, many constitutions have been written and implemented without citizen participation, and the ANC already had an indisputable popular mandate deriving from the elections of 1986. Moreover, it is possible to make the argument that the true institution-building position here would prohibit popular intervention in internal legislative matters. But combined with some of the indicators discussed earlier, resistance to popular ratification points to a more exclusionary attitude on the part of the right. It is also well to recall that this attitude was on display only three years after the transition to democracy, in a crucial "window of opportunity" where elites needed to win popular acceptance for the new regime. The right's comparatively greater resistance to popular participation in the National Congress—the outstanding symbol of popular sovereignty in Brazil, and one that had been subverted by the authoritarian regime of 1964–85—did not appear propitious for the subsequent development of the "representation regime" in the New Republic.

The Right in Congress after the ANC: Results of Survey Research

The constitution written by the National Constituent Assembly was promulgated on October 5, 1988. On that date the ANC ceased to exist, and the

Brazilian National Congress returned to its normal legislative duties for the remainder of the 48th Legislature (1987–91). Thus my 1990 survey tapped the membership of the ANC about eighteen months after the assembly's completion. The 1993 and 1997 replications surveyed the 49th and 50th Legislatures, respectively (Appendix B). One set of questions investigated how politicians spend their time as legislators (Table 6.6).

Returning to our set of theoretical expectations drawn from Weber, and recalling the right's peculiar interaction with political institutions during 1964–85, we should expect the following about the right's time budgeting in Congress: ex-*arenistas* should be less active in parliamentary activities (as measured by the making of speeches, the introduction of bills, and the suggestion of amendments), less oriented toward the actual function of representing social groups (as measured by frequency of contacts with civil society organizations), and more engaged in clientelistic interactions with the state apparatus (as measured by frequency of contacts with federal and local bureaucrats). The self-reported data in Table 6.6 lend support to these hypotheses. Table 6.6 traces six variables across three surveys, for a total of eighteen crosstabulations. In seventeen of the eighteen cases, comparison of the ARENA and opposition cohorts reveals the expected patterns of higher or lower engagement in the legislature in accordance with the aforementioned hypotheses, and in nine of these cases the differences between the two cohorts are statistically significant. In only one case—introduction of bills in the 1997 survey, when the ex-*arenistas* reported higher rates than the ex-oppositionists—did the expected polarity fail to obtain.

These findings reflect patterns established under the former military regime. In 1976 under the dictatorship, for example, ARENA members were making only 36 percent of congressional speeches and introducing 32 percent of the bills, even though the party enjoyed large majorities in Congress (Soares 1979: 119). In the early 1990s, legislators who had passed through ARENA and PDS, by their own admission, were still much less likely than the former opposition to pursue ("frequently") these activities on the floor.

The most interesting indicators in Table 6.6 are those that relate to relations between legislators and the bureaucracy, either at the federal or local level.[16] Members of the ARENA/PDS cohort were more likely to report fre-

16. These figures increased dramatically from the 48th to the 49th Legislatures among all members of Congress. An explanation of this trend must await further research. However, one preliminary hypothesis might be the trend toward intervention in budgetary matters by individual legislators; after the promulgation of the Constitution of 1988, the number of amendments offered to the federal budget began to climb exponentially. See Ames (1995a) for a discussion of this trend toward pork-barrel politics, which eventually culminated in a series

quent contacts with the state apparatus. This finding itself is remarkable, but when combined with the finding of generally lower participation in day-to-day legislative activities, it hints at a fundamental difference in orientation between the right and the opposition cohort in Congress. One group, composed by of the former opposition to military rule, reports *higher* participation in legislative deliberations and *fewer* contacts with bureaucrats; another group, the progovernment coalition under authoritarianism, reports *lower* participation in the legislature and *more frequent* contact with representatives of the federal and local bureaucracies. These data, reported by the legislators themselves, tend to support the distinction between a group with a more institutional orientation and a group with a more clientelistic orientation. This distinction is compatible with—and indeed was foreshadowed by—the qualitative research of scholars such as Jenks (1979), Cammack (1982), and Hagopian (1986, 1992), all of whom emphasized how the institutional emasculation effected by military governments in the 1960s and 1970s led to an expansion of clientelistic practices. The politicians who benefited from clientelism and near-exclusive access to state resources between 1964 and 1985 were the members of ARENA and PDS, who themselves were clients of the military-dominated executive.

My focus here is on the differences in legislative participation between the two cohorts of interest, but there is one aggregate-level finding in Table 6.6 that may augur well for legislative institutionalization in Brazil. Self-reported legislative activity among veterans of the 1964–85 military regime rose broadly and uniformly from 1990 to 1993 to 1997; this was true on all six indicators used. Although there is evidence of the lingering authoritarian-era cleavage between government and opposition, the dramatic rise in participation among *all* veterans of the military regime suggests that democracy has begun to foster the inculcation of pro-institutional parliamentary norms, at least as applies to making speeches, introducing bills and amendments, and consulting with organized civil society. On the other hand, if meetings with bureaucrats are taken as a proxy for clientelistic behavior, they too have increased dramatically since 1990.

How the Right Sees Legislative Life

In the 1990s, personal interviews revealed Brazilian federal legislators, both ex-*arenistas* and others, to be remarkably though not uniformly dissatisfied

---

of corruption scandals and expulsions from Congress in 1994 (Fleischer 1994; Krieger, Rodrigues, and Bonassa 1994).

Table 6.6 Self-reported time usage of federal legislators

Q. "Please tell me if you have participated in the following activities over the past twelve months: frequently, once in a while, rarely, or never" (percentages refer to respondents answering "frequently")

Legislative Activity	1990				1993				1997			
	ARENA/PDS Veterans	Opposition Veterans	All Veterans	Sig.	ARENA/PDS Veterans	Opposition Veterans	All Veterans	Sig.	ARENA/PDS Veterans	Opposition Veterans	All Veterans	Sig.
Address your legislative chamber	34.6	47.5	41.5	.05	47.5	63.1	57.3	.05	52.8	67.6	61.4	.10
Introduce a bill	26.0	44.0	35.8	.01	22.6	43.7	35.8	.01	40.0	36.9	34.1	NS
Present amendments to a bill introduced by someone else	24.8	25.0	24.9	NS	29.3	35.6	33.3	NS	30.8	36.5	34.1	NS
Meet with representatives of the federal bureaucracy	15.9	8.9	12.2	NS	37.1	35.0	35.8	NS	52.7	41.9	46.5	NS
Meet with representatives of the bureaucracy in your state or municipality	33.3	20.8	26.6	.05	46.8	39.2	42.1	NS	44.4	41.3	42.6	NS
Meet with representatives of organizations of civil society (CNBB, FIESP, etc.)[a]	9.6	17.2	13.7	.10	14.8	26.2	22.0	.10	18.2	34.7	27.7	.05
Maximum N in samples[b]	108	128	236	—	63	103	166	—	55	76	131	—

NS = Not Significant

[a] These examples were intended to be even-handed. CNBB is the National Conference of Brazilian Bishops, a corporative organization often consulted by the left; FIESP is the Federation of Industries of the State of São Paulo, the voice of organized business groups.
[b] For the specific questionnaire items cited in this table, the number of valid responses in 1990 ranged from a minimum of 226 to a maximum of 233; in 1993, from 159 to 165; and in 1997, from 126 to 130.

with legislative life. A recurring word was "inefficiency." The National Congress was perceived by legislators as a sluggish, poorly administered, and poorly staffed institution. Several interviewees criticized the *assessoria* (legislative staff) on whom they depended for technical support in drawing up bills and amendments.[17] Others criticized the directing boards (Mesas) of the two houses, as well as the committee structure set up in the aftermath of the ANC.[18] Some complained about a lack of priorities in dealing with legislation—major bills were not sorted out from the mass of impending bills to be considered, and there was no way to predict the importance that Congress would accord any specific initiative. Interviewees confirmed my observer's impression that the agenda of the Brazilian Congress is absolutely unpredictable. As former PMDB deputy Paulo Macarini of Santa Catarina commented to me, legislative initiatives seem to require either a few minutes or a few decades but nothing in between. He gave the example of profit-sharing for workers, first "guaranteed" in the Constitution of 1946. This "guarantee" was finally *regulamentado* (activated and codified via enabling legislation) in 1990, three constitutions and forty-four years later. In contrast, the abolition of the universally hated *selo-pedágio* (an automobile windshield sticker required for travel on federal highways) took all of forty minutes. "The Brazilian Congress is the most inefficient institution in the world," commented Deputy Osmundo Rebouças (PMDB-Ceará).

Recent academic research and public symposia (CEBRAP 1994; Abreu and Dias 1995) on the Brazilian Congress have shed light on some additional reasons for parliamentary dissatisfaction. These range from the lack of resources for individual members, to internal rules, to the inevitably oligarchical power structures in the two chambers, to the city of Brasília itself. Members of Congress, especially those on the right, are also especially critical of the media, which they see as hostile and unfair to the national legislature. "The Brazilian media is controlled by the left," lamented Deputy Stélio Dias (PFL-Espírito Santo). Several deputies who had been members of the Centrão during the ANC complained that the national press had delighted in excoriating the conservative alliance after it took a major role in amending the constitutional draft. Deputy César Cals Neto (PSD-Ceará) went fur-

---

17. For a recent symposium on strengths and weaknesses of the Brazilian staffing system, see Abreu and Dias (1995), especially the contributions by Antônio Carlos Pojo do Rego and Mozart Vianna de Paiva.

18. For discussion of the Mesa and of the Colégio de Líderes (the caucus of party floor leaders, which has significant discretion in shaping the legislative agenda), see the debates transcribed in CEBRAP (1994).

ther, saying that the prestige press of Rio and São Paulo was guilty of *patrulhamento*[19] and of invariably treating conservative legislators in a "pejorative" way. The owners of large newspapers may lean more to the conservative side, said Cals, but the journalists are left of center, and after all it is the journalists who write the stories. Amplifying these comments, the 1997 survey results demonstrated that resentment of the press was strong across the board, but particularly intense among ex-*arenistas*. When presented with the statement that "press coverage of the Congress is unfairly negative," 76.5 percent of all legislators agreed, as did 73.5 percent of legislators active in 1964–85. The percentage of agreement fell to 65.8 percent within the former opposition to military rule, but rose to 87.8 percent among ex-authoritarians (only five of forty-one ARENA/PDS veterans disagreed with the statement). The difference between the two authoritarian-era cohorts was significant at the .01 level.

The alienation of legislators also derives from macropolitical factors. In a series of recent papers, Figueiredo and Limongi (1994a, 1994b, 1995b, 1996) have argued that politics in the New Republic has featured two simultaneous and competing national agendas. The agenda of the executive branch has been macroeconomic stabilization; the agenda of the National Congress has been social action. Given the fiscal crisis of the Brazilian state, the advance of neoliberal reforms in the 1990s that seek to correct this fiscal crisis, and the inevitably zero-sum game of budgetary politics, it is often argued that stabilization and social spending are mutually incompatible goals. The bifurcation of the national agenda is especially dissatisfying for legislators given that the executive agenda invariably takes precedence: the president either gets what he wants (Figueiredo and Limongi 1996), or at the very least dominates the legislative calendar (Power 1998). The profound individualism of Brazilian legislators (Mainwaring 1991b; Novaes 1994; Ames 1995b) leads to collective action problems that no doubt intensify this perception of powerlessness.

Many of the aforementioned issues affect all legislators across the political spectrum. But does the political right have any unique perspectives on congressional life? Similarly to the discussion of party life in Chapter 5, ex-*arenistas* stressed the importance of politics in their home states. Several ex-

19. *Patrulhamento ideológico* (literally "ideological patrol") is an important slang term in Brazilian politics. It is somewhat equivalent to the North American term "political correctness," although the connotation of *patrulhamento* is more harsh. The term is employed in a unidirectional sense: the reputed "thought police" are invariably to the left of their supposed victims.

arenista politicians took time to explain the constellation of political forces in their state of origin, and how their legislative mandate fit into the picture. One influential senator, Jorge Bornhausen (PFL-Santa Catarina), suggested that a vocation for *local* politics was exactly what permitted the ARENA/PDS right to survive the transition from military to civilian rule. He stated flatly that, for a Brazilian politician, "it doesn't matter what your past is— what matters is your political position within your state." He proudly presented his own credentials on this issue, emphasizing that as a senator between 1983 and 1990 he had spent no more than four weekends in the capital. Another deputy, the late Christovam Chiaradia (PFL-Minas Gerais), echoed these observations, stating that his orientation as a federal legislator was essentially local. Calling himself a *deputado municipalista*, he prided himself on his relations with small-town mayors in his electoral stronghold. Again, these conversations are not systematic evidence, but when combined with some of the time-usage data cited earlier, they point to an interesting pattern of legislators' valuing close links with state and local bureaucracies. And if, as Bornhausen suggested, the localistic orientation of ex-authoritarians was the secret of their survival, this bodes ill for the consolidation of a professionalized, nationally oriented legislature.

The other important theme in interviews was nostalgia for executive office. As discussed in Chapter 4, the ARENA/PDS cohort in Congress, due to its trajectory and role under military rule, has more executive experience to its credit than the rest of the membership (see Table 4.6). Ex-authoritarians spoke longingly of their days in the executive branch. Deputy Manoel Castro (PFL-Bahia), a former unelected mayor of Salvador, one of Brazil's largest and most important cities, said "you can't even compare" political service in the legislative and executive branches. Deputy Enoc Vieira (PFL-Maranhão), a lieutenant of the Sarney machine in Maranhão who was one of the unlucky *arenistas* never to hold at least one executive position, expressed executive envy this way: "The deputy is forever asking someone else to do something for his strongholds. His dream is not to have to ask anymore." Deputy Oscar Corrêa Jr. of Minas Gerais, at the time the PFL candidate for governor of his state, was even more blunt in his evaluation of legislative service: "*ser deputado não acrescenta nada à sua vida pública,*" or "being a deputy adds nothing to your political career."

These comments, as well as the data on recruitment presented in Chapter 4, point to one of the great unsolved questions in democratic Brazil: how to transform federal legislative service into an attractive option for rationally minded politicians. Senator Jorge Bornhausen suggested that the adoption of parliamentary rule was the only way to improve recruitment—intuitively plausible, yet vetoed by the electorate in the plebiscite of April 1993. But another former member of ARENA, Deputy Adhemar de Barros Filho (PRP-SP) (in 1990, yet another gubernatorial candidate), disagreed with this view, saying that political recruitment is not a function of the national legislature, it is a function of political parties. In Brazil, with the important exception of the small ideological parties of the left, the weak party organizations fail to structure recruitment in any meaningful way (Mainwaring 1999). Stronger, more disciplined parties could restrict access to candidacies for executive positions, and stop the biannual stampedes for the exit doors of Congress (in each of the municipal-level elections held in 1988, 1992, and 1996, more than 20 percent of sitting deputies attempted to leave Congress for a mayoralty in their home states). The rationalization of candidate selection—a crucial reform—would provide incentives for certain politicians to remain in Congress and make a career of it, thus potentially professionalizing the national legislature.

The Right, the Congress, and Democratization in Brazil

This chapter has reviewed some of the tumultuous changes that have taken place in the Brazilian Congress over the past three decades. The military regime that seized power in 1964 ushered in the era of legislative marginalization. Through the Institutional Acts, the legislative authority of Congress was transferred across the Plaza of the Three Powers to the office of the president. The military remolded the legislative leadership structure in a way that prevented politicians (even those that supported military rule) from using the Congress to develop an independent power base. The disproportionality of representation in Congress, which had its origins in the federal structure of Brazil, was deliberately aggravated by the military in a way that ensured overrepresentation of the more progovernment regions of the country. All of these changes and more turned the Brazilian Congress—which had internal problems even before 1964, to be sure—into a rubber-stamp legislature with little or no decision-making role in the political system.

The emasculation of Congress had a differential impact on the Brazilian political class. During military rule, the ARENA/PDS cohort enjoyed comfortable majorities in the legislature, and yet it was not nearly as active as the opposition party. In 1976, for example, MDB congressmen presented more than twice as many bills as their ARENA counterparts, and MDB senators gave twice as many speeches as ARENA senators (Soares 1979: 119). Today, these differences between the two cohorts are still observable—former members of ARENA are still significantly less active in Congress. Also, under authoritarianism, ARENA/PDS federal legislators were the brokers among the executives of their party, who usually controlled all three levels of government: national, state, and local. Thus, they became accustomed to negotiating with bureaucrats the transfer of state resources among these levels; they were in a favorable position to practice clientelistic politics. The right was socialized in this period to work *outside* the framework of representative institutions, including outside the National Congress.

The data presented in this chapter suggest that in the immediate post-transition years, the Brazilian right retained an orientation that was not propitious for legislative consolidation. This orientation could be described in a number of ways: as pro-executive and anti-legislative, or as pro-clientelistic and anti-institutional. While some may argue that these orientations are generalized throughout the Brazilian political class, the data from the late 1980s show that the ex-authoritarian right clearly stood apart in its lack of institutional loyalties to the National Congress—as was also suggested by the parallel research of Barry Ames, who concluded that the ex-*arenistas* were "pro-executive [and] anti-Congress" (Ames 1995b: 339).

Throughout the National Constituent Assembly of 1987–88, the right consistently voted in greater numbers against initiatives intended to strengthen Congress as a locus of national decision making and popular representation. Some of these initiatives aimed to increase congressional powers and prerogatives; others sought to maximize popular participation in the legislature; and others were introduced with a view to improving the efficiency and image of the National Congress. It is impossible to argue that widespread ex-ARENA opposition to these initiatives was the sole reason for their defeat: even if the entire ex-authoritarian cohort were assembled together, it would be insufficient to pass or defeat any measures on its own (the cohort fluctuated in the range of 210 to 215 *constituintes*, and the ANC rules required an absolute majority, or 280 votes, to pass amendments). But it is certainly true that on a few key initiatives—such as the presidential system, the issue of recall elections, the selection rules for STF justices, and the setting of the congressional quorum—the ex-authoritarian right was *largely* responsible for the outcome. Taking these outcomes together, the pattern revealed is that of a right largely uninterested in building legislative institutions.

In the specific case of presidentialism, it is difficult to underestimate the impact that the choice of presidentialism has had on the political party system, on executive-legislative relations, and on governability itself since 1988. Several analysts consider Brazil's hyperpresidential system either the ultimate source (Lamounier 1994) or a major element (Mainwaring 1993) of the wider syndrome of weak representative institutions in Brazil. On this issue, some 78 percent of ex-*arenistas* endorsed Sarney's March 1988 plea for the maintenance of presidentialism, compared to only 43 percent of legislators who had opposed military rule in 1964–85. Due to its comparatively greater orientation toward parochialism, clientelism, and overall dependency on the state apparatus, the ex-ARENA cohort was more susceptible to Sarney's blatant patronage-based arm-twisting prior to this crucial vote. Adding up the increase in government spending, the concession of radio and TV licenses that went to pro-Sarney legislators, and the costs of direct lobbying that went on prior to the vote, some Brazilian newspapers concluded that the cost of securing the ANC's vote in favor of presidentialism was close to $100 million (Martínez-Lara 1996: 139–42).

Many prolegislative initiatives were doomed from the outset due to opposition by the right. Where prolegislative initiatives succeeded—and many did—they either garnered less support from ex-*arenistas* or were passed in spite of the right. Moreover, the questionnaire data on time usage and on preference for executive office, as well as Ames's research on roll-call voting, point to lower institutional commitments among ex-ARENA members of Congress—although Table 6.6 suggests that these differences have begun to diminish in the second decade of democracy. But especially during the Sarney years, the probability of legislative institutionalization in the New Republic could be seen as inversely proportional to the strength of ex-authoritarians in Congress, and this relationship was at its strongest precisely during the post-transition "critical juncture" for institutional design afforded by the ANC. But does the continued deficiency of the Brazilian Congress matter in the first place? There are several reasons why it does.

First, the impeachment of Fernando Collor notwithstanding,[20] Congress is still unable to counterbalance the traditionally dominant Brazilian

20. Many foreign observers, especially the press, interpreted the removal of Collor as a sign of legislative revitalization in Brazil. This interpretation is erroneous: no serious study of the impeachment process has yet reached the conclusion that executive-legislative relations were permanently altered. Rather, Collor's demise has been explained convincingly as something that he more or less invited upon himself. See Geddes and Ribeiro Neto (1992) and especially Weyland (1993).

presidency—a presidency that Shugart and Carey (1992) classified as the most powerful in the world.[21] While the ANC returned important powers to the legislature, Brazilian presidents still have enormous leverage in setting the public agenda. Elements of presidential power in Brazil include impressive executive privilege, easy media access, and direct control of the executive agencies and parastatal enterprises that are so central to Brazilian development and economic life. Control over the armed forces and ability to negotiate with the state governors are two powers that were used to great effect by the first two postauthoritarian presidents, José Sarney and Fernando Collor, both of whom emerged from the old ARENA/PDS machine. To ensure some balance in executive-legislative relations, the National Congress must expand its oversight and policy-making functions. But the tradition in Brazilian politics is that the executive leads and the legislature follows, as was manifested most clearly in the military-imposed institutions of the *decreto-lei* and *decurso de prazo*. While the ANC eliminated these two examples of "authoritarian debris," it decided to maintain some presidential latitude by creating the *medida provisória*, a form of decree power that has been repeatedly abused.[22] Because of disorganization, inefficiency, and absenteeism, the Congress is ill prepared to deal with the president's decree-driven legislative agenda, and fails to innovate a legislative agenda of its own (Novaes 1994; Power 1998).

Second, Congress awarded itself increased authority in the Constitution of 1988, but the implementation of its new powers has been uneven and at times counterproductive. Oversight privileges go unused; positions created by Congress to advise the executive branch remain vacant. The transfer of budgetary authority to the legislature, seen in 1988 as a congressional victory, has instead turned pork-barrel politics into a source of institutional paralysis. The 1993–94 investigation into corruption on the Joint Budget Committee recommended eighteen legislators for expulsion and turned the files of eleven more over to the police for further investigation. Perhaps not by accident, the ringleader of the corruption racket was the senior ex-*arenista*—the longest-serving supporter of the military regime in Congress—Deputy João Alves (PFL-Bahia).

21. The classification was made as of 1991. In the judgment of the authors, the Russian constitution of 1993 created a presidency that surpasses Brazil's (Matthew Shugart, personal communication).

22. The *medida provisória* is a presidential decree that has the force of law for thirty days. If after thirty days the Congress does not ratify the decree and convert into law, it automatically loses its validity, and the Congress may then rule on the effects it had before expiration (Constitution of 1988, Article 62).

Episodes like these have created the impression that Congress is not prepared to assume its new constitutional responsibilities. Increased legislative powers have been used largely in reactive rather than proactive ways: the percentage of laws originating in the executive branch has changed little since the military regime (Table 6.7). In the first decade of democracy, Congressional inefficiency, absenteeism, and stonewalling torpedoed reform efforts in areas such as social security, taxation, and earmarking of federal revenues. In doing so Congress acquired a schizophrenic image of both overwhelming strength and pitiful weakness: the legislature proved very adept at stymieing permanent constitutional reforms advocated by presidents, while simultaneously allowing the day-to-day administration of the country to be conducted by presidential decree. There is nothing inherently wrong with Congress's exercising its veto power either actively or passively, but when it fails to advance alternatives of its own its contribution to national political life is called into question.

Third, the crisis of the National Congress has worsened the already dismal image of the political class in Brazilian public opinion. A major opinion poll taken in late 1989 showed that only 23 percent of the population had "confidence" in the Congress, with support for the legislature lowest among the young and those with college degrees (Moisés and Venturi, 1990). This finding has been routinely duplicated in newspaper polls every year since. This is a logical outcome of the constant stream of negative publicity for the institution, which emphasizes corruption and failure to meet deadlines and enact laws (or even constitutional provisions). Interviews

Table 6.7 Output and origin of Brazilian legislation, 1964–1992

President(s)	Number of New Laws During Presidential Administration(s)	Percentage of New Laws Originating in Executive Branch[a]
Totals for five military presidents, 1964–85	2,981	75.4
Sarney 1985–90	705	64.3
Collor 1990–92	464	76.3
Franco 1992	148	83.1
Totals for three democratic presidents, 1985–92	1,317	70.6
TOTALS 1964–92	4,298	73.9

SOURCE: Câmara dos Deputados 1993.

[a] Includes laws originating as presidential decrees.

with legislators reveal them to be keenly aware of their poor self-image and resentful of the media, which they see as unfair. Soares (1979) observed a similar phenomenon in the years leading up to the 1964 coup. He found that legislators seemed unaware of the seriousness of their negative image vis-à-vis public opinion; for example, legislators claimed that corruption was a problem of individual legislators rather than a collective problem for the Congress. A similar abdication of collective responsibility exists today. To improve its image, Congress must become more willing to punish members who violate institutional rules and public laws.[23]

Finally, all of the preceding observations have direct implications for democratic legitimation. A recent study of Brazilian political culture shows convincingly that support for the legislature is closely related to support for the regime. In a large-N survey conducted in 1993, Moisés (1994) found that citizens' evaluation of the performance of the National Congress was the second best predictor of overall satisfaction with democracy (which he found to be low). The only stronger independent variable, among two dozen he tested, was the approval rating given to the incumbent government of President Itamar Franco. Such a finding is surprising in the context of a developing country riddled by tremendous socioeconomic inequalities: one would expect instead a more "instrumental" evaluation of democracy, based on individual-level economic satisfaction, leading to "specific support" for—or rejection of—the regime. The centrality of the National Congress in Brazilians' assessment of the political order underscores the relevance of the institution-building approach to democratization.

Finally, the preceding observations tie into the larger question of democratic legitimation. The goal of representative institutions in a process of democratization should be to promote a widespread sense of inclusion and representation, and to do so as fast as possible. Legislatures have an extremely important role in this matter insofar as they are the outstanding symbols of popular sovereignty in democratic regimes (Blondel 1973). A weak Congress, dominated by an activist presidency and mired in scandal, does not advance but rather erodes democratic legitimacy. Without drastic improvements in the qualitative performance of the National Congress, the promise of Brazilian democracy will remain unfulfilled.

23. An excellent journalistic account of the 1993–94 budget scandal (Krieger, Rodrigues, and Bonassa 1994) reveals that despite the visibility of several members' expulsion from Congress, many more members' indiscretions were overlooked.

Conclusions

The inferences drawn here about the Congress are less optimistic than the ones drawn in the preceding chapter about the party system. From the late 1980s to the late 1990s, economic crisis and political immobilism seemed to have some salutary effects in terms of attitudes concerning political parties. The near-universal diagnosis was that parties would have to be strengthened. The authoritarian-era cleavage, in which ex-*arenistas* had harbored antiparty attitudes, began to become somewhat less salient, and significant reforms of the party and electoral systems were proposed. With regard to Congress, however, the diagnosis of a dysfunctional legislature had yet to receive serious proposals for reform. Moreover, in the domain of legislature behavior, the authoritarian-era cleavage maintained its relevance: veterans of ARENA/PDS seemed the least likely to contribute to any legislative renaissance.

There is undoubtedly a connection between the party and legislative arenas. A strengthening of parties would have spillover effects in Congress. Organized, accountable, disciplined, and programmatic parties would cause the Congress to function quite differently from the patterns observed in the first decade and a half of the New Republic. But as long as parties do not shape legislative life, the Brazilian Congress will likely evince the syndrome that we have encountered here: a combination of localism, clientelism, individualism, absenteeism, inefficiency, internal disarray, and subordination to the presidency. These defects are not the exclusive province of ex-*arenistas*, but most elements of the weak-legislature syndrome can be linked—both empirically and theoretically—to the legacy of dictatorship and to specific features of the ex-authoritarian cohort. The implications of this are examined in the concluding chapter.

Collective Action within the ARENA/PDS Cohort, 1987–1999

Introduction

Previous chapters have examined the partisan ancestry of ARENA/PDS, its "afterlife" in the early years after military withdrawal from politics, and the relationship of the ex-*arenista* cohort to parties and Congress under democracy. This brief chapter examines the issue of collective action among ARENA/PDS veterans after 1985. When and how have ARENA/PDS veterans attempted to work together again in Brazilian politics? Why have they done so? And what have been the political consequences of their attempts at collective action?

This chapter focuses on three prominent "class reunions" of ARENA/PDS after 1985: the first as the Centrão (broad center) in the Constituent Assembly of 1987–88, the second as the legislative support base of President Fernando Collor in 1990–92, and the third as part of President Fernando Henrique Cardoso's multiparty alliance after 1995. Although the chapter is largely descriptive, analysis of these efforts at collective action stimulate some theoretical reflection on the individual and collective aspects of political support in Brazil. The analysis also testifies to the impressive staying power of the ARENA/PDS cohort. This generation of conservative political elites, endowed with immense governing experience and durable political machines, has proven remarkably successful at adapting to changing political circumstances and at marketing itself as a guarantor of governability in Brazil.

Stability for Sale: *The Partido de Sustentação* in Brazilian Politics

Prior to 1984 the authoritarian political right was united in the PDS party, but the circumstances of the democratic transition spawned a major diaspora. By 1990 veterans of ARENA/PDS could be found in at least a dozen different political parties, although two large conservative parties, the PDS itself (which changed its name to the PPR in 1993 and to the PPB in 1995) and the PFL, were the largest and most visible heirs to the old ARENA machine. In the 1980s, the governing PMDB—which remained Brazil's largest party for more than a decade after the transition—gained a significant ex-*arena* wing, although the party remained generally in the political center, even retaining many veterans of its left-nationalist incarnation in the 1970s. Other ARENA/PDS veterans founded smaller conservative parties such as the PTB, the PL, the PDC, and the PRN (see Chapter 5). In this book I have largely eschewed attention to these post-1985 partisan affiliations, focusing instead on the ARENA/PDS veterans as if they constituted a "party" of their own.

The ARENA cohort is not literally a party of course, but since 1985 it has functioned informally and continually in two principal ways. First, the cohort reunited as an ideological and tactical movement in the National Constituent Assembly (ANC) of 1987–88 to oppose what it perceived as an extreme leftist bias in the Assembly. This ideological movement, the Centrão, was largely reactive. Almost as soon as it was formally constituted, it promptly disintegrated, revealing interesting obstacles to the formation of a single large conservative political party in Brazil.

Second and more frequently, the ARENA/PDS cohort has functioned as a *partido de sustentação* that executives turned to in time of need. The term *partido de sustentação* can literally be translated as "support party," but has connotations that go beyond this simple phrase. A *partido de sustentação* not only props up the government of the day but also draws substantial nourishment from its privileged position in the orbit of the state. It is a collection of clients whose patron is the president, but who are also patrons themselves in their states, regions, and municipalities. In earlier times this function was exercised by a single party, such as ARENA/PDS itself (1966–82) or the old PSD (1946–60, and intermittently in 1960–64). But in the fragmented multiparty system of post-1985 Brazil, it is unlikely that one party alone can assume the function of *partido de sustentação* (although, admittedly, the PFL has been at the core of all progovernment coalitions). Rather, the pattern has been for several parties, as well as for several semiautonomous individuals and free-floating political machines, to form shifting alliances that aim to perform essentially the same tasks that the more "professional" *partidos de sustentação* carried out in the past. The extreme heterogeneity of progovernment forces, combined with their generally weak ideological profile, can sometimes permit them to be viewed collectively as a single "party of power" (to use the Russian slang denoting the astonishingly diverse coalition arrayed behind former President Boris Yeltsin). "Party of power" may indeed be the most suitable translation for *partido de sustentação*.

Brazilian presidents need *partidos de sustentação* for several reasons: (1) to build congressional support and pass legislation; (2) to obtain downward penetration into existing political machines, particularly in the Northeast and the interior where patronage politics counts most heavily; and (3) to function as a supply of reassuring eminènces grises who, in a clear market exchange, "sell" their ability to generate presidential support while "buying" the right to access state resources and place allies in the state apparatus. The *partido de sustentação* sells "governability" and purchases patronage, which means of course that the president is buying "governability" and selling patronage. This has clear tradeoffs for the quality of democracy.

The two most visible partisan heirs of ARENA/PDS, the PDS/PPR/PPB and the PFL, can each be linked to these two different methods of reconstituting the old authoritarian-era cohort. The PPB has tended to be more of an ideological party, and conformed more to the former pattern of programmatic collective action. The PPB, or the PDS as it was still known then, was very active in the 1987–88 Centrão. The PFL has conformed more to the latter pattern of nonideological, clientelistic *sustentação* of governments, although under President Cardoso it gradually became more identified with the neoliberal policy agenda he propounded.

The Centrão in the ANC, 1987–1988

The origins of the conservative Centrão movement in the Constituent Assembly lie in the unusual elections of 1986. These elections were held during the euphoria of the Cruzado Plan, a short-lived economic stabilization package that gave a tremendous electoral boost to the center-left PMDB. The PMDB also benefited from the spirit of the recent transition to democracy, given that in 1986 the party still represented the historic opposition to authoritarian rule. The election produced an overwhelming victory for the PMDB: the party won twenty-two of the twenty-three governorships and an absolute majority (305 of 559 seats) in the crucial ANC.

Although the PMDB was becoming increasingly heterogeneous due to an influx of opportunistic conservatives, control of the party leadership was firmly in the hands of center-left and progressive forces. In February 1987, the party leader in the newly installed ANC, Senator Mário Covas, used his authority to name numerous left-leaning PMDB figures to the presidencies and *relatorias* (rapporteur positions) of key committees throughout the Assembly. This was especially true of the Integration Committee (Comissão de Sistematização), the "mother of all committees" responsible for putting together the draft constitution: the membership of the Integration Committee was significantly to the left of that of the ANC as a whole (Martínez-Lara 1996: 109). Accusations of ideological "stacking" led to considerable acrimony in the first months of the ANC. Conservatives' fears were confirmed by the release of the first constitutional draft in June, which the right loudly derided as excessively socialist, protectionist, and statist. According to Deputy José Lins (PFL-Ceará), an ARENA veteran and founder of the Centrão, objections to the evolving constitutional draft centered on five points. First, conservatives believed that the text was hostile to private property, especially in the rural sector, and to the principle of economic initiative in general. Second, the expansion of social rights—especially worker's rights such as job stability, severance pay, double pay for overtime, 120 days of maternity leave, and a shorter work week—was deemed to raise prohibitively the cost of hiring workers and thus was expected to aggravate unemployment. Third, the right believed that the text afforded too many economic functions to the state. Fourth, the text contained a strong strain of economic nationalism, creating numerous monopolies and "market reserves" for the state and Brazilian firms. Many (though certainly not all) members of the Centrão viewed this as unnecessarily hostile to foreign capital, and worried about the negative effect on direct foreign direct investment in Brazil. Fifth, the mounting tax burden in the Integration draft was viewed as incompatible with a vigorous private sector (*Correio Braziliense*, November 7, 1987). Although most of these arguments were emanating from the main conservative parties, approximately 125 members of the PMDB (or about 40 percent of the party) were known to be dissatisfied with their party's leadership and willing to side with the conservatives on specific issues.

Conservatives' efforts to amend the constitutional draft quickly ran up against the *Regimento Interno*, the internal rules of the Assembly. Originally written by then-Senator Fernando Henrique Cardoso (PMDB-São Paulo), the bylaws were highly favorable to protecting the Integration Committee's draft. The *Regimento* specified that in order to modify any aspect of the draft, it would be necessary to muster an absolute majority (280 votes out of 559 members) of the ANC. Data from the ANC show that the average attendance during roll-call votes was only 402 members, meaning that the magic number of 280 would represent around 70 percent of members present on a typical vote. The burden of mustering votes thus fell on *opponents* of the Integration Committee draft. In a series of meetings held in September and October 1987, conservative and centrist forces in the ANC concluded that the only way to pursue their ideological goals would be to amend the *Regimento Interno*, reversing the rules to put the burden of mustering votes on *defenders* of the Integration draft. This procedural rebellion was the origin of the Centrão.

In October, the Centrão emerged as a large, informal, somewhat amorphous movement with no single leader. Rather than anoint leaders, the Centrão selected thirty whips, each responsible for mobilizing small groups of ten *constituintes* (*Correio Braziliense*, November 5, 1987). On November 5, Centrão organizers handed ANC president Ulysses Guimarães (PMDB-São Paulo) a petition with 315 signatures—35 more than necessary—asking for a vote on the proposed changes in the internal rules (*Jornal da Tarde*, November 6, 1987). On November 24, the Centrão won only 271 votes and failed in its attempt to amend the *Regimento Interno*. However, the Centrão regrouped in late November and early December, a period in which the Brazilian press focused on the exhaustive efforts (including faxes, telegrams, and borrowed corporate LearJets) that were necessary to marshal the conservative troops in Brasília. Finally, in a raucous second vote held on December 3 (featuring a dramatic walkout of the left and center-left led by Mário Covas), the Centrão was able to garner 290 votes in favor of its substitute *Regimento*. With the Centrão's procedural victory, the allegedly leftist draft written by the Integration Committee was in jeopardy. The new rules would allow any article to be separated out for a special vote (*destaque para votação em separado*), in which case it would have to then win the absolute majority of 280 votes to be *maintained* in the Constitution.

During its brief lifetime, the Centrão used the new rules to force a small number of clear programmatic changes in the evolving constitutional draft. The three most important of these were the adoption of a presidential system (discussed in Chapter 6), the confirmation of President Sarney in a five-year term in office, and the dilution of the agrarian reform language that had prevailed in the Integration draft. But on many other issues, the Centrão could not remain united (Martínez-Lara 1996: 117–18). Beyond its three

major victories, the Centrão only really succeeded in obstructing or post-
poning controversial issues. By creating numerous procedural impasses, the
Centrão transformed many of the contested constitutional articles into non–
self-executing provisions (provisions that would have to be enabled by a
vote of a subsequent Congress) and pushed for a top-to-bottom review of
the Constitution five years later in 1993—the idea being that the right
would live to fight its battles another day. In the end, the Centrão's impact
on the Integration draft was limited. As Martínez-Lara concluded: "Among
the leaders of the left and progressive sectors, the new constitution was seen,
on the whole, as a victory" (1996: 119). Leaving aside the policy changes
engineered by the Centrão, it is more important for this analysis to examine
the Centrão as a "class reunion" of ARENA/PDS, and subsequently to assess the collective action problems revealed by the Centrão's rise and fall.

Analysis of the Centrão's victory in the rules fight reveals the important
role played by conservative parties. Breaking down the 290 "centrists" by
party reveals the following: the alternative *Regimento* received favorable
votes from 130 members of the PMDB (out of 306), 104 members of the
PFL (of 132), 30 members of the PDS (of 37), 14 members of the PTB (of
23), and 5 members of the PL (of 6) (*Jornal de Brasília*, December 6, 1987).
The two main ARENA successor parties, PDS and PFL, were the most com-
mitted to the Centrão, but the numerous dissidents from the PMDB (called
the "Democratic Center" within that party) were indispensable to the victory. Examining the link between ARENA and the Centrão, a Brazilian
journalist, Aglaé Lavoratti, found that 162 of the 290 "centrists" (56 percent) had roots in ARENA or PDS before 1985 (*Jornal do Brasil*, December
13, 1987). Put another way, of the entire ARENA/PDS cohort in the ANC,
about 75 percent could be considered members of the Centrão in 1987–88.

Queried about the Centrão's origins, the movement's top whip, Deputy
Daso Coimbra (PMDB-Rio de Janeiro), said that ideologically speaking he
was still in ARENA—which was, in his view, "clearly a party of the center."
He continued:

> This is the moment for the reconstitution (*reaglutinação*) of ideologies.
> Each *constituinte* is sovereign in his will, and the parties no longer have
> any importance. . . . In the making of the Constitution, there are no
> parties. They only existed through the committee phase because the
> members of the committees were named by party leaders. Now we are
> on the floor, which allows for the reunion of common forces. ARENA
> is a point of reference, and there is no problem with that. (Quoted in
> *Jornal do Brasil*, December 13, 1987)

Senator José Fogaça (PMDB-Rio Grande do Sul), a longtime opponent of military rule, added that "[w]hen we had democratization and the campaign for direct elections, the conservative forces were dispersed. The *Constituinte* is becoming the forum for the reconstitution of these forces, which represent nothing other than ARENA and PDS" (quoted in ibid.)

Within two months of its major rules victory, serious fault lines began to emerge within the Centrão. The movement had been united over the rules change and on several major programmatic points, but this unity concealed strong intergroup rivalries and jockeying for power. Most of its major victories came in February and March 1988—the adoption of presidentialism and the awarding of five years—but these were actually interpreted as victories of the Sarney government itself, not as sovereign decisions of a working majority in the ANC. According to the Centrão's legal specialist, federal deputy and 1985 PDS vice-presidential candidate Bonifácio de Andrada (Minas Gerais), by the time the second round of roll-call voting began in July 1988, the Centrão barely existed (interview, Brasília, October 19, 1990). Only about 100 members remained, and the movement was no longer a force in the ANC.

Press reports and interviews with leading Centrão figures suggest the following reasons for the movement's rapid demise.[1] First, local, regional, and personalistic tensions—key reasons behind Brazil's extreme party fragmentation—quickly became visible in the Centrão. The decision to create a leaderless, decentralized movement reflected these tensions. Second, beyond an abstract ("high politics") commitment to private property and free enterprise, Centrão members could not agree on the fine details of many of the complex administrative and policy ("low politics") issues that consumed the ANC's attention. Third, a public counteroffensive by the Central Única dos Trabalhadores (CUT), a radical labor federation linked to the leftist PT, was effective in causing wavering members to drop out of the Centrão. Beginning in January 1988, the CUT distributed posters in the large cities that featured photographs and phone numbers of major Centrão figures, who were dubbed "traitors of the people." Fourth, although the Centrão represented a broad continuum from center to right, several of its self-anointed spokesmen, including the most visible ones, were drawn from the far right. These included deputies Amaral Netto (PDS-Rio de Janeiro), José

---

1. I interviewed a number of the Centrão's most visible leaders, including Affonso Camargo, Álvaro Valle, Bonifácio de Andrada, Carlos Sant'Anna, and Daso Coimbra, in addition to many other ANC members who opposed the Centrão.

Lourenço (PFL-Bahia), and Roberto Cardoso Alves (PMDB-São Paulo), all of them highly theatrical conservatives.[2] Finally, given that several of the prime movers within the Centrão were closely linked to President Sarney, the Centrão began to be viewed as a Trojan horse for the presidential palace. The desire of several Centrão leaders, particularly Cardoso Alves and Carlos Sant'Anna, to place the Centrão at the service of the Planalto led to major disputes within the movement.

All of these factors revealed the Centrão to be an ephemeral alliance of convenience. As Delfim Netto (PDS-São Paulo), a leading luminary of the military regime, put it to the conservative newspaper *O Estado de São Paulo*: "The *Centrão* does not exist. Don't be fooled. The *Centrão* was a mechanism of organization for voting on the changes in the *Regimento Interno* of the *Constituinte*. It was the cry of the majority marginalized by the minorities." In its editorial, the *Estadão* agreed, criticizing the Centrão for knowing what it was against, but not what it was for. "As long it knew what it didn't want, great. But at the very moment when it had to send a message and formulate a positive option in favor of doctrine or ideological principles, the divergences emerged and the front just fell apart" (*Estado de São Paulo*, February 18, 1988).

The experience of the Centrão in 1987–88 reveals the many difficulties of reconstituting a single large conservative political party in Brazil. Such a party existed in 1966–79 when the military forced it to exist (as in the phenomenon of "cohesion via coercion" discussed in Chapter 5), but disintegrated shortly after the party system was liberalized. The Centrão was formed in reaction to a perceived threat from the left in the ANC, but when it had to move to the next phase and behave as a proactive agent in legislative politics, it too disintegrated.

The Collor Support Coalition, 1990–1992

Just as the origins of the Centrão can be traced to the lopsided legislative elections of 1986, a second "class reunion" of ARENA/PDS can be traced to the closely fought presidential election of 1989. In that election, the candidates of the two parties that had dominated the 1986 elections, the PMDB

2. The late Cardoso Alves, popularly known as Robertão ("Big Bob"), was particularly colorful. His February 1988 plea to ANC members to support the Sarney government has gone down in the annals both of Brazilian political folklore and of the comparative study of clientelism. In his pursuit of his colleagues' votes, Robertão's exhortation took the form of a quote from Saint Francis: "*É dando que se recebe*" (give, that you may receive). See Geddes and Ribeiro Neto (1992).

and the PFL, were virtually irrelevant. Instead, the election came down to the two candidates who campaigned most strenuously against the incumbent Sarney government: Luis Inácio Lula da Silva of the PT and Fernando Collor of the PRN. Lula was a leftist labor leader who promised major redistributive change in Brazil. Collor was a scion of a traditional conservative family (his father, Senator Arnon de Mello, was a founder of ARENA), and had himself begun his political career as a mayor and federal deputy for the PDS of Alagoas.

Although Collor was running for president as an antiparty populist and claimed he would be beholden to no one, the specter of a leftist government led by Lula was enough to cause many conservative elites—despite their misgivings about Collor's independent streak—to fall in line behind Collor. The closeness of the December 1989 runoff, in which Lula received a surprising 47 percent of the votes, ensured that Collor's presidency would begin with the political right in his debt. Collor had, after all, saved conservative elites from their worst nightmare. At his inauguration in March 1990, Collor became the seventh consecutive Brazilian president to have been a member of ARENA/PDS. The stage was set for a second reunion of the ARENA/PDS cohort, but it did not occur immediately.

Collor's first cabinet illustrated his attitude toward the conservative parties in Congress—he would accept their support but would not necessarily reward them with major positions in his government. Collor initially resisted a strong identification with the legislative right. He drew his ministers from a variety of sources and parties: some were unknowns pulled from universities, some from the private sector and moderate labor unions, some from the centrist PMDB, and a few from the ARENA/PDS cohort. The PFL, a party that had supported the very same Sarney government so vilified by Collor, ended up with the education, agriculture, and communications ministries, and PFL politicians such as Senator Marco Maciel and Deputy Ricardo Fiúza (both of Pernambuco) became key interlocutors of the government in Congress. But Collor also angered many in Congress by awarding the government floor leaderships to two minor figures from his own miniscule PRN, Senator Ney Maranhão (Pernambuco) and Deputy Renan Calheiros (Alagoas). These early appointments illustrated Collor's suspicion toward traditional politicians: his intent was to maximize his own autonomy by governing "above" the parties (Weyland 1993).

Collor's early attitude toward the legislative right—which could be described as one of studied dismissiveness—was possible in the first months of his presidency for three main reasons. First, Collor enjoyed the political legitimacy and tremendous personal prestige conferred by his winning of 35 million votes in Brazil's first popular presidential election since 1960. Collor clearly viewed his election victory as a mandate for considerable (even para-constitutional) latitude as president, a situation conforming closely to O'Donnell's model of "delegative democracy" (O'Donnell 1994). (The president believed that the legitimacy of Congress, having been elected in 1986 and now in the final year of its session, was clearly inferior to his own, given his fresher electoral mandate.) He aggressively pushed his program of modernizing neoliberal reform, a major departure from the economic policy of the preceding decades. Second, the hyperinflationary spiral of 1989–90 gave Collor essentially carte blanche to do what he could to stop the crisis. The situation was so dire that even Collor's controversial blocking of 80 percent of the currency in circulation, as part of the "Collor Plan" intro-duced on his second day in office, met with initially strong popular ap-proval. Third, like Sarney before him, Collor was equipped with considerable authority to implement his policies by decree powers; in 1990, he issued a presidential decree on average every forty-eight hours (Power 1998).

All three of these factors, combined with elements of Collor's personal-ity and populist style, led the telegenic forty-year-old president to believe that he could dispense with a traditional reliance on the parties in Congress. However, each factor was to have a boomerang effect by the time Collor had completed six months in office. Collor's go-it-alone populism was soon perceived as arrogance. Governors and legislators began to criticize his in-sensitivity to the routine give-and-take of politics, and his pedantic messian-ism was increasingly lampooned by the print media. More importantly, the draconian Collor Plan was deliberately recessionary, and as the economy contracted and unemployment mounted Collor began to feel the backlash. His efforts to implement his program by decree created severe tensions in executive-legislative relations, and at one point in June 1990 the Supreme Court intervened to prevent him from re-issuing rejected decrees.

Due to the nonconcurrence of elections at the time, Collor faced the unusual prospect of legislative and gubernatorial elections in October and November 1990, occurring less than seven months into his term. Initially believing that these would take place in a honeymoon period, Collor soon watched his support erode due to the mounting recession and several com-pounding political factors. The largest party in Congress, the PMDB, which initially provided only tepid opposition, turned more strongly against him during the economic contraction. The recession provided an opportunity for left and center-left candidates to run hard against Collor. Conservative parties expressed their dissatisfaction with the one-way street of Collor's governing style, in which the PFL and others were expected to support him without receiving the customary clientelistic gratification in return. A series of blunders by his cabinet members—including the confrontational style of his economics minister, and her later involvement in an extramarital affair with the minister of justice—made his government appear undisciplined and incompetent. The large number of ministerial novices led Brasília insiders to complain that *nesse governo, falta cabelo branco*—"there is not enough gray hair in this government." All of these factors, but most importantly the deepening recession, led to disappointing results in the 1990 elections. Although the opposition made only moderate gains in the Congress, Collor's preferred candidates for governor were defeated in every one of the seven most important and economically developed states of the South and Southeast. Given the importance of governors in Brazilian politics, these results were widely viewed as a humiliation for the president.

The humbling experience of the electoral defeat led Collor to rethink his strategy. Immediately after the October elections, Collor made it clear that he would seek a new convivium with the incoming Congress. This was to be achieved in two ways: by the appointment of a "political coordinator" to oversee relations with both progovernment and opposition political parties, and by the construction of a supraparty bloc for political support in Congress. As his *articulador político* and bridge to Congress, Collor chose Senator Jarbas Passarinho (PDS-Pará), awarding him the prestigious post of Minister of Justice in mid-October. Passarinho, a conservative seventy-year-old retired colonel and the only person to have held three ministerial portfolios during the military regime, was perhaps the most widely respected veteran of ARENA/PDS. His age and expertise—providing the *cabelo branco* lacking in the first cabinet—gave an entirely new look to the Collor government. Passarinho was entrusted with the task of building a supraparty coalition in Congress, and in doing so he drew on his extensive contacts in the ARENA/PDS cohort.

Passarinho first attempted to convince the leaders of the two main ARENA/PDS successor parties, PDS and PFL, that they should fold back together into a single party in support of the Collor government. The two parties, he claimed, "have the same origin and the same ideology" (*Folha de São Paulo*, November 6, 1990). When this failed due to predictable opposition by the party leaders, Passarinho aimed instead for a multiparty coalition, and convened a meeting of PDS, PFL, PTB, PDC, and PRN leaders on November 7. (Astonishingly, all five party leaders at the time were ARENA veterans like Passarinho himself.) The meeting quickly degenerated into an opportunity for the progovernment parties to vent their dissatisfaction with the president and their suspicion of his attempts to unite them in a single bloc. "We need to know if this will be a bloc to support the government or a bloc to participate in the government," insisted the leader of the PTB, Gastone Righi of São Paulo (*Jornal do Brasil*, November 8, 1990). "If a party participates in the government, it has to sit at the table where decisions are made," warned PFL leader Ricardo Fiúza (*Folha de São Paulo*, November 8, 1990). The main theme of the floor leaders was that the government needed to allocate more ministerial positions to the allied parties. A week later, the message was reinforced when the PDS and PTB voted against Collor on a veto override, with their leaders warning publicly that the president had not consulted them sufficiently on the distribution of *cargos* (government appointments) (*Folha de São Paulo*, November 15 and 18, 1990).

With Collor's personal intervention in December, Passarinho finally succeeded in creating the desired progovernment bloc in Congress. This was the first such bloc created under the Constitution of 1988, which explicitly permitted the formalization of legislative coalitions (see Chapter 6). Called the Movimento Parlamentar Social Liberal but known simply as the Bloco, it was based formally on the PFL and PRN, but also received informal support from the PDS, PTB, PDC, and several microparties. The Bloco was inaugurated in February 1991 along with the new 49th Legislature. It remained intact until shortly after the eruption of the Collorgate corruption scandal in May 1992, which led to Collor's impeachment and removal from office in September of that year. During the existence of the Bloco, the PFL emerged as the dominant support party for Collor. Numerous PFL deputies and senators passed through the Collor cabinet during this period, and Collor's own PRN party became less important as he relied increasingly on the PFL. The PFL, and the Bloco more widely, reflected the characteristic *partido de sustentação*, and observers commented on the strong resemblance of the Collor support coalition to the Centrão in the ANC (for example, Carlos Castello Branco in the *Jornal do Brasil*, December 8, 1990).

In essence, Collor capitulated to reality. He began his term in office with ill-disguised hostility toward traditional political elites, but as his position weakened in late 1990, he found himself articulating the revival of the ARENA/PDS cohort. The PFL and all of the smaller parties in his support bloc were dominated by and formally led by ex-*arenistas*, all of whom who knew the rules of the game far better than Collor. Collor entered into an informal bargain with these experienced elites. They would support him in return for control of government ministries, access to state resources, and the prestige that comes with being able to return to one's home region and announce the support of the President of the Republic. In return, they would provide Collor with a basis of support for his legislative program in the Chamber and Senate. In so doing, the ex-*arenistas* were doing what they knew best, and were simply acting on the impulses they acquired in the 1960s and 1970s, when they exercised exactly the same roles under the military regime.

The PFL in particular showed its astonishing capacity to support the government of the day: the party has supported all four presidents under democratic rule, and its core leadership has an unbroken record of serving every president dating back to 1964. Pointing to their experience and their extensive political machines, they offered Collor expertise and "governability," and Collor purchased these items at the price of ministries. When asked why presidents turn to the PFL in time of need, Collor responded: "Today in this country, one does not govern without the PFL. . . . They [PFL notables] know how to wield power. . . . These people are *professionals*" (interview, Brasília, November 29, 1994). But in the end, even the ex-*arenistas'* much-ballyhooed "professionalism" could not save Collor from himself.[3]

The Cardoso Support Coalition, 1995–1999

Collor's impeachment left the presidency to Itamar Franco, the reclusive and moody vice president from Minas Gerais. A former PMDB senator with no party affiliation in 1992, Franco was a veteran of the opposition to military rule, and was indeed the first non-*arenista* president after 1964. Lacking both the charisma and the ideological convictions of Collor, Franco at first groped unsuccessfully for a political identity, surrounding himself with an astonishingly heterogeneous cabinet ranging from Marxist feminists like Luiza Erundina (PT-São Paulo) to billionaire bankers like José Eduardo Andrade Vieira (PTB-Paraná). Franco relied less on the ARENA/PDS cohort than any democratic president before or since, awarding only two ministries (communications and regional integration) to the PFL. His main support parties were the PMDB (five ministries) and the PSDB (three), with the latter

---

3. For analysis of the impeachment process, and for an overview of the Collor period more generally, see Weyland (1993).

participating officially in a cabinet for the first time. Most revealingly, Franco awarded five cabinet posts to personal friends from Minas Gerais. With inflation once again raging, Franco's government seemed more like a caretaker cabinet intent on holding down the fort until presidential elections in 1994. He had virtually no role in the April 1993 plebiscite in which Brazilians ratified the ANC's choice of the presidential system. Franco's first three Finance Ministers had an average tenure of eighty days, while inflation hovered in the range of 30 percent monthly. His fortunes began to change somewhat in May 1993 when he appointed his fourth finance minister, Senator Fernando Henrique Cardoso (PSDB-São Paulo), and effectively withdrew from most day-to-day decision making. Functioning as a de facto prime minister, Cardoso spent the next year laying the groundwork for the Plano Real, the historic currency reform implemented in July 1994. With its early success at reducing inflation, the Plano Real launched Cardoso as a natural candidate for president in the elections of October 1994.

Like Collor, Cardoso had a clear idea of what he wanted to achieve for Brazil, but unlike Collor, he was a congressional insider equipped with excellent negotiation skills. By now far afield from his origins as a Marxist sociologist, Cardoso had become convinced of the need for a thorough overhaul of the state and economy. Influenced by promarket European social democrats such as Mário Soares, Felipe González, and Michel Rocard, Cardoso aimed to implement liberal economic policies under the rubric of reformist social democracy.[4] Although Cardoso downplayed the similarities to Collor's reforms, many observers commented that his proposals aimed to revive and accelerate the neoliberal adjustment initiated unevenly by Collor in 1990.

But before Cardoso could implement his ambitious plans, he had to win the presidency first. As he resigned from the finance ministry in April 1994 to begin his campaign, he knew that he faced several daunting obstacles. First, his own party, the PSDB, held less than 10 percent of the seats in Congress, and its electoral appeal was largely restricted to São Paulo and the urban middle class of the South and Southeast. Second, Cardoso had no penetration at all in the vast and impoverished Northeast, and indeed—as a comfortable *paulista* intellectual—had very little idea of how to campaign

---

4. For an overview of Cardoso's intellectual transformation (seen as consistent with a lifelong tendency toward pragmatism), see the flattering biography by Leoni (1997). A similar appraisal, with more attention to macropolitical trends in Brazil, is that of Goertzel (1999). For additional insights on Cardoso's reformist social democracy, see the interview of Cardoso conducted by former Portuguese president Mário Soares (Cardoso and Soares 1998).

in the hinterland (Dimenstein and Souza 1994: 161–74). Third, the PT's Lula was planning to run again for president in 1994, and he consistently bested Cardoso in all the trial heats. Division among the anti-Lula forces might play into the PT's hands. Fourth, even if Cardoso were to win the election, he would not have much of a governing base were he to rely on the PSDB alone. An alliance would be necessary, both to win the election and to govern Brazil after 1995.

Cardoso was painfully aware of his own political limitations, and like Collor before him, he knew where he might look for a remedy. However, unlike Collor, Cardoso had strong reasons for resisting an entente with the ARENA/PDS cohort. Cardoso had been exiled by the military in the 1960s, and had returned to fight authoritarianism by joining the MDB of the 1970s. He became one of Brazil's most eloquent voices in favor of a transition to civilian rule. As a PMDB senator after 1983, Cardoso fought bitterly against the PDS in the Diretas Já campaign and against the Centrão in the ANC. In the *Constituinte*, Cardoso pushed aggressively for the removal of what he called the "authoritarian debris," the institutional vestiges of dictatorship, many of which were defended by the ex-*arenistas*. He had impeccable democratic credentials, and the ex-*arenistas* did not.

Moreover, Cardoso was known to loathe *fisiologismo*, the clientelistic exchange of favors, and the conservative parties that practiced it. In 1988, he led a defection from the PMDB centering on dissatisfaction with the rightward turn of the Sarney government and the naked practice of patronage politics by President Sarney and by the wily PMDB governor of São Paulo, Orestes Quércia. (This revolt led to the creation of the PSDB in June 1988.) When asked in 1990 to define the Brazilian right, Cardoso cited two prime characteristics: *arbítrio*, which he defined as a "permanent desire to support the government," and *clientelismo*, which he described as "the practice of constantly dealing in favors" (author interview, Brasília, August 29, 1990). When Fernando Collor invited the PSDB to join his cabinet, Cardoso refused, citing the presence in Collor's government of the notoriously clientelistic PFL: "The PFL is the very incarnation of backwardness. It symbolizes everything that is wrong with this country" (quoted in Dimenstein and Souza 1994: 66).

However, even though Cardoso had been on the opposite side of history from the *arenistas* and disdained their political practices, he shocked the political world in 1994 by announcing an electoral alliance with the PFL. (Later, the alliance was broadened to include the PTB, a party that was much smaller than the PFL but whose clientelistic reputation was nearly as intense.) The PSDB and PFL would take the top of the ticket, with Cardoso as the presidential candidate and Senator Guilherme Palmeira (PFL-Alagoas) in the number two slot. Later, a campaign finance scandal forced Palmeira to drop out, and the PFL substituted Senator Marco Maciel (Pernambuco), a well-placed ally of every president since Geisel in 1974. The success of the Plano Real and Cardoso's enormous popularity facilitated the replication of this alliance in a large number of Brazil's twenty-seven states. Within three weeks after the July 1 introduction of the Plan, Cardoso passed Lula in the polls and never looked back. He won election outright on October 3, his 54 percent of the popular vote obviating the need for a runoff like the one in 1989.

The fact that Cardoso was elected on the success of the Plano Real led many to wonder whether the alliance with the PFL had been necessary in the first place. However, Cardoso did not have the luxury of knowing whether the Plan would work, and made the deal before the new currency was introduced. But Cardoso maintained that the alliance would have been necessary anyway in order to facilitate executive-legislative relations and governability after his inauguration on January 1, 1995. In the end, the PFL obtained only three ministries (energy and mines, social security, and environment) in the first Cardoso cabinet, about on par for what it was accustomed to under Franco and Collor—though fewer posts than it had enjoyed under Sarney. But the PFL presence was still very strong in the government, given Maciel as vice president and Senator Antônio Carlos Magalhães (Bahia) as the government's chief interlocutor in the Senate (of which he was president in 1997-98). ACM's son, Luis Eduardo, was to become the most important architect of Cardoso's first-term legislative successes, and was elected president of the Chamber of Deputies in 1995–96. (Widely touted as a potential successor to Cardoso, Luis Eduardo died of a heart attack at the age of 43 in April 1998, leaving a major void in the Cardoso coalition.) Although the PSDB rank and file had greatly resented Cardoso's initial decision to ally with the PFL, the two parties generally cooperated peacefully in Congress after 1995.

Although Cardoso largely got what he wanted out of the PFL—a legislative support base—there were clear costs to his Northeastern strategy. As Cardoso knew well before running for president, the patronage-dependent politicians from these regions are pathologically pro-government, tending to support virtually any incumbent president and his initiatives. The PFL, as Cardoso lamented when spurning Collor's entreaties, is the *partido de sustentação* par excellence. Weyland (2000) has argued that Cardoso achieved many of his legislative goals at the price of maintaining clientel-ism—but did so cleverly, trading small clientelistic favors for larger struc-tural reforms. If Weyland is correct, Cardoso has elected to prey on the suicidal shortsightedness of these politicians, using their inability to defer clientelistic gratification to his own long-term benefit—and perhaps under-mining the entire equation of patronage politics well into the future. But only time will tell if this is a brilliant ploy or a counterproductive wink to *fisiologismo*.

Immediately upon taking office, the Cardoso coalition embarked on an ambitious plan of neoliberal reforms. In order to pass his economic reforms, Cardoso had to amend heavily the constitution that had been promulgated only seven years earlier, and his efforts to do so provided much of the day-to-day action in Brazilian politics beginning in 1995. As in neighboring countries, the radical shift in the development model was vigorously con-tested by the political left, by public employees, and by various rent-seeking social forces weaned on the developmentalist state. Although Cardoso's governing coalition had expanded to include the PMDB, PPB, and PL, thus ostensibly controlling up to 75 percent of the seats in Congress, opposition forces colluded with the less enthusiastic of Cardoso's allies to slow the process of constitutional reforms. By late 1996, Cardoso had concluded that a single four-year term would be insufficient to complete his program, and he authorized his supporters to push for a constitutional amendment allow-ing presidential reelection. The amendment passed in 1997, paving the way for Cardoso to run again. He and Maciel replicated their 1994 ticket, and were reelected with 52 percent of the vote in the first round in October 1998, once again besting the PT's Lula. The PSDB-PFL had not only suc-cessfully maintained a governing alliance for four years, but had also de-cided to stick together for four more.

Unlike the three presidents before him, Cardoso had a strong un-derstanding of the institutional deficiencies of Brazilian democracy. For example, Cardoso was and is still one of the strongest proponents of parlia-mentarism and party reform in Brazil. His election raised hopes that he would shepherd major institutional reforms of the party system, electoral system, and national legislature. However, Cardoso did little in his first term to advance the institution-building agenda. Rather, the president focused most of his political energies on two items: first, getting his macroeconomic constitutional amendments through Congress, and second, passing the re-election amendment. Cardoso's inaction was costly for Brazilian democ-racy. In June 1995, apparently believing that Congress was too distracted by Cardoso's economic agenda to concern itself with political and electoral reform, the independent Supreme Electoral Court (TSE) took the unprecedented step of announcing its own package of party-strengthening proposals. These included a German-style mixed electoral system with a national threshold, a return to party fidelity, and sanctions against politicians who change parties. This sweeping agenda was never viable *in toto*, but it did stimulate legislative debate. Three months later, Congress passed a new political parties statute (Law 9096 of September 19, 1995) that contained several mini-reforms. Parties can no longer be legally chartered without demonstrating national penetration (*caráter nacional*), defined as the winning of at least 0.5 percent of the national vote for the Chamber of Deputies (with at least 0.1 percent in one third of the states). This is still permissive in comparative terms, but it will eliminate some of the *legendas de aluguel* (literally, parties for rent) that spring up at every election and award their nominations in exchange for money or votes. To win official recognition in Congress (*funcionamento parlamentar*, necessary for leadership and committee privileges), parties must now win 5 percent of the national vote, with at least 2 percent in one third of the states. Legislators who switch parties will now automatically lose their parliamentary privileges (but not their seat). As for party fidelity, the new law authorizes sanctions against transgressors, but does not make them mandatory.

Although this law does not go nearly as far as the original TSE proposals, it does represent an advance over the extreme permissiveness in the party and electoral arenas that prevailed between 1985 and 1995 (Porto 1995). But there is a limit to how far Brazilian politicians will go in delegating power to parties: even if the mixed electoral system is adopted, which now appears to be likely in the near future, the proportional side will probably remain open-list. The two key remaining reforms are the ones that the TSE proposed and Congress ignored: party fidelity and a national vote threshold for legislative representation. But such a threshold would have little effect on party fragmentation if the law maintains the current practice of allowing multiparty alliances in PR elections (Nicolau 1993: 108).

As Cardoso's proposed political reform amendments are only now taking shape in 1999, it is too early to speculate on these provisions. But data presented in Chapters 5 and 6 show that Cardoso's own party, the PSDB, is much more favorable to institution-building than his coalition partner, the PFL—the party he once despised for its *arenista* origins and it clientelistic proclivities. Moreover, Cardoso's personal inaction on institution-building proposals, reflecting his desire to put economic reform ahead of political reform, is worrisome from the perspective of democratic consolidation. Institutional reform has been postponed many times in the New Republic, and the results of this procrastination have never been kind to democratic sustainability.

Conclusion: Class Reunions Compared

Since 1987, the ex-*arenistas* have attended three major "class reunions." The first, as the Centrão in the Constituent Assembly, was an uneven effort that revealed many of the obstacles to the permanent reconstitution of the ARENA/PDS party structure. The second class reunion, as the Collor support coalition in 1990–92, marketed "governability for sale" in Brasília. With trouble swirling around him, a young and inexperienced president turned to his ARENA elders to stabilize his government and lubricate the executive-legislative relationship. In the third reunion, a pragmatic presidential candidate chose to ally with a notoriously clientelistic party, gambling that the benefits of this strategy would outweigh the costs. Once again, the nucleus of the ARENA/PDS cohort sold itself to a president as a *partido de sustentação*.

From this review of ex-ARENA collective action in the New Republic, several conclusions emerge. First, at an abstract level, the "class reunions" illustrate the impressive capacity for political survival of the ARENA/PDS cohort. Second and more specifically, when the cohort attempts to unify as a proactive, ideological movement, failure is likely. Factional and regional tendencies limit the ability of the cohort to cohere as it did under military rule, and this sort of collective action allows the cohort to be painted again as the right, something that individual ex-*arenistas* wish to avoid at all costs. Third, when elements of the cohort offer themselves to presidents as subordinate, understated, coalitional partners, success is likely. The "professionals" of the PFL have been remarkably successful in marketing themselves as a solution to governability problems. Their domination of the Northeast, their extensive political machines, their downward penetration into society, and their considerable administrative experience are all major assets.

A final and more tentative conclusion relates to the Cardoso era. In their alliance with a popular president identified with "modern" economic ideas, many ex-*arenistas* have been able to reshape their identities. Cardoso's successes have permitted Brazilian conservatism to alter its connotations, evolving from a disreputable association with authoritarianism in the

1980s to a more "respectable" association with neoliberalism in the 1990s. Should this trend continue, and should the ARENA/PDS cohort maintain the quieter "insider" strategy that it adopted after the demise of the Centrão, the cohort may yet survive as a *partido de sustentação* without the baggage of authoritarianism.

The Impact of Conservative Democratization   8
Legacies and Lessons in the Brazilian Case

Introduction

This chapter synthesizes the foregoing material about the Brazilian political right, restates some of the findings and conclusions, and places them in theoretical and comparative perspective. It is divided into three sections. I begin by discussing how the Brazilian political system is colored by the persistence and survival of the authoritarian-era right. One important question in this section concerns how we might assess the "democraticness" of the ARENA/PDS cohort in the New Republic. The second section goes beyond the subject of the right to look at the "big picture" in Brazil, a country that faced severe economic and social crises in the first decade of its new democracy. Analysis of the right cannot be completed without a look at the macrolevel "costs" of Brazil's political predicament.

The final section of the chapter presents the study's theoretical conclusions. In it, I consider two ways in which I might approach the question of *why* the Brazilian right has retarded the partial regime of representative institutions—and by logical extension, the consolidation of the full regime of democracy—in the New Republic. I conclude by addressing a question that was first raised in Chapter 1 and which is of interest to students of comparative democratization: What are the advantages and disadvantages of the Brazilian pathway from authoritarianism? Is a conservative form of transition, such as the one Brazil has experienced, conducive to continued democratization, or does it make consolidation more difficult to attain? The argument I make cites the experience of the Brazilian right as illustrative of the costs and drawbacks of a conservative process of democratization.

The Place of the Right in Brazilian Politics

This book has appraised the process of democratic consolidation in Brazil by focusing on the role of the ARENA/PDS right. My approach to this problem, outlined in Chapter 2, established the "partial regime" of national representative institutions as a key entry point to the study of democratic sustainability. Because modern, mass democracy requires mediating structures between the state and civil society—or more specifically, between political elites and ordinary citizens—contemporary polyarchies feature formal institutions such as elections, parties, and legislatures, all of which seek at their most basic level to enhance the level of vertical accountability in politics. In the context of a transition away from authoritarian rule, such as the one Brazil has recently experienced, the construction of effective democracy demands that these institutional arenas—which were emasculated or perverted under military authoritarianism—reemerge and establish themselves as privileged and fundamental axes of political life. Therefore, to assess the Brazilian right's impact on the new democracy I examined its impact on representative institutions.

Two case studies—on the party system in Chapter 5 and the national legislature in Chapter 6—examined the politics of (formal) democratic institutionalization in the New Republic. The focus was on the "critical juncture" immediately after the transition to democracy, a period that provided a unique opportunity for reshaping the institutional framework of the polity. Both case studies revealed a weaker commitment on the part of the right to the privileging and strengthening of parties and parliament, but this phenomenon was most intense in the immediate posttransitioin period. In the case of the party system, after several years of institutional paralysis the right began to revise its orientation toward weak, undisciplined parties; a similar phenomenon occurred in the case of the National Congress, although in that institution the right's pro-executive and anti-legislative orientation appeared somewhat more enduring. Even with the evidence of attitudinal change in the 1990s, a critical window of opportunity had been missed during the ANC. On issues such as legislative power, the adoption of the presidential system, the defeat of recall elections, and issues of congressional efficiency and popular participation, the ex-ARENA right succeeded in maintaining institutional features guaranteeing a lower-intensity democracy. The evidence suggests that an important challenge obstacle to Brazilian democracy in its early years was the right's fragmentary or ambivalent commitment to formal representative structures.

This story of the right's ambivalent relationship to institutions is an important one, but it is only one of many that could be told about the overall role of the ARENA/PDS cohort in the New Republic. The institutional "partial regime" is only one of several in which the political right pursues its interests simultaneously. Even within this arena we must recognize that political parties and the national legislature, while visible and crucial, are still only two subsystems of democratic politics. To broaden the analytical framework and preface the general conclusions, I now step beyond the original research design to present a few observations about the "larger picture" of rightist engagement in politics. Apart from the travail of representative institutions narrowly understood, what does it mean for Brazil in the 1990s to afford so much space in the political system to the ARENA/PDS right? What is the right's impact on the *nature* of contemporary Brazilian politics?

The Chaotic Polity

Observers of Brazilian politics have continually pointed to the system's comparatively low level of institutionalization. The Brazilian polity is seen as amorphous and fluid, with weakly drawn ideological lines and minimal organizational density.[1] The term *geléia geral* ("general jelly"), coined by the songwriter Gilberto Gil in the 1960s to characterize the daily chaos and fluidity of Brazilian society, would, in this view, be a fair and immediately recognizable description of the country's political life.

It is worth noting that such characterizations have been made of Brazilian politics regardless of the prevailing political regime. In the 1950s, under the democracy of the Second Republic, a foreign observer examined Brazil's party system and pronounced it to be "institutionalized confusion" (Peterson 1962). In the 1970s, under military authoritarianism, Peter McDonough wrote of the "unideological, experimental gloss" of Brazilian politics (McDonough 1981: 236). Another keen observer, Douglas Chalmers, in a seminal article drawing heavily on the Brazilian experience, used the term "politicized state" to refer to a political system that is fluid and malleable, and in which representative institutions are sidestepped in favor of an in-

---

1. These observations on politics are often applied to Brazilian society as a whole by sociologists and anthropologists. For an influential interpretation, see DaMatta (1991).

strumental, pragmatic, outcome-oriented view of politics (Chalmers 1977b). In the post-1985 New Republic, newer research has once again made similar observations about the new democracy's weak institutionalization and seeming lack of direction.[2] Such characterizations as Souza's "invertebrate centrism" (Souza 1989), O'Donnell's "coalition of all for all" (O'Donnell 1992), and Pang's "democratic cacophony" (Pang 1989) echo these earlier analyses. Over time, these assessments of Brazilian politics evoke an image of a country where such things as transparency in politics, elite accountability, the posing of clear political alternatives, and the effective use of representative institutions are more or less foreign to political life.

Regardless of the name we give it—whether it be "politicized democracy," "general jelly," or whatever—this phenomenon of an amorphous, weakly institutionalized polity is inimical to political democracy. Democracy consists of participation and contestation (Dahl 1971), of the posing of political alternatives and the exercise of political accountability, none of which can take place outside of minimally developed institutional structures. The inability of the Brazilian political system to move away from its uninstitutionalized traditions—from a "chaotic" polity—is synonymous with its difficulty in consolidating democracy. But does the collective actor profiled in this book—the political right—really have all that much to do with the preservation or prolonging of this disordered mode of politics? Admittedly, the evidence for the Weberian hypothesis discussed in Chapter 2 is somewhat mixed, and was certainly stronger in the 1980s than after some apparent resocialization of the right in the 1990s. But without denying the multidimensional nature of this complex problem, there are two reasons why the right's role stands out as a crucial factor in the quality of Brazilian democracy. Both reasons have been introduced in prior chapters, but it is worth returning to them at some length.

The impact of the "abashed right." Chapter 4 presented empirical evidence of Brazil's *direita envergonhada*, an "abashed right" that refuses to acknowledge its very existence. My survey research supported earlier findings by political sociologist Leôncio Martins Rodrigues, whose 1987 study of federal deputies found that only 6 percent would classify themselves as being ideologically right of center. As Rodrigues remarked wryly: "Judging

2. Analyses of the New Republic include Smith (1987), Hagopian and Mainwaring (1987), Souza (1989), Power (1991), O'Donnell (1992), Martínez-Lara (1996), and Mainwaring (1999).

from the political self-definition of the deputies, Brazil is a country without a right" (1987: 99). In researching this book, I encountered one perplexing methodological problem: how to approach a political animal that pretends not to exist. I began with an experiential definition of the right—basing it on an individual's commitment to authoritarian rule before 1985—and then went on to demonstrate that veterans of ARENA/PDS not only conform to more traditional definitions of the right (they are politically conservative beyond question), but also that this cohort of politicians fills the illusory void at the rightmost end of the Brazilian political spectrum.

In the New Republic, former ARENA/PDS politicians shun the labels "right" and "conservative" and prefer instead to masquerade as "centrists." *Centro* is the label of choice because it allows the ex-*arenistas* to avoid association with Brazil's authoritarian past as well as dodge culpability for persistent socioeconomic inequalities. The left and center-left, who long ago arrogated the "correct" values of democracy and equality, see no need to flee from the political labels that fit them. Unlike the right, their political project[3]—at least at this historical juncture in postauthoritarian Brazil—is wrapped in an aura of legitimacy, and they openly proclaim their progressivism. This is just another way of saying that in Brazilian elite political culture, the left has appropriated the popular struggle, and the right is always "guilty" of being on the *contramão da história* (swimming against the tide of history). Among the politically informed during the early years of democracy, this distinction was taken as an article of faith—much to the irritation of (not all, but most) conservative public figures, who were continually uncomfortable, apologetic, and generally squirming in the presence of journalists and intellectuals. The CUT's *traidores do povo* campaign, for example, was effective in causing defections from the Centrão and forcing many legislators to deny that they belonged to the "right" (Chapter 7). This perception of a qualitative difference between a "righteous" left and a "pitiable" right was elucidated in an interview with a Communist deputy. He pointed out that in Brazilian elections—as any observer can easily verify—both the left and the right employ poor people as their campaign workers in the streets. But he asserted that when it come to the recruitment of these workers, there is a fundamental difference between the left and the right. The impoverished

---

3. I am being careful to say "political project" and not "economic project." The sectors of the left that still propose state socialism in Brazil (for example, the PC do B [Partido Comunista do Brasil] and some sectors of the PT) have seen their economic proposals become almost completely irrelevant to the national debate in the 1990s.

campaign workers of the left donate their time, but "the right has to pay theirs!" (interview with Deputy Augusto Carvalho, Brasília, July 17, 1990).

The mass migration of conservative politicians to an imaginary center underlies Souza's notion of "invertebrate centrism," which she defines as a "vast center whose boundaries . . . are unknown" (M. Souza 1989: 355). The reason that the center's boundaries are unmarked is that the political right has engaged in ideological obfuscation. Sensitive to the negative connotations of the label *direita*, and avoiding forms of collective action (such as party formation) that would subject itself to easy identification by voters, the right denies its own existence and confuses the ideological contours of the Brazilian political system.

The right's self-denial contributes to the perpetuation of the "chaotic polity." The right's strategy is nothing less than a frontal attack on political identities, which are crucial to the posing of political alternatives inherent in polyarchy. The strategy is no doubt a conscious one. Rightist politicians are undoubtedly sensitive to the low level of political information among the Brazilian citizenry, because (as demonstrated in Chapter 4) these politicians tend to come from precisely those regions where levels of information are lowest. By adopting a democratic discourse and claiming the political "center" for its own, the right attempts to make it difficult for voters to determine precisely who among the political class supported military authoritarianism, who is politically conservative, who supports the socioeconomic status quo, and so on. This strategy of obfuscation, which diminishes the ability of voters to identify such political tendencies and then either reward or punish them, is clearly destructive of political accountability in Brazil.

The impact of the undermining of representative institutions. As is abundantly clear in the literature, and as is visible in even a cursory examination of its most recent incarnation, Brazilian democracy suffers from weak, nonconsolidated representative institutions. The case study of the party system supported the prevailing view that Brazilian parties are extraordinarily underdeveloped, but went on to demonstrate that one of the phenomena frequently cited to explain party weakness—the putative antiparty, individualistic orientation of the Brazilian political class—was in the critical period of the 1980s far more pronounced among former *arenistas* than within any other segment of the political elite. The partisan diaspora of the ARENA/PDS cohort after 1984, as well as its voting record on issues of party and electoral reform in the Constituent Assembly, illustrate how these anti-institutional attitudes have been transformed into concrete anti-party actions. Similarly, the case study of Congress revealed that the right in the ANC showed little interest in building a representative institution that is of central importance to any political democracy. Instead, during the ANC—the window of opportunity for institutional redesign—the right showed a preference toward maintaining a highly executive-centered form of national government in Brazil, in which the president acts and the Congress reacts. Despite the right's frequent opposition, however, the Congress did indeed acquire some significant new powers in the 1988 Constitution—but prospects for their successful deployment were dimmed early on by the right's low level of interest and participation in legislative affairs. The early survey data suggested that rightist federal legislators were more interested in personal autonomy and the chance to deal one-on-one with state officials than they were in the collective action necessary to strengthen and consolidate the National Congress. More recently, the right's level of engagement in Congress has begun to "catch up" to that of the former opposition to military rule (see Table 6.6), yet many of the patterns and folkways of the institution continue to echo both the military's emasculation of the institution in the 1970s and the right's attempts to preserve executive dominance in the 1980s.

In exploring what the right's presence means to the nature of Brazilian politics, it is apparent from the foregoing observations that one potential answer to this question is the following: the right makes Brazilian politics *conservative*. Here I do not use "conservative" in the sense of a predominant ideological tendency or temporary political majority. Such an assertion would lead to a circular argument, that is, "Brazil has long had a conservative political system, which permits the ongoing survival of the right; and given the overwhelming presence of the right, Brazilian politics is heavily conservative" (true, but tautological). Rather, I mean that the right makes Brazilian politics conservative by depriving it of many of the institutional mechanisms that could promote change. Returning to the theme of democratic quality discussed in Chapter 2, I draw attention to the relationship between functional political institutions and the ability of social actors to pursue the normative goals of high-intensity democracy: participation, contestation, and especially *accountability*. In so doing, I am coming close to the idea expressed by Maurice Duverger in his often-cited maxim: "A regime without parties is of necessity a conservative regime" (Duverger 1954: 426). If we substitute *institutions* for *parties* in Duverger's famous dictum, we have a concise yet compelling characterization of Brazil's New Republic.

How Democratic is the Right?

This book has examined the ARENA/PDS cohort in the New Republic by studying its relationship to formal institution building. It is appropriate to ask at this point whether we may classify the Brazilian right as a democratic actor, as an antidemocratic actor, or somewhere in the gray area in between.

There are three principal ways that scholars have assessed the "democraticness" of political actors during Latin America's transition to democracy. One typical way has been to examine whether the actors support or reject substantive socioeconomic reform; the "antidemocratic" actors are those that resist such change, that is, industrialists and large landowners in many countries. A second method is to apply the label "antidemocratic" to those sectors in the armed forces who prefer a return to direct military rule, and to those civilians who explicitly or implicitly appeal to the generals to act on their interventionist impulses. A third classification gauges the "democraticness" of political actors by assessing their commitment to democratic practices. Because the first of these yardsticks leads us too far afield from the procedural definition of democracy outlined in Chapter 2, I shall focus on the second and third approaches.

Civil-military relations. This is an important issue, given the past political trajectory of the right. In 1964, conservative political elites endorsed the overthrow of a democratically elected government. Subsequently, the ARENA/PDS cohort collaborated with military rulers for two decades. Given its past association with dictatorship, it is reasonable to suspect that the right may constitute an antisystem—or, as Juan Linz (1978) put it, a "disloyal"—actor under democracy. Attempting to classify an actor as democratic or antidemocratic in this way is not overly simplistic, even given the complexies of democratic consolidation. Potential disloyalty *matters* for the simple reason that the consolidation of democracy is only one of several possible outcomes in a postauthoritarian political situation: consolidation is *never* preordained, in Brazil or anywhere else (Valenzuela 1992; Przeworski 1992). In fact, consolidation entails first and foremost the avoidance of the worst-case scenario, an authoritarian retrogression (O'Donnell 1985).

The question of renewed military intervention in Brazil has heretofore been absent from the present study, because in the New Republic the possibility of a military coup has *mostly* seemed remote.[4] The one (arguable) exception to this rule was in late 1993 and early 1994, when the paralysis of the Itamar Franco government, combined with the demonstration effect

---

4. The 1990 survey asked whether legislators agreed that "the Brazilian armed forces are more pro-democratic in 1990 than in 1980." Some 84.6 percent of all veterans agreed. Agreement stood at 81.7 percent among the opposition cohort and at 89.9 percent among ex-*arenistas,* and the difference of means was not significant. Due to the high level of consensus on this question, I did not replicate the question in 1993 or 1997.

of the 1992 presidential *autogolpe* in Peru, led to a brief spate of rumor-mongering about possible *fujimorização* in Brazil).[5] Academic studies of civil-military relations in the aftermath of the 1985 transition argued that the army's influence was still overwhelming (Stepan 1988); a more recent analysis suggests that this influence was eroded significantly by the mid-1990s, mostly via the cumulative effect of rational civilian politicians pursuing micro policy and budgetary goals in a competitive framework (Hunter 1997). However, these studies tell us little about the likelihood of a coup, simply because the military's degree of influence in political life is not the same thing as its decision to attempt a coup d'état. This was demonstrated amply in Chile in 1973 and in Venezuela in 1992—in both cases, military coups were launched against two of the most "consolidated" (by virtually any definition of the term) democratic regimes that ever existed in Latin America. Therefore, I shall say nothing definitive about the probability of return to military rule in Brazil. Rather, my objective is more modest: I shall examine how the political right views its former allies, the armed forces.

In the Constituent Assembly of 1987–88, democratic reformers tried repeatedly to scale back some of the impressive institutional prerogatives of the Brazilian military. Progressive legislators introduced amendments that proposed granting amnesty to officers purged by the 1964 coup, restoring their commissions, giving them back pay, and so on. Other amendments attempted to establish official recognition of the illegality of military decrees and Institutional Acts. All such amendments fell pathetically short of achieving the absolute majority of 280 votes in the ANC. A review of the roll-calls showed that the ARENA/PDS cohort was impressively united—usually on the order of 80 percent to 90 percent—in supporting the armed forces' position on these controversial amendments, while the opposition veterans were often divided.[6] The military was widely seen as a beneficiary of the constitutional deliberations: Article 142 of the 1988 Constitution guarantees the right of the armed forces to intervene to preserve internal order.

The 1990 and 1993 surveys found the ARENA/PDS cohort to be highly supportive of the military's continuing right to intervene, with more than 70 percent support in each survey, although this diminished somewhat to about 57 percent in 1997 (Table 8.1). Not surprisingly, the opposition co-

---

5. For a discussion, based largely on alarmist reporting by the journalist Elio Gaspari, see Linz and Stepan (1996: 178).

6. See *Diário da Assembléia Nacional Constituinte*, June 15–16, 1988, and August 27, 1988.

Table 8.1 Indicators of civil-military relations and authoritarian nostalgia (percentage agreeing)

Question or Statement	1990				1993				1997			
	ARENA/PDS Veterans	Opposition Veterans	All Veterans	Sig.	ARENA/PDS Veterans	Opposition Veterans	All Veterans	Sig.	ARENA/PDS Veterans	Opposition Veterans	All Veterans	Sig.
Support or oppose the (1988) "constitutional provision granting the Armed Forces the right to intervene to maintain internal order"	72.5	35.3	52.5	.001	70.0	44.9	54.4	.01	56.6	34.7	44.0	.05
"Instead of having several military ministries, Brazil should have a single Ministry of Defense"	52.8	78.6	66.8	.001	70.5	78.2	75.3	NS	83.3	82.4	82.8	NS
"If the Ministry of Defense is created, the minister should be a civilian"	57.0	68.3	63.2	.10	57.9	69.9	65.3	NS	59.3	72.6	66.9	NS

"Authoritarian regimes are better equipped than democratic regimes to stimulate economic growth"	17.8	11.9	14.6	NS	26.7	10.0	16.3	.01	18.5	5.3	10.8	.05
"In Latin America, it has been easier for authoritarian governments than for democratic governments to maintain social order"	50.0	46.8	48.2	NS	57.4	43.9	49.1	.10	40.4	25.7	31.7	.10
Maximum N in samples[a]	108	128	236	—	63	103	166	—	55	76	131	—

NS = Not significant

[a] For the specific questionnaire items cited in this table, the number of valid responses in 1990 ranged from a minimum of 221 to a maximum of 233; in 1993, from 150 to 162; and in 1997, from 126 to 130.

hort has been much less favorable to the idea. Despite the right's recent shift toward a less interventionist posture, the difference of opinion between the two cohorts was still at more than 20 percentage points, and still statistically significant, in 1997. This distribution of preferences says nothing about the likelihood of a new coup nor whether the ex-authoritarians would support one if it came. It simply indicates that the right wishes to retain the Brazilian military in its historical role as the ultimate arbiter of unrest. Article 142 specifies that the military may not intervene without the "initiative" of one of the three branches of government—but it is unclear what constitutes an emergency situation, or how an invitation for military intervention would be properly formulated. To the extent that the constitutional text would have any importance at all in such a grave situation, Article 142 clearly grants substantial latitude to the armed forces. By giving strong support to this clause, the right demonstrates that it is (at the very least) amenable to future direct military intervention in politics.

What about military influence short of a coup? Several survey questions sought the right's reaction to a number of reforms that have been proposed to reduce the military's sphere of influence. One such reform was to reduce the number of military ministries (in the Sarney administration, military-controlled portfolios made up six of the twenty-three cabinet positions). This idea was first proposed in the ANC, but went nowhere; later, it was resurrected in the Collor and Cardoso governments, with Cardoso finally creating the Ministry of Defense in 1999.[7] In considering the statement "instead of having various military ministries, Brazil should have a single Ministry of Defense," only 52.8 percent of the right supported this reform in 1990, a figure that rose to 70.5 percent in 1993 and to 83.3 percent in 1997—by which time there was virtually no difference in the opinions of ex-authoritarians and ex-oppositionists. The statement that "if the Ministry of Defense is created, the Minister should be a civilian" had stable ex-ARENA support averaging about 58 percent in each survey, and stable ex-opposition support averaging about 70 percent. Similar figures resulted when respondents were queried about the infamous National Intelligence

---

7. Brazil's first civilian Minister of Defense, named by Cardoso in early 1999, was Élcio Álvares, a recently retired PFL senator. Revealingly, Álvares had excellent credentials within the ex-ARENA cohort, having been a vice-leader of the governing PDS in the Chamber of Deputies in 1971–73, and later serving as the "bionic" governor of Espírito Santo between 1975 and 1979. Press reports suggested that his political trajectory made him acceptable to the military. Álvares assumed his full authority as minister in June 1999, when the Army, Navy, and Air Force ministries were finally abolished.

Service (Serviço Nacional de Informações, or SNI), the most important element of the military's repressive apparatus in the 1960s and 1970s. In 1990, some 53.7 percent of ex-*arenistas* supported the abolishment of the SNI, compared to 79.2 percent of the opposition cohort.[8] The responses to these three questions demonstrate that the opposition cohort (much of which endured repression in the 1960s and 1970s) consistently and decisively favored a rollback of military influence in the 1990s, while ex-authoritarians—initially divided and ambivalent—slowly began to follow suit.

For any randomly selected civilian politician, it is plausible that his or her orientation toward future military intervention would be based on his or her experience under military rule in the past. Guillermo O'Donnell made a similar point when he advanced a counterintuitive argument about democratic consolidation. Contrary to expectation, consolidation may be more difficult in situations where the outgoing authoritarian regime was more economically successful and less politically repressive. In these Brazil-like scenarios, elites are less likely to have suffered personally under dictatorship, and are therefore not well "vaccinated" against authoritarian retrogressions (O'Donnell 1992). For this reason, the survey research endeavored to capture any potential "nostalgia" for authoritarianism by measuring elites' orientation toward military rule in the abstract.

The statement that "authoritarian regimes are better equipped than democratic regimes to stimulate economic growth" did not have much currency among politicians active in 1964–85: overall agreement was only 14.6 percent in 1990, 16.3 percent in 1993, and 10.8 percent in 1997. There was no statistically significant difference in the attitudes of ex-*arenistas* and the opposition cohort in 1990, but there was in 1993, when the right's agreement rose to 26.7 percent. The cleavage remained significant in 1997 (see Table 6.1). As for the statement that "in Latin America, it has been easier for authoritarian governments than for democratic governments to maintain social order," the level of agreement was much higher, with the entire sample agreeing at almost identical levels of 48.2 percent in 1990 and 49.1 percent in 1993. But overall agreement fell sharply in 1997 to only 31.7 percent. Again, it is striking that there was no statistically significant differ-

8. The 1990 survey was conducted during the presidential transition from Sarney to Collor, during which Collor had announced his intention to do away with the SNI and replace it with a civilian-run intelligence service. The new organ, created in 1990, is called the Secretariat for Strategic Affairs (Secretaria de Assuntos Estratégicos, or SAE). For this reason the SNI question was not repeated in the 1993 and 1997 surveys. For a discussion of Collor's intelligence reforms, see Hunter (1997: 60–66).

ence between the two cohorts in 1990, but such a difference had emerged by 1993 and remained significant in 1997 From the first to the second survey ex-opposition agreement fell by 2.9 percentage points, while ex-ARENA agreement rose by 7.4 points.

The results here are intriguing: the "nostalgia cleavage" within the political class apparently became sharper rather than weaker as the years of democracy wore on. The most plausible explanation for this is assessment of the democratic regime's performance. From 1990 to 1992 the Brazilian economy contracted, and the political system was characterized by scandal, mass protests, and presidential impeachment. Although growth resumed in 1993, at the time of the survey this was not yet apparent—and at that moment the incumbent government of Itamar Franco was a pitiful sight, beleaguered and adrift, with hyperinflation on the horizon. It is likely that the dismal performance of Brazilian democracy in the early 1990s reawakened some authoritarian nostalgia within the ex-ARENA cohort, but this nostalgia then diminished somewhat in 1997 after three years of relatively successful economic management by Fernando Henrique Cardoso. Ex-opposition sympathy for authoritarianism, always low to begin with, fell uniformly across the three surveys, while ex-*arenista* nostalgia spiked upward then moderated downward. The survey results, in which rightist attitudes showed erratic movement but ex-opposition attitudes did not, suggests that at least some of the ARENA/PDS veterans are "fair-weather democrats."

The problem of fair-weather democrats—or in the jargon of political culture, "specific" (performance-based) rather than "diffuse" (value-based) support for democracy—is equally relevant to Brazil's economic elite, whose interests the ex-*arenistas* ostensibly defend. During the political crises preceding the coup of 1964, conservative political parties in Brazil—most notably the UDN—allied with the business community in demanding military intervention to overthrow João Goulart. The precedent of the political right willingly serving as the conduit for business elites' pro-coup exhortations remains an alarming one for contemporary democratic consolidation. In her research on business elites in the New Republic, Leigh Payne suggested several reasons why capitalists in the 1990s are less likely than their 1960s predecessors to favor an authoritarian reversal: they have greater confidence in government competence and legitimacy, they sense greater influence over government policy in the neoliberal era, and their increasing diversity makes them less likely to mobilize collectively (Payne 1994: 152–60). However, she also found that business elites greatly mistrusted political parties and the national legislature as potential vehicles for representation of their interests. Only 29 percent cited federal legislators as dependable representatives of business interests, and only 12 percent described parties in this way (interestingly, "lobbying by individual firms" was as popular a response as political parties). Some 70 percent felt that the best vehicle for representation was lobbying by sectoral associations (Payne 1994: 118). These findings suggest that although capitalists are more satisifed with democracy than they were in the populist Second Republic, they do not view the institutional incarnations of their natural allies, the political right, as effective channels for processing their demands. This raises the specter of renewed praetorianism should democracy fall short of capitalists' expectations in the future. Therefore, a major goal of democratic sustainability discussed in Chapter 1—the "institutional incorporation of the right"—seems to be unrealized with regard to both the political and the "social" right in Brazil.

These findings may be troubling, but they must must be put into perspective. It is true that since 1985 the ARENA/PDS cohort has not burned any bridges between itself and the military. Much to the contrary, the right has at times vociferously supported the military's demands, as in the ANC debates over amnesty. The military's most visible champions in the political class are almost uniformly drawn from the old ARENA/PDS party structure.[9] But it is important to point out that none of these individuals—nor any other major politician in Brazil, for that matter—has yet openly called on the military to take power. *Golpismo* (coup incitement) has been notable for its absence in the New Republic. While it is probable—as O'Donnell's (1992) analysis would suggest—that the political right would find it easy to reestablish a convivium with the military in the event of a new authoritarian regime, to date there has been no evidence that ex-*arenistas* desire this.

Commitment to democratic practices. If we use the criterion of "knocking on the barracks door" to gauge the democraticness of political actors in the New Republic, we would have to conclude that the ARENA/PDS cohort is not a disloyal or antisystem actor. However, if we use the alternative criterion of commitment to democratic practices, a different picture emerges.

Any meaningful definition of actors' commitment to democratic practices must necessarily bring us back, full circle, to the theme of representa-

---

9. These include former president José Sarney, Deputy Ricardo Fiúza (PFL-Pernambuco), former senator and retired colonel Jarbas Passarinho (PDS/PPR/PPB-Pará), and the late Deputy Amaral Netto (PDS/PPR/PPB-Rio de Janeiro),

tive institutions. As set out in the Huntingtonian definition used in Chapter 2, institutions are "stable, valued, recurring patterns of behavior." The process of institutionalization is one in which "organizations and procedures *acquire* value and stability" (Huntington 1968: 12; emphasis added). Because the political legacy confronting Brazil is widely perceived as one of weak representative institutions—this would be the consensus not only of scholars of Brazilian politics, but also its practitioners—then for these practitioners it is reasonable to define "commitment to democratic practices" as *active* participation in the process of institutionalizing the new democratic organizations and procedures. Again, such a definition builds on openly normative standards of democratic quality. If we operationalize a commitment to democratic practices in this way, drawing attention to the necessity of politicians' *promoting* the value of representative institutions and thus helping to move Brazil away from the status quo ante, the performance of ARENA/PDS veterans has been dismal. Case studies of the party system and the National Congress illustrated that the in the ANC, the right generally did *not* contribute to the consolidation and privileging of these institutions. Despite some evidence of the gradual institutional resocialization of the right presented in Chapters 5 and 6, the cumulative record of the right since 1985 is not very encouraging on this score: in its best moments, the right has dragged its feet on institutional reform, or ignored it; in its worst moments, the right has obstructed or torpedoed institution-building proposals. With the important exception of direct popular elections, which are highly regular in the New Republic, it is doubtful that any representative institutions can be said to have acquired additional "value" and "stability" by virtue of the right's engagement in their redesign during the ANC.

This study did, however, uncover some evidence of political learning on the part of the ex-authoritarian cohort. The data presented in Chapter 5 demonstrated that from the 1987–91 legislature to the 1991–95 legislature, the political class as a whole evinced increasing support for the idea of strengthening Brazil's political parties, and the greatest upswing occurred among ex-*arenistas*. Although there was a slight decline in support for strong parties in the 1995–99 legislature, this support still remained higher than what was registered in the baseline 1990 survey. Turning to legislative institutions, Chapter 6 suggested that although still lower among the ARENA/PDS cohort, parliamentary participation was increasing across the board in the 1990s. The results suggest that most political learning—the revising of attitudes—occurred in the early 1990s, after the ANC was concluded and the Constitution of 1988 was in place.

By the beginning of the 1990s, Brazilian elites had largely recognized the importance of institutional redesign in resolving the crisis of governability. Of course, the survey data presented in this book can be interpreted as saying essentially the same thing, so I confront a potential tautology here: we need *independent* confirmation of a sea change in elite attitudes toward strengthening political institutions in the 1990s. There is an abundance of such evidence. The institutional paralysis that accompanied the slow death of the Sarney administration (1985–90) generated widespread calls for political party reform and party-strengthening rules. Politicians, journalists, and political scientists participated equally in this dialogue. (The print media in particular emphasized the weak-institutions angle. If one was reading the prestige press of Rio, São Paulo, or Brasília during the 1990s, it was virtually impossible in any given week not to see at least one op-ed piece lamenting Brazil's political institutions.) The national debate preceding the 1993 plebiscite on a proposed switch to parliamentary rule was revealing: the desired strengthening of political parties was the number one reason cited by the proponents of parliamentary government. It became increasingly common in the early 1990s to hear politicians quote foreign political scientists as they argued for more effective parties. Dozens of bills and constitutional amendments were presented concerning electoral and party system reform. But the survey research revealed the ex-ARENA right still to be disproportionately favorable to weak parties and a strong presidency.

Overall assessment. The answer to the question of whether the right is a democratic collective actor depends on the criteria used for "democraticness." An approach that focuses on the unrealized potential for *golpismo* and system disloyalty paints the ARENA/PDS cohort in a favorable light. Alternatively, an approach that emphasizes commitment to democratic institutions and the promotion of "quality" standards of democratic consolidation (especially accountability) shows the right in a generally unfavorable light. It could be argued, then, that by virtue of not knocking on the barracks door, the right is not *actively* antidemocratic; but by its omission and uninterest in the process of institutional consolidation, it is *passively* antidemocratic. It may be objected that this assessment is too harsh, that judging the right by what it is *not* doing is unfair. However, Brazil's twin political legacies—weak institutions and recurrent military intervention—are reminders that the stakes in this game of democratic consolidation are high indeed.

The Costs of Conservative Democratization: The Brazilian Crisis in the 1990s

I have argued in this book that the right bears disproportionate responsibility for the underdevelopment of representative institutions in the New Republic. But what are the wider implications of this for Brazil and for Brazilians? In focusing mainly on the ARENA/PDS right, I been unable to paint a complete picture of the crisis of post-1985 Brazilian democracy. In its first decade and a half, Brazilian democracy's failure to consolidate representative institutions and to develop a set of more or less permanent "rules of the game" had devastating effects all over the political landscape.[10]

Two features of Brazilian politics widely commented upon in recent years have been a generalized lack of accountability and an increasing fragmentation of political power. This is a deadly combination, which has further amplified the (always considerable) political space available for clientelism or outright corruption (Weyland 1993). The intensification of these practices has had an incalculable social cost. As the press amply documented during the Sarney and Collor administrations, millions of dollars in public monies have been squandered or have mysteriously vanished. Some of the most egregious (and audacious) examples of kleptocracy came to life in the infamous "Collorgate" scandal of 1992, which ultimately led to the impeachment and resignation of Brazil's first democratically elected president in twenty-nine years.[11] With Collor's spectacular political demise, the New Republic was robbed of a potentially important psychological milestone: Collor failed in his bid to become only the third Brazilian president in history to have been democratically elected and serve a complete term in office.[12]

By the early 1990s, the prestige of politicians and of political life in general had reached all-time lows. The legitimacy of democracy in Brazil was low by regional and cross-national standards (Linz and Stepan 1996). Weak legitimacy appeared causally related to the dismal public image of parties and Congress (Moisés 1994, 1995). Popular impatience was directed at failures and delays on many substantive reforms, including agrarian reform and the updating of labor legislation (Hagopian and Mainwaring 1987), or taxation and social policy (Weyland 1996), many of which were

10. Treatments of this and related topics are found in Hagopian and Mainwaring (1987), Pang (1989), Schneider (1991), Power (1991, 2000), O'Donnell (1992) and Weyland (1993).

11. In December 1992, Collor was permanently replaced by his vice-president, Itamar Franco. A former leader of the MDB/PMDB in his home state of Minas Gerais, and a federal senator from 1975 to 1990, Franco was a consistent opponent of the military regime. He became the first president since 1964 to have never been a member of ARENA/PDS.

12. Fernando Henrique Cardoso achieved this milestone when he completed his first term in office in January 1999. The two prior presidents to have have done so were Eurico Dutra in 1946–51 and Juscelino Kubitschek in 1956–61. Kubitschek and FHC are the only civilians ever to have achieved this feat.

traceable to unstable legislative coalitions or to high turnover at the ministerial level. The failure of Congress to enable (*regulamentar*) many important articles of the 1988 Constitution was also widely deplored. When Congress attempted a thorough overhaul of the constitutional text in 1993–94 (a revision after five years had been mandated by the ANC in 1988), it found itself evaluating many constitutional provisions that had never been enacted in the first place. More than 30,000 amendments were presented to the so-called Congresso Revisor, but the special assembly died quickly due to three factors: the "Budgetgate" corruption scandal, determined obstructionism by the left, and the approaching elections of 1994. Of the 30,000 amendments presented, only 5 were adopted. A sixth amendment, the Social Emergency Fund (Fundo Social de Emergência, or FSE), which consumed much of the special assembly's energy, was not even on the Revisão agenda to begin with; rather, it was championed by the Franco government as a means for emergency fiscal stabilization.

The costs of weak institutions are also evident in the state of relations between the executive and the legislative branches. In other presidential systems, this relationship is generally structured by the party system, which shapes the necessary channels for dialogue and political support. But because the contemporary Brazilian party system is so fragmented, it has proved difficult for the postauthoritarian presidents to achieve a stable majority in Congress. In response, presidents have taking to ruling by emergency measures (*medidas provisórias*)—a favorite tool of President Fernando Henrique Cardoso, who in 1995 and 1996 averaged one decree per day. The emergency measures replicate two features of the authoritarian regime, in that they (1) grant the political initiative to the president and (2) lend an unwelcome aura of arbitrariness to political life. The Congress is often thrown off balance by these measures, as it is constitutionally obligated to convene and rule on the legality of each (a requirement the legislature finds hard to meet, because of its notorious inefficiency). Thus far in the New Republic, it seems that in the game of executive-legislative relations, no one wins and everyone loses (Power 1998).

These observations on politics and institutions have to be put back into the context of economic and social crisis in Brazil. A country long accustomed to spectacular growth and development slid backwards in the 1980s and early 1990s. Annualized inflation was close to 2000 percent for a good part of this period, and the foreign debt climbed to more than $130 billion. In March 1990, as President Sarney yielded office to President Collor, inflation reached 80 percent monthly and the cruzeiro was being devalued at 3 percent per day. Collor's efforts to stem inflation in 1990 and 1991 proved futile; he was replaced in October 1992 by Itamar Franco, who went through three failed Finance Ministers in his first six months in office. A study by the Brazilian Census Bureau showed that 90 percent of the Brazilian population became poorer between 1981 and 1990 (*Istoé Senhor*, March 20, 1991). After the "Lost Decade" of the 1980s, most major Latin American economies turned the corner beginning in 1991—but Brazil's GDP actually contracted that year. For several years into the 1990s, the country was cited as the economic laggard of the Latin America, and concern grew that Brazil was becoming ungovernable.

Brazil finally began its own turnaround in 1993, when President Franco appointed Senator Fernando Henrique Cardoso as his fourth Finance Minister. Functioning as a de facto prime minister, Cardoso first implemented a fiscal adjustment that was then followed in July 1994 by the Plano Real currency reform. The success of the *Real* in taming inflation led not only to a consumer spending boom and renewed growth, but was the major factor in Cardoso's presidential election victory in 1994. Cardoso's first term in office was characterized by moderate economic expansion and reasonable—though uneven—progress toward structural adjustment. But while the economic context changed rather drastically beginning in 1994, the political equation had changed little by 2000. The problems of a weak legislature, party system fragmentation, and precarious executive-legislative relations persisted. Economic reform has detracted attention from political reform, and—with a capable president and his state-shrinking proposals dominating the headlines—many observers fail to notice the institutional fault lines that still crisscross the Brazilian political system. The preoccupation with "governability" that consumed Brazil analysts as recently as 1993 has diminished under Cardoso, and this is a great error—because the problems of political and institutional development remain fundamental and of controlling importance to democratic sustainability.

The question of "governability" was and is a reflection of the problems with political institutionalization. Because of the weak party system and the fragmented Congress, it was difficult in the first decade of democracy to build political and societal support for any of the numerous economic stabilization plans. More effective and functional political institutions would not by themselves guarantee economic recovery, but they would at least create more favorable conditions for experimentation with different solutions. Brazil's dismal roller-coaster ride between 1985 and 1993 should not be forgotten so quickly. The negative consequences of democracy's first decade point to the tremendous costs of weak institutions in Brazil, and by extension, to some drawbacks of its peculiar form of conservative democratization.

The Right and Conservative Democratization in Brazil: Implications for Theory

This book approached the problem of democratic consolidation by means of an actor-centered, institutionally focused study, focusing on the political right in postauthoritarian Brazil. Employing the idiographic method, this study is not explicitly comparative; however, the material presented here raises questions and hypotheses that are of theoretical and comparative importance. An assessment of the theoretical implications of this study raises two central questions for reflection. First, *why* did the Brazilian right support weak representative institutions in the early years of the New Republic? An examination of this question can tell us something about the importance of authoritarian-era legacies in new democracies. The second question, which also addresses the issue of legacies, gets to the heart of this study's contribution to the evolving theory of political democratization: are "conservative" transitions from authoritarian rule conducive to democratic consolidation?

Why Does the Right Behave As It Does?

This book explained Brazil's difficulties with democratic consolidation via reference to the anti-institutional orientation of the ARENA/PDS right. This is a causal generalization. The central argument merits three comments, each of which is true of all causal explanations in the social sciences. First, the argument advanced here is a *partial* explanation; the preservation of the ARENA/PDS cohort is certainly not the only reason why Brazil has had difficulty institutionalizing democracy, but it is an important one, and one that has not received the attention it deserves. Second, as is often the case in social research, finding a satisfying "answer" to any puzzle often raises an additional set of questions, and sometimes these are more perplexing than the original research question itself. Third, the theoretical value of any explanation increases if we act on this perplexity by taking the causal chain one step further. In the case at hand, it may be intuitively plausible to state that Brazilian democratic consolidation is imperiled because the right is uninterested in representative institutions, but what, in turn, explains that? An explanation for the Brazilian right's anti-institutional orientation is *not* intuitive—the phenomenon cannot be explained away by referring to the individualism of the Brazilian political class, because we have found this trait to be most pronounced on the right—and so I build one by drawing on two prominent hypotheses.

The socialization argument. A first explanation is inspired by the Weberian hypothesis referred to in Chapter 1. In his study of early Weimar Germany, Max Weber stressed the importance of authoritarian-era legacies as challenges to the new parliamentary democracy. His point of entry into this subject was how Bismarck had intentionally marginalized the early German parliaments.[13] In doing so, Bismarck weakened the recruitment and overall quality of the German political class, a process that left the Weimar Republic without the wherewithal to develop strong democratic institutions. Weber's description of "Bismarck's legacy" is highly reminiscent of trends under the Brazilian military regime of 1964–85. An authoritarian executive packed parliament with its cronies, left them with no serious political responsibilities, and ruled instead through a rapidly expanding bureaucracy. Over time, the influence of politicians diminished vis-à-vis the state apparatus:

> What then was Bismarck's legacy, as far as we are here interested in it? He left behind him a nation *without any political sophistication,* far below the level which in this regard it had reached twenty years before. . . . A *completely powerless parliament* was the purely negative result of his tremendous prestige. . . . The level of parliament depends on whether it does not merely discuss great issues but decisively influences them; in other words, its quality depends on whether what happens there matters, or whether parliament is nothing but the unwillingly tolerated rubber stamp of a ruling bureaucracy. (Weber 1978: 1392; emphasis in original)

What happens when weak, elected politicians become subordinated to strong, unelected bureaucrats? When politicians are denied any policy-making or oversight role in national administration, their political survival depends on their learning to successfully intervene with state officials in order to deliver patronage resources to their constituents (or to themselves). Apart from status and prestige, there would seem to be no other reason why politi-

13. It is clear from Weber's essay that he intended both "parties" and "parliament" to denote not just these formal organizations per se, but also to refer more generally to the German political class. In this discussion I follow Weber's convention.

cians would be attracted to service in a "powerless parliament." As Weber explicitly states, over time such politicians begin to care little about the identity of the executive, as long as their established channels to state resources are kept open. Political and institutional loyalties take a back seat to opportunism and convenience. Weber's description of the Conservatives' abandonment of Bismarck in 1890 bears remarkable resemblance to events in Brazil in the mid-1980s. The following passage could easily have been written about the Party of the Liberal Front, the splinter party of ARENA/PDS whose defection from the generals brought about the transition to democracy in 1985:

> Bismarck had plenty of reason for thinking lowly of his peers. For what happened to him when he was forced out of office in 1890? . . . Conservative lackeys occupied the chairs of Prussian ministers and sat in the Federal offices. What did they do? They sat it out. "Just a new superior"—that was the end of the matter. . . . What words of sympathy did they find for the departing creator of the *Reich*? They did not utter one word. Which of the big parties constituting his following demanded any account of the reasons for his dismissal? They did not bestir themselves, they simply turned to the new sun. (Weber 1978: 1386)

There is nothing mysterious about this phenomenon in Weimar Germany or in contemporary Brazil: it can be described quite accurately as the primacy of personal/individual interests over collective/institutional interests. By promoting a weak parliament populated by clientelists, whose interests in politics were narrowly and individually defined, Bismarck increasingly left himself open to the possibility of an opportunistic abandonment of his government. This is exactly the pattern followed in the Brazilian bureaucratic-authoritarian regime. Weber's argument is that Bismarck's strategy was irresponsible in that it saddled Germany with a political class poorly suited for democratization. Germany paid the price: *"Bismarck tragically reaped his own harvest, for he had wanted—and deliberately accomplished—the political impotence of parliament and the party leaders"* (ibid.; emphasis added). This book examined the similar Brazilian harvest of the 1980s and 1990s.

The genius of Weber's argument is that it illuminates not only the collapse of authoritarian governments, but also the difficulties created for the subsequent process of democratization. In short, Weber's is a major contribution on the role of "authoritarian legacies." Applying his insights to the problems with democratic consolidation in Brazil's New Republic, we can more easily comprehend the anti-institutional behavior of politicians who supported the military regime. In this vein, Eli Diniz, who wrote extensively on the practice of patronage under authoritarianism (Diniz 1982), also cited the relevance of Weber's arguments in an essay on the postauthoritarian party system. "Inoperative parties," Diniz wrote, "go hand in hand with the absence of governing functions." A lack of serious responsibilities encourages party politicians to turn to clientelistic pursuits, which further delegitimates party politics. In the New Republic, "personalism, lack of seriousness and competence, and the irresponsible use of public resources" are characteristics often associated with the parties (Diniz 1989: 85). The data presented in Chapter 5 showed that at the outset of the New Republic, correlates of an antiparty orientation—such as electoral personalism, suspicion of organizational authority, and a closer relationship to the federal bureaucracy—were more common among politicians who supported the military regime.

All of this suggests that an argument can be made that rightist politicians in Brazil were *socialized* to an anti-institutional orientation by means of their political trajectory under authoritarianism. In making the same argument about Germany in 1918, Weber was quite explicit about the direction of the causal arrow. Parliament under authoritarianism, he wrote, was not "deservedly powerless because of the low level of parliamentary life"— rather, it was the powerlessness of parliament that engendered a decline in the quality of politicians (Weber 1978: 1392). This explains not only their eventual opportunistic abandonment of their patron, but also their lack of suitability—what Brazilians might call their *preparação*—for democratic politics, especially as relates to representation and accountability. Weber's socialization argument is compatible with the story told here about the Brazilian right in the New Republic, and is a plausible explanation for the right's lack of loyalty to representative institutions.

Weber's analysis seems to account for the behavior of ex-authoritarians in the contemporary Brazilian Congress. However, Weber implies that the anti-institutional socialization process was generalized across the German political class, whereas I have linked it only to one sector of the Brazilian political class, the ARENA/PDS cohort. There is an apparent tension in my argument, because I have left some major players out of the picture. What about the former opposition to the military regime of 1964–85? Would not marginalization and lack of responsibilities also have affected the former anti-authoritarian cohort and its many veterans in the New Republic? Though the MDB veterans cannot have escaped all of the debilitating effects of the military's emasculation of parties and Congress, the data show the ex-opposition cohort to possess an orientation that is—however unevenly distributed and implemented—much more conducive to institution building than the corresponding attitudes and behavior of the political right. What explains this cleavage in the postauthoritarian political class?

The reason for the differential impact of socialization can be found in the logic of opposition to authoritarian rule. Because the military regime left open some channels for political contestation, the MDB *had* to use the "democratic" institutions of elections, parties, and Congress to push for political liberalization. For a decade after the coup of 1964, this strategy was fruitless, until a surprising opposition victory in the elections of 1974 changed the political dynamic. An awakening occurred within the legal opposition, generating a strategy that was ultimately successful: using the preserved representative institutions, the "Achilles' heel" of Brazilian authoritarianism, to delegitimate and eventually bring down the regime (Lamounier 1984, 1989; Kinzo 1988). Therefore, the attainment of the common goal of opposition forces—an end to military rule—became identified with their *utilization of and participation in representative institutions.* When the logic of opposition is understood in this way, it becomes less surprising that the MDB cohort would arrive to the New Republic more prepared than the right for constructive engagement in institutional life.

A rational choice perspective. While the socialization argument, holds that the right acquired its anti-institutional orientation through a political learning process under authoritarianism, an alternative hypothesis would posit that anti-institutional behaviors can be explained via the aggregate individual-level preferences of rational politicians. Such an approach would focus on the relationship between individual politicians and the rules or constraints to which they are subjected in political life, and in particular on the crucial moment of rulemaking—the consious design of future rules of the political game—that unfolded in the Constituent Assembly of 1987–88.

According to George Tsebelis's concept of "nested games," political actors are constantly playing a number of simultaneous games in multiple arenas (Tsebelis 1990). Their actions, choices, and behaviors can be studied by the observer in accord with the rules in effect at a given point in time, but that is only part of the story. Actors often think and act simultaneously at another level, which is that of *institutional redesign*—they enlarge their strategic focus to consider how the rules of the game themselves might be changed in order to produce a more optimal outcome at a later point in time. Their behavior is shaped by their preexisting information and expectations about the game at hand, a set of reasoning tools for which Tsebelis uses the shorthand "priors." Priors subsume what we have referred to in this study as political experience and political learning. The importance of priors is not constant across actors, because their intensity varies with age and experience. Older actors have stronger priors, and have more difficulty "revising their attitudes." Tsebelis remarks that "the stronger the priors, the less they are modified by conflicting information" (ibid., 23, note 7).

The application of such a perspective to the problem at hand requires an understanding of the rules of the game to which the Brazilian right is accustomed. While to a certain extent this was an underlying theme of the entire book, a few examples are given here to clarify the utility of the rational choice approach. The question to keep in mind is what kind of behavior the "rules of the game" would encourage on the part of the ARENA/PDS cohort—would they encourage behavior oriented toward institutional redesign, or toward defense of the status quo ante?

In attempting to explain the political right's anti-institutional orientation in the New Republic, a rational choice model would emphasize the relative freedom that politicians enjoyed in subnational politics during the authoritarian regime. The military executive rarely intervened in politics below the level of the governors; a bargain was struck whereby ARENA/ PDS politicians maintained their local bases in return for support for the generals at the national (federal) level. Over time, especially in the interior and the less developed regions of Brazil, these bases were solidified: traditional politicians of the pre-1964 period retained their old turf, while newer clients of the dictatorship established their own political machines based on state patronage. In the New Republic, the interest of rational politicians would be in nurturing these local political networks and machines. Such politicians should be expected to show little interest in consolidating formal representative structures, which would not only draw their attention toward national issues but also occasionally subordinate the interests of their constituents to a party platform or a legislative agenda designed by others.

A rational choice model would also emphasize the institutional constraints that shape politicians' dealings with the state apparatus. These interactions are highly individualistic. As Lamounier and Meneguello point out, in Brazil "the federal structure and the financial preponderance of the central power force professional politicians to consider above all their role as *procuradores* for their respective states and municipalities" (1986: 59). Lamounier and Meneguello present this phenomenon as a historical constant, but there is no doubt that it was intensified under authoritarianism—

especially so for the pro-regime politicians, who had little else to do. As one prominent former deputy, Nelson Jobim (PMDB-Rio Grande do Sul), is fond of pointing out, during the military regime federal legislators were little more than glorified *despachantes*.[14] Politicians whose livelihood depends on individual transactions with state officials should, according to a rational choice model, seek to maintain these patterns of interaction, rather than permit a formal organization (such as a political party or a legislative caucus) come between themselves and the state. The rational choice approach would stress that rightist politicians have strong "priors" with regard to this issue—what they would see as good reasons for resisting the advent of disciplined parties or a highly professionalized legislature in the New Republic. Rightist behavior is consistently oriented toward the preservation of the status quo ante.

These observations are supported by both country-specific and theoretical literature. Earlier political science research on Brazil (Cammack 1982; Ames 1995b; Hagopian 1996) suggested that the right in Brazil is pro-executive and pro-clientelistic, while this case study finds the right anti-legislative and anti-institutional. Recent work on comparative presidentialism by Shugart and Carey (1992) draws interesting theoretical connections among these orientations. Shugart and Carey begin by observing an association between strong presidencies and weak parties, with Brazil serving as an extreme example of each tendency. The weak Brazilian parties are the products of extreme localism and of an electoral system that provides not only for personal voting within parties, but contains several other mechanisms that weaken the control of party leadership (Mainwaring 1991b). The locally based party system creates an incentive for politicians to adopt pork-seeking strategies as federal legislators: they seek to bring resources back to their home regions in order to further their political careers (Ames 1995b). Not mentioned by Shugart and Carey, yet strengthening their argument, is the fact that the Brazilian state retains great control over economic resources: an environment of centralized "state capitalism" (Hagopian 1996) only aggravates the institutional incentives toward clientelism (Geddes and Ribeiro Neto 1992).

According to Shugart and Carey, when constitutional conventions are

14. In Brazil, *despachantes* are professional "go-betweens" who are paid to intercede with the bureaucracy, for example to obtain a permit or license, etc. Hiring a *despachante* is the usual end result of frustrating experiences with delays and red tape. Jobim used the metaphor of Brazilian legislators as *despachantes* in several press reports and in an interview with me (Brasília, December 6, 1990).

dominated by localistic/clientelistic politicians, "the institutional arrangement that emerges is one permitting these representatives . . . to *free themselves* of direct involvement with broader national policy matters by creating a central, accountable agent to handle such matters without impinging on their ability to attend to constituent needs" (Shugart and Carey 1992: 187). Such politicians should be expected to strive to maintain a strong presidency and a permissive legislative environment—behavior that conforms closely to the patterns observed among ex-authoritarians in the Brazilian Constituent Assembly of 1987–88. The Shugart and Carey argument is applicable to our analysis only to the extent that the right can be identified as the axis of localism and clientelism in Brazilian politics, yet there is abundant evidence to support this claim.[15]

These observations are consistent with recent studies that emphasize the individualistic nature of Brazilian politicians and employ rational choice models to study their behavior (Geddes 1994; Ames 1995a, 1995b; Hunter 1997; Mainwaring 1999). One of the contributions of the present study has been to show that *highly individualistic, anti-institutional orientations are not evenly distributed across the political class* but are in fact clustered disproportionately on the right. To the extent that rationality-based explanations of politicians' autonomy have been successful—and I believe that they have, given the rich insights discussed above—they have been most successful in explaining the ARENA/PDS cohort, because it is precisely within this cohort that the antipathy toward formal institutionalization is the greatest.

Once again, as in the case of the Weberian socialization hypothesis, a rational choice explanation forces us to recognize the exceptionalism of the former opposition (MDB) cohort. Lacking the direct access to state resources that *arenistas* enjoyed under military rule, it is likely that MDB politicians were less molded to the role of *despachante* or go-between. Data presented in Chapter 6 show that in the New Republic, the former opposi-

15. The overlap between the ARENA/PDS cohort and clientelistic/localistic elites is considerable. Shugart and Carey see Brazilian institutional architecture as the predictable outcome of a constitutional convention "whose representation ran along regional, clientelistic lines" (1992: 190). The right by itself was not quite large enough to make up such the "clientelistic majority" referred to by Shugart and Carey, and certainly no one would argue that the right has a perfect monopoly on clientelism. The point is that localism-clientelism is clustered disproportionately within the right, so that without the ex-authoritarians no such "majority" would have existed. As Chapter 4 demonstrates, Brazilian legislative representation is not proportional to population and drastically overrepresents the poorer states where clientelism is more pervasive. If Brazil were to adopt a system whereby national legislative representation were purely proportional to population, the size of the congressional right would immediately be reduced by a third or more.

tion politicians report generally lower levels of personal interaction with both federal and local bureaucrats than do rightists. Therefore, the former oppositionists have less to lose by permitting their interactions with the state to be mediated by representative structures; they are not so dependent on personal contacts. Another reason for MDB exceptionalism is, once again, the logic of opposition to authoritarian rule. Building representative institutions requires that individual politicians surrender some individual power to formal organizations such as parties and Congress. The contemporary right resists this today, but their former antagonists in the MDB have already experienced this to some degree in the past. I stress again that the former opposition was compelled to *utilize* emasculated "democratic" institutions in order to contest and ultimately remove the authoritarian regime. The *emedebistas'* "priors" were fundamentally different from those of their rightist counterparts: theirs was a logic of cooperation and institution building, which may explain why they are today more tolerant than the ex-*arenistas* of collective authority and of rules in general.

The two explanations of why the right behaves as it does—the first resting on a socialization argument, the second on a rational choice model—come to us from very different traditions in the social sciences. Weber's concept of socialization—the process that inculcates deep-seated value commitments in individuals and groups—diverges both temporally and substantively from Tsebelis's notion of learning, which may be described as the periodic updating of probability assessments by rational actors. But although the two approaches have dissimilar theoretical origins, when applied to the case at hand they are not incompatible but complementary perspectives. The former (Weberian) approach explains the acquisition of a distinct set of preferences and priors; the latter (rational choice) approach focuses on the crucial role of these orientations in Brazil's process of institutional redesign in the 1980s and 1990s. Each approach informs the other, and together they suggest the possibility of a path dependence of major theoretical and comparative importance. Max Weber's insights about the dangers of marginalizing parliament are not threatened by a rationality-based explanation of politicians' anti-institutional behavior. Conversely, only a hopelessly ahistorical rational choice theorist would fail to take into account the experience of authoritarianism—the right's collective "priors"—in determining politicians' preference ordering in the New Republic.

In essence, these two complementary approaches both draw heavily on the notion of political learning. Weber might argue that Brazilian rightists acted extra-organizationally because the institutions they long inhabited (the ARENA party and the authoritarian Congress) never had any serious responsibilities, and because they (unlike their MDB counterparts) never had any real reason for attempting to resuscitate them. A rational choice theorist might cite this learning process as a reason why the maintenance of individual autonomy and resistance toward institution building are highly ranked preferences for former *arenistas*. The former approach attempts a macropolitical and macrosociological analysis of the relationship between politicians and institutions; the latter approach sheds light on the micro-foundations of actual outcomes. These two theoretical frameworks taken together contribute to our understanding of Brazilian right's behavior in the New Republic.

Before concluding on this issue, it is worthwhile to comment on whether these hypotheses are applicable to other cases of conservative de-mocratization. I believe that they are, with a few qualifications. The longer the duration of the authoritarian experience, and the greater the role of the state in political and economic development (in both Brazil and Germany, bureaucratization far outstripped the pace of historical trends toward de-mocracy), the more relevant are Weber's insights. If Weber was correct that service in a rubber-stamp parliament drives politicians toward practices that uniquely disqualify them as institution builders, then the Weimar or Brazil-ian patterns should be observable in other postauthoritarian regimes. Brazil is only one of many cases where politicians socialized to marginal represen-tative institutions now find themselves participating in "the real thing." Not long ago in Eastern Europe and Russia, the current leaders of Communist successor parties were mid-level apparatchiks or delegates to fictional legis-lative bodies. Bereft of decision-making capabilities, subservient to a huge state bureaucracy, and often functioning as a political link between the cen-ter and the periphery within their countries, they were subject to many of the same incentives that drove ARENA/PDS politicians to individualistic clientelism. It is not unreasonable to expect that the anti-institutional syn-drome may be detected among these politicians as well. This proposition awaits comparative research in other new democracies.

The rational choice approach emphasized how individual preferences are embedded in a web of preexisting institutional constraints. With this approach we must also take a step back to see how the sum of these individ-ual preferences affects overall macropolitical outcomes. Within the Brazilian political class, anti-institutional impulses and abdicant orientations summed together outweigh the sum total of conscious institution-building efforts. The result that is that the "partial regime" of national representative institutions has languished, as have the principles that democratic theory assigns to this arena (representation and accountability). The sheer size of the ARENA/PDS cohort during the Constituent Assembly in 1987–88 (at least 40 percent of the membership) meant that only a few cognates—clientelistic, autonomous, even conservative politicians—needed to be drawn from the non-ARENA cohort in order to form, in conjunction with the right, an anti-institutional political majority during the ANC. (Ten years later, the ex-*arenistas* still comprised one quarter of the National Congress, as Chapter 4 demonstrates.)

In contrast to Brazil, in other conservative transitions to democracy the number of political elites who were products of authoritarian sponsorship has either started out smaller or has been reduced by the right's defeat in elections (that is, a defeat that changes the rules of the game by reconfiguring the distribution of power among actors). In Spain, for example, the number of Franco-era elites in parliament declined dramatically in the pivotal elections of 1982. Spain is also an example of the other way to avert a Brazilian-style fate: by emphasizing early on the necessity for pactmaking and constitutionalism in order to establish clear rules for the political game.[16] In transitions with heavy formal negotiation, such as the Spain in the late 1970s, and in cases where prior elite political learning has played a significant role, such as Venezuela in the late 1950s and early 1960s (Levine 1973), micropolitical rationalities have been overcome in favor of a consensus on the importance of practicing politics exclusively through democratic institutions. In Brazil this consensus has not yet been achieved, at least as measured by the outward performance of elites.

Are Conservative Transitions Conducive to Stable Democracy?

The second theoretical implication of this book concerns a central issue in the study of political democratization, which is the debate over "continuous" versus "discontinuous" modes of transition. The debate over the nature and desirability of conservative transitions was partially introduced in Chapter 1, but a few additional observations are appropriate here.

16. I do not intend to suggest that Brazil could simply have imitated the Spanish pattern of *pactos*. Several factors in the Spanish transition led to a clear necessity for elite negotiation, among them the pressing need to negotiate the autonomy of subnational regions and the desire to impress on the European Community that democratization would be swift and authentic. One factor of particular importance was the comparatively greater salience and strength of Spanish political parties. The more effective Spanish parties meant that elites could usually "deliver" their followers, whereas in Brazil the lack of vertical representative linkages made a pact-based strategy less viable.

I have used the term "conservative" to refer to processes of democratization where continuities from the outgoing authoritarian regime remain extraordinarily high. The most important variable in this regard is the fate of authoritarian elites. In conservative transitions, authoritarian elites are responsible for the initial decision to liberalize their regime, as Brazil's General Ernesto Geisel did in 1974. Authoritarian elites also control the pace of the political opening to an impressive degree. In Brazil, Geisel and his successor, General João Figueiredo (1979–85) were able to steer the transition in their preferred direction until early 1984; the sheer length of this process illustrates the degree of their control. In conservative transitions, the gradual and "continuous" nature of liberalization and democratization ensures that many political elites of the authoritarian regime will survive the shift to civilian rule. By virtue of certain circumstances of the transition—for example, the manipulation of electoral rules or genuine retention of electoral support—the authoritarian elites are simply not dislodged from positions of effective political power. Therefore, these elites retain impressive influence in the postauthoritarian regime. These patterns are observable in Brazil since 1985, but they have also been noted in other transitions: Spain between 1975 and 1979, Turkey since 1983, and South Korea since 1987. In each case, two results of the transition were that (1) the executive branch remained in the hands of a trusted ally of the military dictatorship, and (2) that the party or parties that supported authoritarianism did well in the first elections under democracy.

Other processes of democratization have followed a different path, where authoritarian elites have not fared so well. In discontinuous transitions, elites do not lay the groundwork for liberalization and democratization. Therefore, when their government collapses for whatever reason (and the reasons have been numerous, including economic distress, defeat in war, or overwhelming popular mobilization), elites are swept aside. A new democratizing coalition takes power and promotes a clear break with the policies and practices of the defeated regime. Costa Rica in 1948, Argentina in 1983, and Czechoslovakia in 1989 (which, excepting the special situation of the former East Germany, had the most discontinuous transition of any post-Communist regime) are all examples of the *ruptura* pattern of transition. Exclusionary elites in Costa Rica, vainglorious military officers in Argentina, and Communist apparatchiks in Czechoslovakia did not do too well in their country's first democratic elections. Their dismal performance in these "founding elections" does not imply that such forces cannot eventually become reintegrated into democratic politics—they may indeed reappear, and perhaps even recoup electoral strength in the long run. But their relative weakness in the early years of democratic rule means the business of democratic consolidation can get under way without much interference by potentially antisystem or disloyal actors.

Modes of transition are certainly not restricted to "continuous" versus "discontinuous"; in fact, several analysts have constructed typologies of transitions to democracy that range from three subtypes (Share and Mainwaring 1986) to ten (Stepan 1986). But allowing for some simplification in my review, it is clear that one of the major debates in the literature on democratization has been over the relative merits of political continuities in the transition process. Typically, this debate has gone beyond empirical analysis to touch on issues of scholarly preferences and biases about what is to be expected from postauthoritarian politics. After the initial transition to civilian rule, should the democratizing coalition bring about significant political and socioeconomic transformations even at the risk of an authoritarian retrogression? Or should democrats moderate their politics, recognizing a tradeoff between the "survivability" and the "deepening" of democracy? In studying Latin American democratization in the 1980s, scholars made various suggestions. The most influential comparative work on democratization (O'Donnell and Schmitter 1986) suggested that transition processes may be solidified if political forces loyal to the outgoing authoritarian regime (which in all of their cases turns out to be the civilian political right, the pattern followed in Brazil) emerge victorious—or at the very least, not annihilated—in the founding election of the new democracy (ibid., 62–63). The thrust of their argument is that former authoritarian elites should not be provoked or marginalized too early on in the new regime. If these elites are spared an early defeat, they may learn that democracy is not a great threat to their interests, and they may decide to go along and play the game of competition and elections.

> Put in a nutshell, parties of the Right-Center and Right must be "helped" to do well, and parties of the Left-Center and Left should not win by an overwhelming majority. This often happens either "artificially," by rigging the rules—for example, by overrepresenting small districts or small peripheral constituencies—or "naturally," by fragmenting the partisan choices of the Left (usually not a difficult task) and by consolidating those of the Center and Right (sometimes possible

thanks to the incumbency resources of those in government). (ibid., 62)[17]

This prescriptive generalization, had it emerged in another work, might have escaped notice. But O'Donnell and Schmitter based their "tentative conclusions" on the findings of their many collaborators, who produced two dozen case studies of transitions on two continents. Thus it is fair to say that the proposition under consideration here—that conservative transition processes may lead to be more resilient democratic regimes—is a dominant hypothesis in the literature on Latin America.[18] It may be implicit, it may be carefully worded, but it is definitely embedded in the literature. This led some scholars to claim that the democratization literature possessed a conservative bias (for example, Petras 1988).

In a highly critical review of O'Donnell, Schmitter, and Laurence Whitehead's *Transitions from Authoritarian Rule*, Daniel Levine (1988) took the opposite tack. He disagreed with others' criticism that the transitions literature suffered from a conservative bias; in fact, he argued precisely the opposite point of view, saying that the literature had not been favorable enough to conservative transition processes. Much of his polemic, in which the *Transitions* collaborators are unfairly portrayed as socialist discontents who turn up their noses at "procedural" democracy, is not appropriate for review here. But Levine's review did have the value of making a very bold, explicit statement about conservative transitions to democracy. "They [the *Transitions* editors] are unwilling to draw the obvious lesson from experience: that *conservative transitions are more durable*" (Levine 1988: 392; emphasis added).

To be fair, Levine concerns himself with only one type of conservative transition, which is the subtype involving explicit pacts and elite accommodation. Such elite-led and pacted transitions have been heavily criticized by some authors as inherently exclusionary and undemocratic (Peeler 1985,

17. It is worthwhile to note the relevance of these observations to the Brazilian case. The right in Brazil was certainly "helped" by overrepresentation of small districts and rural areas (see Chapter 3), but this is a constant in republican history, not an outcome of the transition to democracy in the 1980s. What is artificial and temporary in other countries is a relatively permanent feature in Brazilian politics.

18. The *Transitions from Authoritarian Rule* project was in final form a half-decade before the fall of the Berlin Wall. Some of its findings from Latin America and Southern Europe are currently being appropriated for research on the former East Bloc countries, but this particular proposition—which, transposed to the East would seem to prescribe a victory by former Communists—may not fare too well there. I suspect that the proposition is better suited to former authoritarian elites than to former totalitarian elites.

Karl 1986). Levine takes these authors to task for failing to recognize the importance of representation, that is, that elites are linked to mass publics. Elites can engage in mutual accommodation because they are tied to their followers "through political parties, trade unions, and secondary associations of all kinds" (Levine 1988: 385). He goes on to say that "the editors underscore the manipulative and exclusionary nature of pacts, but they rarely ask why the political leaders had elite status in the first place. This question would require serious attention to the social foundations of political parties, and to how leaders find roots in the transformations through which parties and other mediating structures emerge and take hold" (388). In essence, Levine assumes accountability.

Levine fails to consider that there could be a kind of conservative transition that is *not* pacted, and in which leaders are generally *not* tied to their followers through institutional channels. Influenced perhaps by the Venezuelan case in which pacts and continuities were stabilizing factors in democratization, Levine seems never to entertain the notion that there can be a conservative transition in which there are continuities (for example, in the political class), in which electoral outcomes are favorable to formerly authoritarian elites (that is, the right does well), but in which authoritarian elites retain a high degree of autonomy due to the absence of institutional mechanisms promoting representation and accountability. What if there were a conservative transition to democracy and such mechanisms were hardly to be found? There has been such a transition: Brazil in the 1980s and 1990s.

Postauthoritarian Brazil is an anomaly among the set of conservative transitions to democracy, because the role of elites has been fundamentally different. In other conservative transitions, as Levine correctly states, elites were the guarantors of the process, but their permanence as elites depended on their performance as negotiators. In Brazil, the political right has acted extra-institutionally, has demonstrated little awareness of the concept of political accountability, and is protected from retribution by voters through some of the "artificial" mechanisms that O'Donnell and Schmitter referred to above. Brazil does not conform to Levine's idealized notion of a conservative transition to democracy. He favors a conservative transition based on pacts, but Brazil's is conservative democratization without pacts. He argues for elite-led transitions with representation, but Brazil's is an elite-led transition with extremely precarious channels of representation. He claims that conservative transitions are more durable, yet Brazil's experience casts serious doubts on that claim. While Brazil's new democracy has not met a "sudden death," that is, an authoritarian involution, neither has it moved significantly toward consolidating some of the major representative institutions, a shortcoming that exposes the New Republic to the possibility of a "slow death" (O'Donnell 1992). The first decade of the new regime demonstrated beyond doubt that a dominant hypothesis of the literature on democratization—that conservative transitions are conducive to democratic stability—is flawed. The costs of conservative transitions have been explored on a theoretical level by Przeworski (1992); the specific implications for Brazilian democratization have been addressed by Hagopian (1990, 1996), Hagopian and Mainwaring (1987), and O'Donnell (1992).

The "outlier" of the Brazilian transition cannot and should not obviate the many insights we have gained about continuities in political democratization. Rather, this prominent hypothesis about conservative transitions should be revised to reflect the Brazilian experience. Such a revision might occur along the following lines. A conservative transition to democracy promotes the eventual consolidation of democracy only when former authoritarian elites meet all of three necessary conditions: (1) they are not electorally destroyed in the early years of democracy, (2) their interest in democratization is reflected in explicit negotiation with the democratizing coalition about the contours of the new regime, both procedural and substantive in nature, and (3) these elites are actually representing actors other than themselves, and they are tied to their constituencies through representative channels that (a) demonstrate that they accept the general principle of accountability and (b) will permit them to be rewarded, punished, removed, or replaced as the circumstances warrant. The third condition did not obtain in Brazil. The ARENA/PDS cohort emerged in the New Republic as a powerful political force operating with a great degree of autonomy, overrepresented and protected by archaic electoral laws, and generally uninterested in institutional reforms that would change this status quo by expanding representation and accountability.

What is the lesson for other countries undergoing processes of democratization? The lesson is to avoid a "continuous" or conservative transition in the absence of some minimal rules and institutions promoting accountability. A conservative transition in the context of weak institutions means that authoritarian elites are carried over from the old regime into the new democracy accustomed to a high degree of autonomy. The next step for the new regime, according to our "partial regime" approach to democratic consolidation, is to get to work on consolidating the principal representative institutions such as parties and Congress. But the former authoritarian elites can logically be expected to oppose this. Moreover, their opposition to the institutionalization of democratic norms and procedures costs them very little, because in the absence of accountability there is no way for the new regime to dislodge them. This leads to a perverse situation in which, instead of the right accommodating itself to the rules of the new democracy, the rules of the new democracy must accommodate the right.

These observations, if correct, raise interesting counterfactuals. Would it have been "better" for Brazil if the right had been electorally eliminated in the first moments of the transition? The answer is unclear. Certainly the right's defeat would have created great anxiety on the part of the armed forces, who witnessed their colleagues being put on trial for human rights abuses in neighboring countries, and who would have likely feared the country's rapid swing to the left. The electoral marginalization of the right would have alarmed conservative politicians suddenly cut off from their lifeblood, access to state resources. The more irresponsible members of the ARENA/PDS cohort might have considered resurrecting the civilian-military alliance of 1964. But it is also possible that more moderate members of the PMDB, who always held sway over the democratizing coalition, could have maintained their control and allayed some of the fears of the right. In fact, as with all hypothetical arguments, there are multiple scenarios with varying costs and benefits. My own view is that an crushing electoral defeat of the right was and remains impossible, due to the resilience of the right's local power bases in the less developed regions, and to the fact that these regions remain heavily overrepresented in national politics. It is likely that this overrepresentation is "frozen" in place, because the right has the votes to stop any redistribution of seats in Congress. It has used, and will continue to use, its voting power to thwart this and other institutional reforms.

Conclusions: The Costs of Conservative Democratization

This study of the political right in postauthoritarian Brazil has cast doubts on, and proposes a revision of, one of the major hypotheses in the literature on democratization: that conservative transitions are conducive to stable democracy.

The study illustrates the crucial position that authoritarian elites retain through the process of democratization. The question is not just whether they do or do not play by the rules of the game; if they choose not to, democracy will likely collapse anyway. The more interesting question is when they choose to stay in the game: do they work to consolidate those rules, or do they show little interest in them? This book has focused on the Brazilian right's relationship to representative institutions, principally the parties and the national legislature, in the postauthoritarian era. Case studies of these institutions showed that the right—especially in the window of opportunity in the 1980s—contributed little to their consolidation, and has at times obstructed reforms aimed at increasing the power of these institutions and thereby promoting the idea of political accountability. Because of the sheer dimensions of the right's continuing presence in politics, the right has been able to obstruct and retard the consolidation of democracy in the New Republic.

Since the mid-1980s, Brazil has faced a dilemma that confronts other postauthoritarian and posttotalitarian regimes around the world. Without a minimum of participation by forces of the authoritarian past, *democracy* is not possible; but with excessive participation by these forces, *change* is not possible. The elusive goal has been, and remains, the reconciliation of democracy with change. The experience of the political right in democratic Brazil sheds light on the tradeoffs, paradoxes, and drawbacks of a conservative transition to democracy.

Brazilian Federal Legislators, 1987–1999

This book presents data on Brazilian federal legislators who served in the 48th Legislature (1987–91), the 49th Legislature (1991–95), and the 50th Legislature (1995–99).

Between February 1987 and October 1988, the 48th Legislature sat simultaneously in a constitutional convention called the National Constituent Assembly (Assembléia Nacional Constituinte, or ANC). The total membership of the ANC and of the first half of the 48th Legislature was 559 legislators (487 deputies and 72 senators). Of these 559 *constituintes*, some 536 were elected in the national elections of November 15, 1986. The remaining 23 members were federal senators who had been elected in 1982 under the military regime, and whose terms did not expire until 1990. (Despite a protest by progressive legislators on the first day of the ANC, these senators were permitted to participate in the constitutional convention.) During the twenty months of constitutional deliberations, some 18 alternate members (*suplentes*) were admitted to the ANC for various lengths of time, as some of the original members left for federal, state, and local cabinet positions, or died in office. Therefore, while the number of seats was held constant at 559, the total number of individuals who participated in the ANC was actually 587. Later, with the creation of the state of Tocantins in 1989, the number of congressional seats was increased to 570 for the remainder of the 48th Legislature.

Beginning with the 1990 elections, the size of the Senate was increased to 81 members with the inclusion of three senators each from the new states (formerly federal territories) of Amapá and Roraima. With new deputies elected from these states and from Tocantins, the size of the Chamber of Deputies rose to 503, and thus in the 49th Legislature the total number of seats in Congress rose to 584. In 1994, in an effort to reduce the disproportionality that works principally against the state of São Paulo, this state was permitted to increase its Chamber delegation from 60 to 70 seats. Thus, in the 50th Legislature the size of Congress increased to 594. Each of these legislatures contained a large number of *suplentes*, especially in the second half of the session, after mid-term elections caused some members of Congress to give up their seats to become mayors.

Criteria for Inclusion in the ARENA/PDS Cohort

In accordance with the definition of the political right discussed in Chapter 1, the objective was to identify those legislators who had an individual and institutional commitment to the authoritarian regime of 1964–85. The criteria for inclusion in the rightist cohort revolved around individual commitment to the progovernment party (ARENA until 1979, and PDS thereafter). When I used biographical sources, a federal legislator in 1987–99 was included in the ex-ARENA cohort if he or she

(1) was a candidate, either successful or unsuccessful, for elective office on the ARENA or PDS ticket between 1964 and 1985;
(2) was nominated to serve the ARENA/PDS party in one of the public offices for which direct elections were suspended at various times between 1964 and 1985 (president, vice president, senator, governor, vice governor, or mayor of a capital city or "national security" municipality); or
(3) served on the National Executive Committee of either ARENA or PDS between 1964 and 1985.

These three criteria are intended to measure the individual's commitment to the perpetuation of military-authoritarian rule. As discussed in Chapter 2, this is admittedly not a perfect definition of the contemporary Brazilian right, but is probably the best available.

It is important to stress that this definition *underrepresents* the presence of the Brazilian right in the National Congress in at least three ways. First, an ideological definition of the right would probably identify many individuals who are socially and politically conservative, yet who never made an institutional commitment to the authoritarian regime. Second, political analysis at the local level would probably identify politicians who (for whatever reason of personal or political convenience) always belonged to opposition parties, yet who collaborated with the national government or otherwise reached some modus vivendi with the authoritarian regime. Third, my criteria do not include as part of the right those individuals who served the authoritarian regime in a technical or administrative capacity, for example as upper-echelon federal bureaucrats or even as state-level cabinet ministers in ARENA/PDS governments. While escaping direct involvement in the ARENA/PDS party apparatus, they may well have sympathized with the authoritarian regime. The Brazilian Congress contains a substantial number of such technocrat-turned-politicians, whom I did not classify as being of the ARENA/PDS right.

Methodology and Sources for Classification

When I used biographical data (as in Chapter 4), I was fortunate in that there exist many handbooks and guides to the congressional membership. My principal sources for biographical data were the guidebooks published by the Câmara dos Deputados, the Senado Federal, and the ANC. I also relied on some independent studies, especially Coelho and Oliveira (1989), DIAP (1988), Rodrigues (1987), and SEMPREL (1989), as well as newspaper accounts.

When I worked with my survey data (as in Chapters 5, 6, and 8), my method was different: I relied on the self-reported party affiliations of the respondents. The 1990, 1993, and 1997 survey questionnaires (see Appendix B) contained questions about past party affiliation in the party systems of 1966–79 and 1979–85. Those who reported having been a member of ARENA or PDS at any time were classified as part of the rightist cohort, even if they also belonged to an opposition party at some other time in their past. Those who reported membership in an opposition party but never joined ARENA/PDS were classified in the "opposition" cohort. Respondents who had no record of either progovernment or opposition party affiliations in 1964–85 were considered censored cases and were not reported in the data analyses (see Chapter 2 for further discussion).

In 1990, the survey results contained 108 ex-*arenistas* (43.4 percent of all respondents), 128 ex-oppositionists (51.4 percent), and 16 censored cases (5.2 percent), from a total of 249 responses. In 1993, there were 63 ex-authoritarians (34.1 percent of responses), 103 members of the opposition cohort (55.7 percent), and 19 censored cases (10.3 percent), from an N of 185. In 1997, the equivalent figures were 55 ex-*arenistas* (34.0 percent of total), 76 opposition veterans (46.9 percent), and 31 censored cases (19.1 percent), from a total of 162 responses.

The first survey was conducted in March and April of 1990, more than three years after the inauguration of the ANC, and after the expansion of the Congress to 570 seats. The second survey was conducted in May–June 1993, approximately two and a half years after the last legislative elections, and the third was conducted in May–June 1997, again two and a half years after the 1994 elections. Therefore, in all three cases, at the moment of the survey the membership of the Congress was significantly different from its composition on the opening day of the legislative session; in each case, there were as many as 30 new faces in the legislature by the time of the survey. Estimates of ARENA cohort size made via biographical research are therefore not identical to those achieved by survey research; this is attributable not only to potential sampling error but also to minor, ongoing changes in the composition of Congress.

Methodology

The 1990, 1993, and 1997 surveys took the form of mail questionnaires sent to every incumbent federal legislator in both houses. Each respondent received a cover letter explaining the research project in general terms as a study of political institutions and democratization in Brazil. The introductory letter was accompanied by the survey instrument itself and a return envelope. Legislators who did not respond within an initial three-week window were contacted in three subsequent waves of reminder letters. Although I promised anonymity to the respondents, my impression was that only a handful of legislators cared about this. The majority of respondents returned the questionnaire in personalized business envelopes, usually including greeting cards or business cards, and a fair number signed the questionnaires or wrote comments on them. Despite the fact that the anonymity guarantee did not seem important to the respondents, I have maintained it in processing the data.

The first survey was begun in March 1990 and was largely complete by the end of April, although some responses continued to arrive in May. The second survey was conducted principally in May and June 1993, with the last responses arriving in late August of that year. The third survey was begun in March 1997, with most survey responses arriving in May and June.

Some commentary about the political context of these surveys is in order. Although the Brazilian party system has been in flux and the country has drifted from crisis to crisis in the New Republic, the three surveys were conducted at relatively "stable" moments at which the reliability of responses can be presumed to be high. The 48th Legislature served concurrently as the ANC and promulgated Brazil's current constitution in October 1988. The pressures of the Assembly led to internal divisions within the main parties, as numerous *ad hoc* supraparty alliances were built around single issues or themes; moreover, in 1987–88 President José Sarney intervened repeatedly in the Assembly's deliberations through blatant vote-buying and reliance on military intimidation. At the time of my first survey in March 1990, however, the Assembly had been over for eighteen months, the new Constitution was in force, the party system already reflected the changes induced by divergences in the Assembly, and the country was in a presidential transition. This political "time out" was an opportune time for survey research, a fact that—combined with my guarantee of anonymity to the respondents—allows for a high degree of confidence in the attitudinal data. The same was true in the May 1993 replication, which fortunately took place between two extended paralyses of the Brazilian legislature: the first in 1992, which resulted in the impeachment of President Fernando Collor de Mello on corruption charges, and the second in 1993–94, which resulted in the expulsion of eighteen legislators for similar reasons. The 1997 survey took place in a nonelection year during unremarkable political conditions.

Characteristics of the Sample

The characteristics of the respondents correspond closely to those of the Brazilian Congress as a whole, as can be seen in the following tables.

Table B.1 1990 survey: Profile of respondents by political party

Party	Number of Seats January 1990	Percentage Seats January 1990	Number Responding	Percentage of Sample
PMDB	200	35.1	77	30.9
PFL	108	19.0	45	18.1
PSDB	61	10.7	37	14.9
PDT	35	6.1	17	6.8
PDS	32	5.6	15	6.0
PRN	24	4.2	7	2.8
PTB	26	4.6	8	3.2
PL	19	3.3	9	3.6
PT	16	2.8	7	2.8
PDC	17	3.0	8	3.2
PSB	8	1.4	3	1.2
PC do B	6	1.0	3	1.2
PCB	3	0.5	3	1.2
Others/none	15	2.6	6	2.4
No response	—	—	4	1.6
TOTALS	570	100.0	249	100.0

Table B.2 1990 survey: Profile of respondents by region

Party	Number of Seats	Percentage of Seats	Number Responding	Percentage of Sample
North	72	12.6	26	10.4
Northeast	178	31.2	80	32.7
Center-West	53	9.3	23	9.2
Southeast	181	31.8	77	30.9
South	86	15.1	39	15.7
Unknown	—	—	4	1.6
TOTALS	570	100.0	249	100.0

Table B.3 1993 survey: Profile of respondents by political party

Party	Number of Seats June 1993	Percentage Seats June 1993	Number Responding	Percentage of Sample
PMDB	128	21.9	38	20.5
PFL	104	17.8	28	15.1
PPR	77	13.2	27	14.6
PSDB	53	9.1	17	9.2
PDT	39	6.7	16	8.6
PP	44	7.5	10	5.4
PT	37	6.3	17	9.2
PTB	31	5.3	7	3.8
PRN	20	3.4	6	3.2
PL	14	2.4	5	2.7
PSB	10	1.7	3	1.6
PC do B	7	1.2	3	1.6
PPS	3	0.5	2	1.1
Others/none	17	2.9	6	3.2
TOTALS	584	100.0	185	100.0

Table B.4 1993 survey: Profile of respondents by region

Party	Number of Seats	Percentage of Seats	Number Responding	Percentage of Sample
North	86	14.7	24	13.0
Northeast	178	30.5	50	27.0
Center-West	53	9.1	16	8.6
Southeast	181	31.0	65	35.1
South	86	14.7	30	16.2
TOTALS	584	100.0	185	100.0

Table B.5 1997 survey: Profile of respondents by political party

Party	Number of Seats June 1997	Percentage Seats June 1997	Number Responding	Percentage of Sample
PFL	126	21.2	40	24.7
PMDB	120	20.2	33	20.4
PSDB	99	16.7	32	19.8
PPB	92	15.5	19	11.7
PT	56	9.4	17	10.5
PDT	28	4.7	5	3.1
PTB	28	4.7	5	3.1
PSB	12	2.0	2	1.2
PL	10	1.7	3	1.9
PC do B	10	1.7	3	1.9
PPS	3	0.5	2	1.2
Others/none	10	1.7	1	0.6
TOTALS	594	100.0	162	100.0

Table B.6 1997 survey: Profile of respondents by region

Party	Number of Seats	Percentage of Seats	Number Responding	Percentage of Sample
North	86	14.5	26	16.0
Northeast	178	30.0	47	29.0
Center-West	53	8.9	12	7.4
Southeast	191	32.2	44	27.2
South	86	14.5	33	20.4
TOTALS	594	100.0	162	100.0

Portuguese Text of 1990 Survey Questionnaire

Questionário n° __/__/__ (Para uso da tabulação. Não preencher.)

Seu partido atual _____   Seu estado _____

Legenda pela qual foi eleito ao Congresso _____

Em quantas legislaturas já foi membro do Congresso Nacional? _____

Sua idade: _____ anos

O Sr. será candidato a um cargo eletivo nas eleições deste ano?
_____ será candidato a uma cadeira do Senado ou da Câmara
_____ será candidato a um cargo executivo
_____ não será candidato a nenhum cargo eletivo

A que partido (ou partidos) o Sr. foi filiado no período 1980-1985?
_____ PDS   _____ PMDB   _____ PP   _____ PDT
_____ PT   _____ PTB   _____ outro   _____ nenhum partido

A que partido (ou partidos) o Sr. foi filiado no período 1966–1979?
_____ ARENA   _____ MDB
_____ outro   _____ nenhum partido

Nos últimos anos tem havido um grande debate a respeito do sistema eleitoral. O Sr. é favorável ao sistema de representação proporcional, ao sistema distrital majoritário ou ao sistema misto (proporcional para uma parte das cadeiras e distrital-majoritário para as restantes)?
_____ sistema proporcional   _____ sistema misto
_____ sistema distrital majoritário

Se o Brasil mantiver o sistema de eleições proporcionais, o Sr. preferiria que a ordem de candidatos na lista fosse determinada pelo partido ou preferiria uma lista aberta (como existe agora)?
_____ lista aberta   _____ lista determinada pelo partido

Gostaria de saber sua opinião a respeito de dois temas que foram debatidos na Assembleia Nacional Constituinte de 1987-1988. O Sr. está a favor ou contra:
À inclusão do dispositivo que assegura às Forças Armadas o direito de intervenção para garantir a ordem interna
_____ favor   _____ contra

À instituição do regime parlamentarista de governo

_____ favor _____ contra

Se favorável:

_____ ao sistema misto (com eleição direta do presidente)

_____ ao sistema puro (com eleição indireta do presidente)

_____ ou a qualquer um deles

Como o Sr. julgaria a capacidade dos seguintes partidos políticos para atuar de acordo com as regras do jogo democrático e contribuir à estabilidade democrática?

	nenhuma									máxima
PMDB	1	2	3	4	5	6	7	8	9	10
PFL	1	2	3	4	5	6	7	8	9	10
PDS	1	2	3	4	5	6	7	8	9	10
PSDB	1	2	3	4	5	6	7	8	9	10
PRN	1	2	3	4	5	6	7	8	9	10
PDT	1	2	3	4	5	6	7	8	9	10
PTB	1	2	3	4	5	6	7	8	9	10
PT	1	2	3	4	5	6	7	8	9	10
PL	1	2	3	4	5	6	7	8	9	10
PC do B	1	2	3	4	5	6	7	8	9	10
PDC	1	2	3	4	5	6	7	8	9	10
PCB	1	2	3	4	5	6	7	8	9	10
PSB	1	2	3	4	5	6	7	8	9	10

O Sr. acha correto o partido fechar questão e usar o recurso da fidelidade partidária?

_____ sim _____ não

O Sr. acredita que, na atividade parlamentar, em geral um parlamentar deve votar como o partido indica, ou de acordo com o que ele acredita?

_____ como o partido indica _____ de acordo com o que ele acredita

Imagine que os eleitores exijam que um parlamentar lute por uma coisa a que ele pessoalmente se opõe. O que o Sr. acha que ele deve fazer?

_____ o que os eleitores querem _____ fazer aquilo em que ele acredita

Em quem o Sr. votou no primeiro turno da eleição presidencial de 1989?

_____ Collor _____ Lula _____ Camargo _____ Maluf

_____ Brizola _____ Covas _____ Freire _____ Caiado

_____ Ulysses _____ Aureliano _____ Afif _____ outro
_____ nulo/branco

E no segundo turno? _____ Lula _____ Collor _____ nulo/branco

Se o Sr. tivesse que escolher um Ministério federal que é da maior importancia para seu estado ou região, qual seria? (Por favor escreva o nome de um dos 23 ministérios que existiram durante o governo Sarney.) _____

Agora vamos supor que nesta reta o número 1 corresponde a esquerda, o número 5 ao centro, e o número 10 a direita. Como o Sr. está vendo, uma pessoa que fosse muito de esquerda estaria no número 1, uma muito de direita, no número 10. Onde é que o Sr. se colocaria?

esquerda				centro					direita
1	2	3	4	5	6	7	8	9	10

E onde é que o Sr. colocaria cada um dos seguintes partidos em âmbito nacional? Como o Sr. classificaria o. . . .

	esquerda				centro					direita
PMDB	1	2	3	4	5	6	7	8	9	10
PFL	1	2	3	4	5	6	7	8	9	10
PDS	1	2	3	4	5	6	7	8	9	10
PSDB	1	2	3	4	5	6	7	8	9	10
PRN	1	2	3	4	5	6	7	8	9	10
PDT	1	2	3	4	5	6	7	8	9	10
PTB	1	2	3	4	5	6	7	8	9	10
PT	1	2	3	4	5	6	7	8	9	10
PL	1	2	3	4	5	6	7	8	9	10
PC do B	1	2	3	4	5	6	7	8	9	10
PDC	1	2	3	4	5	6	7	8	9	10
PCB	1	2	3	4	5	6	7	8	9	10
PSB	1	2	3	4	5	6	7	8	9	10

Alguns parlamentares são eleitos por causa de sua sigla partidária—isto é, o poder de organização do partido ou o perfil que ele tem na opinião pública. Outros são eleitos devido a sua capacidade individual para a organização ou a sua atuação pessoal na política. No seu caso, qual foi mais importante?

_____ o partido _____ seus esforços pessoais

O Sr. já serviu em um ou mais dos seguintes cargos públicos? Marque todos.

_____ vereador _____ deputado estadual _____ senador

_____ dep. federal   _____ prefeito/vice   _____ governador/vice

_____ Ministro   _____ secretário estadual

Algum parente seu já exerceu um dos cargos acima nos últimos 50 anos?

_____ sim   _____ não

Muitos parlamentares tem especialização em uma área específica do governo federal e na legislação referente a essa área. Em sua trabalho como parlamentar, em que área governamental o senhor atua mais ou tem o maior nível de conhecimento? Marque apenas uma (a principal).

_____ na área de política exterior (e.g., Itamaraty)

_____ na área econômica (e.g., Fazenda, Planejamento, Banco Central, etc.)

_____ na área militar (e.g., EMFA, Gabinete Militar, SNI, Exército, etc.)

_____ na área de infra-estrutura (e.g., Transportes, Comunicações, Minas e Energia, etc.)

_____ na área de ação social (e.g., Saúde, Educação, Trabalho, Previdência Social, etc.)

Há algum órgão governamental que o senhor conhece especialmente bem? (Por favor escreva o nome de um ministério, secretaria, órgão ou estatal de que o senhor tem especial conhecimento.) _____

Por favor, indique se o Sr. tem participado das seguintes atividades nos últimos 12 meses: frequentemente, de vez em quando, raramente, ou nunca.

	frequentemente	de vez em quando	raramente	nunca
Introduzir um projeto de lei	_____	_____	_____	_____
Apresentar emendas a um projeto de lei introduzido por outra pessoa	_____	_____	_____	_____
Tomar a palavra em sua casa legislativa	_____	_____	_____	_____
Participar de reuniões de uma Comissão de sua casa legislativa	_____	_____	_____	_____
Reunir com a Executiva de seu partido	_____	_____	_____	_____
Discutir temas de interesse nacional com oficiais das Forças Armadas	_____	_____	_____	_____
Reunir com representantes da burocracia federal	_____	_____	_____	_____

Reunir com represent-
antes da burocracia em
seu estado ou município   _____   _____   _____   _____

Reunir com diretores de
órgãos da imprensa   _____   _____   _____   _____

Reunir com represent-
antes de organizações
corporativas (CNBB,
FIESP, etc.)   _____   _____   _____   _____

Reunir com José Sarney
Costa   _____   _____   _____   _____

Reunir com Fernando
Collor de Mello   _____   _____   _____   _____

Por que o Sr. acredita que os eleitores votaram no Sr. nas últimas eleições? Usando
um escala que vai de 1 (menos importante) até 10 (mais importante), por favor
indique o peso relativo dos seguintes fatores.

	menos imp.									mais imp.
Suas declarações e promessas	1	2	3	4	5	6	7	8	9	10
A organização de seu partido	1	2	3	4	5	6	7	8	9	10
O apoio de interesses econômicos	1	2	3	4	5	6	7	8	9	10
Suas possibilidades de êxito	1	2	3	4	5	6	7	8	9	10
O desgaste de outros concorrentes ou siglas	1	2	3	4	5	6	7	8	9	10
O apoio de grupos de base	1	2	3	4	5	6	7	8	9	10
A campanha eleitoral que o Sr. fez	1	2	3	4	5	6	7	8	9	10
Tradição familiar/lealdades históricas	1	2	3	4	5	6	7	8	9	10
Seu carisma pessoal	1	2	3	4	5	6	7	8	9	10

Finalmente, gostaria de saber se o senhor concorda ou discorda com as seguintes
frases. Por favor, use um dos seguintes códigos para indicar sua opinião:

    1 = concorda, plenamente
    2 = concorda, em termos
    3 = discorda, em termos
    4 = discorda, plenamente

Os regimes autoritários tem mais condições de estimular o crescimento econômico
que os regimes democráticos.   1   2   3   4

Na América Latina, tem sido mais difícil para os governos democráticos manter a
ordem social que para os governos autoritários.   1   2   3   4

As Forças Armadas brasileiras são mais pró-democráticas
em 1990 do que em 1980.   1   2   3   4

Em vez de ter vários ministérios militares, o Brasil deve ter
um único Ministério da Defesa.   1   2   3   4

Se for criado o Ministério da Defesa,
o Ministro deve ser um civil.   1   2   3   4

O Serviço Nacional de Informações (SNI) deve ser extinto.   1   2   3   4

Um partido político deveria expulsar um parlamentar
que vota contra as determinações do partido.   1   2   3   4

Os partidos políticos devem ter o direito de indicar candidatos
que são membros de outros partidos.   1   2   3   4

Um parlamentar deve perder o mandato se trocar
de partido depois das eleições.   1   2   3   4

Qual foi sua principal ocupação nos últimos anos? Marque apenas uma (a principal):

_____ fazendeiro—grande proprietário (lavoura ou pecuária)   _____ advogado

_____ fazendeiro—médio proprietário (lavoura ou pecuária)   _____ farmacêutico

_____ fazendeiro—pequeno proprietário (lavoura ou pecuária) _____ médico

_____ trabalhador rural (não propietário de terras)   _____ dentista

_____ grande comerciante (mais de 30 empregados)   _____ contador

_____ comerciante médio (de 11 a 30 empregados)   _____ engenheiro

_____ pequeno comerciante (até 10 empregados)   _____ agrônomo

_____ grande industrial (mais de 500 empregados)   _____ comerciário

_____ médio industrial (de 50 a 500 empregados)   _____ industriário

_____ pequeno industrial (até 50 empregados)   _____ militar

_____ professor secundário   _____ prof. univ.

_____ professor primário   _____ estudante

_____ servidor público (federal, estadual, ou municipal), ocupante de cargo de direção, chefia, ou similares

_____ servidor público—outros cargos

_____ outra. Qual? _____

Desde já, agradeço sua especial colaboração na pesquisa.

Portuguese Text of 1993 Survey Questionnaire

Seu partido atual _____

Seu estado _____

Legenda pela qual foi eleito ao Congresso _____

Em quantas legislaturas já foi membro do Congresso Nacional? _____

Sua idade: _____ anos

A que partido (ou partidos) o Sr. foi filiado no período 1980–1985?
_____ PDS _____ PMDB _____ PP _____ PDT _____ PT _____ PTB
_____ outro _____ nenhum partido

A que partido (ou partidos) o Sr. foi filiado no período 1966–1979?
_____ ARENA _____ MDB _____ outro _____ nenhum partido

Nos últimos anos tem havido um grande debate a respeito do sistema eleitoral. O Sr. é favorável ao sistema de representação proporcional, ao sistema distrital majoritário ou ao sistema misto (proporcional para uma parte das cadeiras e distrital-majoritário para as restantes)?

_____ sistema proporcional _____ sistema misto _____ sistema distrital majoritário

Se o Brasil mantiver o sistema de eleições proporcionais, o Sr. preferiria que a ordem de candidatos na lista fosse determinada pelo partido ou preferiria uma lista aberta (como existe agora)?

_____ lista aberta _____ lista determinada pelo partido

Gostaria de saber sua opinião a respeito de dois temas que foram debatidos na Assembléia Nacional Constituinte de 1987-1988. O Sr. está a favor ou contra:
À inclusão do dispositivo que assegura às Forças Armadas o direito de intervenção para garantir a ordem interna _____ favor _____ contra
À instituição do regime parlamentarista de governo _____ favor _____ contra

Como o Sr. julgaria a capacidade dos seguintes partidos políticos para atuar de acordo com as regras do jogo democrático e contribuir à estabilidade democrática?

	nenhuma									máxima
PMDB	1	2	3	4	5	6	7	8	9	10
PFL	1	2	3	4	5	6	7	8	9	10
PPR	1	2	3	4	5	6	7	8	9	10
PSDB	1	2	3	4	5	6	7	8	9	10
PP	1	2	3	4	5	6	7	8	9	10
PDT	1	2	3	4	5	6	7	8	9	10
PRN	1	2	3	4	5	6	7	8	9	10
PTB	1	2	3	4	5	6	7	8	9	10
PT	1	2	3	4	5	6	7	8	9	10

PL	1	2	3	4	5	6	7	8	9	10
PPS	1	2	3	4	5	6	7	8	9	10
PC do B	1	2	3	4	5	6	7	8	9	10
PSB	1	2	3	4	5	6	7	8	9	10
PSTU	1	2	3	4	5	6	7	8	9	10

Agora vamos supor que nesta reta o número 1 corresponde a esquerda, o número 5 ao centro, e o número 10 a direita. Como o Sr. está vendo, uma pessoa que fosse muito de esquerda estaria no número 1, uma muito de direita, no número 10. Onde é que o Sr. se colocaria?

esquerda				centro					direita
1	2	3	4	5	6	7	8	9	10

E onde é que o Sr. colocaria cada um dos seguintes partidos em âmbito nacional? Como o Sr. classificaria o. . . .

	esquerda				centro					direita
PMDB	1	2	3	4	5	6	7	8	9	10
PFL	1	2	3	4	5	6	7	8	9	10
PPR	1	2	3	4	5	6	7	8	9	10
PSDB	1	2	3	4	5	6	7	8	9	10
PP	1	2	3	4	5	6	7	8	9	10
PDT	1	2	3	4	5	6	7	8	9	10
PRN	1	2	3	4	5	6	7	8	9	10
PTB	1	2	3	4	5	6	7	8	9	10
PT	1	2	3	4	5	6	7	8	9	10
PL	1	2	3	4	5	6	7	8	9	10
PPS	1	2	3	4	5	6	7	8	9	10
PC do B	1	2	3	4	5	6	7	8	9	10
PSB	1	2	3	4	5	6	7	8	9	10
PSTU	1	2	3	4	5	6	7	8	9	10

Alguns parlamentares são eleitos por causa de sua sigla partidária—isto é, o poder de organização do partido ou o perfil que ele tem na opinião pública. Outros são eleitos devido a sua capacidade individual para a organização ou a sua atuação pessoal na política. No seu caso, qual foi mais importante?

_____ o partido _____ seus esforços pessoais

O Sr. acredita que, na atividade parlamentar, em geral um parlamentar deve votar como o partido indica, ou de acordo com o que ele acredita?

_____ como o partido indica _____ de acordo com o que ele acredita

O Sr. acha correto o partido fechar questão e usar o recurso da fidelidade partidária? _____ sim _____ não

O Sr. já serviu em um ou mais dos seguintes cargos públicos? Marque todos.

_____ vereador   _____ deputado estadual   _____ senador

_____ dep. Federal   _____ prefeito/vice   _____ governador/vice

_____ Ministro   _____ secretário estadual

Algum parente seu já exerceu um dos cargos acima nos últimos 50 anos

_____ sim _____ não

Em quem o Sr. votou no 2° turno da eleição presidencial de 1989?
_____ Collor _____ Lula _____ nulo/branco

Por favor, indique se o Sr. tem participado das seguintes atividades nos últimos 12 meses: frequentemente, de vez em quando, raramente, ou nunca.

	frequentemente	de vez em quando	raramente	nunca
Introduzir um projeto de lei	_____	_____	_____	_____
Apresentar emendas a um projeto de lei introduzido por outra pessoa	_____	_____	_____	_____
Tomar a palavra em sua casa legislativa	_____	_____	_____	_____
Reunir com a Executiva de seu partido	_____	_____	_____	_____
Reunir com representantes da burocracia federal	_____	_____	_____	_____
Reunir com representantes da burocracia em seu estado ou município	_____	_____	_____	_____
Reunir com representantes de organizações corporativas (CNBB, FIESP, etc.)	_____	_____	_____	_____

Nos últimos anos tem havido um grande debate sobre reformas políticas e institucionais em geral. Alguns dizem que as reformas institucionais são necessárias para tirar o Brasil da crise. Outros dizem que as razões da crise são mais profundas, encontrando-se na sociedade e na cultura, e que as reformas políticas não adiantam. Qual é a sua opinião a respeito da importância das reformas políticas e institucionais?

Usando uma escala que vai de 1 (menos importante) até 10 (mais importante), por favor indique a sua opinião.

	menos imp.							mais imp.		
As reformas políticas e institucionais são:	1	2	3	4	5	6	7	8	9	10

Por que o Sr. acredita que os eleitores votaram no Sr. nas últimas eleições? Usando uma escala que vai de 1 (menos importante) até 10 (mais importante), por favor indique o peso relativo dos seguintes fatores.

	menos imp.							mais imp.		
Suas declarações e promessas	1	2	3	4	5	6	7	8	9	10
A organização de seu partido	1	2	3	4	5	6	7	8	9	10
O apoio de interesses econômicos	1	2	3	4	5	6	7	8	9	10
Suas possibilidades de êxito	1	2	3	4	5	6	7	8	9	10
O desgaste de outros concorrentes ou siglas	1	2	3	4	5	6	7	8	9	10
O apoio de grupos de base	1	2	3	4	5	6	7	8	9	10
A campanha eleitoral que o Sr. fez	1	2	3	4	5	6	7	8	9	10
Tradição familiar/lealdades históricas	1	2	3	4	5	6	7	8	9	10
Seu carisma pessoal	1	2	3	4	5	6	7	8	9	10

Finalmente, gostaria de saber se o senhor concorda ou discorda com as seguintes frases. Por favor, use um dos seguintes códigos para indicar sua opinião:

1 = concorda, plenamente
2 = concorda, em termos
3 = discorda, em termos
4 = discorda, plenamente

A não coincidência das eleições parlamentares e municipais, ou seja, o fato de que as eleições municipais são realizadas no meio de uma legislatura, dificulta os trabalhos parlamentares. 1   2   3   4

No Brasil, é preciso dar ao presidente da República o poder das medidas provisórias. 1   2   3   4

Os regimes autoritários têm mais condições de estimular o crescimento econômico que os regimes democráticos. 1   2   3   4

Na América Latina, tem sido mais difícil para os governos democráticos manter a ordem social que para os governos autoritários. 1   2   3   4

Em vez de ter vários ministérios militares,
o Brasil deve ter um único Ministério da Defesa. 1   2   3   4

Se for criado o Ministério da Defesa, o Ministro deve ser um civil. 1   2   3   4

Um partido político deveria expulsar um parlamentar
que vota contra as determinações do partido. 1 2 3 4

Em geral, ocupar um cargo executivo é melhor do que ter um mandato parlamentar. 1 2 3 4

Sob a Constituição de 1988, os presidentes da República têm abusado
do poder das medidas provisórias. 1 2 3 4

Deve haver coincidência de todas as eleições e mandatos, a todos os níveis de governo. 1 2 3 4

Desde já, agradeço a sua especial colaboração na pesquisa.

Portuguese Text of 1997 Survey Questionnaire

Seu partido atual _____

Seu estado _____

Legenda pela qual foi eleito ao Congresso _____

Em quantas legislaturas já foi membro do Congresso Nacional? _____

Sua idade: _____ anos

A que partido (ou partidos) o Sr. foi filiado no período 1980–1985?
_____ PDS   _____ PMDB   _____ PP   _____ PDT   _____ PT   _____ PTB
_____ outro   _____ nenhum partido

E no período 1966–1979? _____ ARENA _____ MDB
                          _____ outro   _____ nenhum partido

Nos últimos anos tem havido um grande debate a respeito do sistema eleitoral. O
Sr. é favorável ao sistema de representação proporcional, ao sistema distrital majoritário ou ao sistema misto (proporcional para uma parte das cadeiras e distrital-
majoritário para as restantes)?
_____ sistema proporcional _____ sistema misto _____ sistema distrital majoritário

Se o Brasil mantiver o sistema de eleições proporcionais, o Sr. preferiria que a ordem
de candidatos na lista fosse determinada pelo partido ou preferiria uma lista aberta
(como existe agora)?
_____ lista aberta   _____ lista determinada pelo partido

Gostaria de saber sua opinião a respeito de dois temas que foram debatidos na
Assembléia Nacional Constituinte de 1987–1988. O Sr. está a favor ou contra:

À inclusão do dispositivo que assegura às Forças Armadas o direito de intervenção para garantir a ordem interna _____ favor _____ contra
À instituição do regime parlamentarista de governo _____ favor _____ contra

Como o Sr. julgaria a capacidade dos seguintes partidos políticos para atuar de acordo com as regras do jogo democrático e contribuir à estabilidade democrática?

	nenhuma									máxima
PMDB	1	2	3	4	5	6	7	8	9	10
PFL	1	2	3	4	5	6	7	8	9	10
PPB	1	2	3	4	5	6	7	8	9	10
PSDB	1	2	3	4	5	6	7	8	9	10
PDT	1	2	3	4	5	6	7	8	9	10
PTB	1	2	3	4	5	6	7	8	9	10
PT	1	2	3	4	5	6	7	8	9	10
PT	1	2	3	4	5	6	7	8	9	10
PPS	1	2	3	4	5	6	7	8	9	10
PC do B	1	2	3	4	5	6	7	8	9	10
PSB	1	2	3	4	5	6	7	8	9	10

Agora vamos supor que nesta reta o número 1 corresponde a esquerda, o número 5 ao centro, e onúmero 10 a direita. Como o Sr. está vendo, uma pessoa que fosse muito de esquerda estaria no número 1, uma muito de direita, no número 10. Onde é que o Sr. se colocaria?

esquerda				centro					direita
1	2	3	4	5	6	7	8	9	10

E onde é que o Sr. colocaria cada um dos seguintes partidos em âmbito nacional? Como o Sr. classificaria o. . . .

	esquerda				centro					direita
PMDB	1	2	3	4	5	6	7	8	9	10
PFL	1	2	3	4	5	6	7	8	9	10
PPB	1	2	3	4	5	6	7	8	9	10
PSDB	1	2	3	4	5	6	7	8	9	10
PDT	1	2	3	4	5	6	7	8	9	10
PTB	1	2	3	4	5	6	7	8	9	10
PT	1	2	3	4	5	6	7	8	9	10
PL	1	2	3	4	5	6	7	8	9	10
PPS	1	2	3	4	5	6	7	8	9	10
PC do B	1	2	3	4	5	6	7	8	9	10
PSB	1	2	3	4	5	6	7	8	9	10

Gostaria de saber a sua avaliação geral de vários aspectos da democracia brasileira desde 1985. Usando uma escala que vai de 1 (avaliação mais negativa) até 10 (avaliação mais positiva), indique sua opinião sobre os seguintes itens:

O governo de José Sarney
O governo de Fernando Collor
O governo de Itamar Franco
O governo de Fernando Henrique Cardoso
O desempenho do Congresso Nacional desde 1985
O sistema partidário pós-1985
A descentralização fiscal introduzida pela Constituição de 88
A desestatização da economia nos últimos anos

Alguns parlamentares são eleitos por causa de sua sigla partidária—isto é, o poder de organização do partido ou o perfil que ele tem na opinião pública. Outros são eleitos devido a sua capacidade individual para a organização ou a sua atuação pessoal na política. No seu caso, qual foi mais importante?
_____ o partido _____ seus esforços pessoais

O Sr. acredita que, na atividade parlamentar, em geral um parlamentar deve votar como o partido indica, ou de acordo com o que ele acredita?
_____ como o partido indica _____ de acordo com o que ele acredita

O Sr. acha correto o partido fechar questão e usar o recurso da fidelidade partidária?
_____ sim _____ não

O Sr. já serviu em um ou mais dos seguintes cargos públicos? Marque todos.
_____ vereador _____ deputado estadual _____ senador _____ dep. federal
_____ prefeito/vice _____ governador/vice _____ Ministro _____ secretário estadual

Algum parente seu já exerceu um dos cargos acima nos últimos 50 anos?
_____ sim _____ não

Por favor, indique se o Sr. tem participado das seguintes atividades nos últimos 12 meses: frequentemente, de vez em quando, raramente, ou nunca.

	frequentemente	de vez em quando	raramente	nunca
Introduzir um projeto de lei	_____	_____	_____	_____
Apresentar emendas a um projeto de lei introduzido por outra pessoa	_____	_____	_____	_____

Tomar a palavra em sua casa legislativa	_____	_____	_____	_____
Reunir com a Executiva de seu partido	_____	_____	_____	_____
Discutir temas de interesse nacional com oficiais das Forças Armadas	_____	_____	_____	_____
Reunir com representantes da burocracia federal	_____	_____	_____	_____
Reunir com representantes da burocracia em seu estado ou município	_____	_____	_____	_____
Reunir com diretores de órgãos da imprensa	_____	_____	_____	_____
Reunir com representantes de organizações corporativas (CNBB, FIESP, etc.)	_____	_____	_____	_____

Na sua opinião, que tipo de sistema econômico seria mais adequado para o Brasil? Marque apenas uma opção.

1   Uma economia predominantemente de mercado com a menor participação possível do Estado
2   Um sistema econômico em que houvesse uma distribuição eqüitativa entre uma parte de responsabilidade das empresas estatais e outra das empresas privadas
3   Uma economia em que as empresas estatais e o Estado constituíssem o setor principal mas sem que a participação da economia do mercado fosse eliminada
4   Uma economia em que o capital privado fosse totalmente afastado dos principais setores econômicos, passando as grandes empresas para o controle estatal

Por que o Sr. acredita que os eleitores votaram no Sr. nas últimas eleições? Usando uma escala que vai de 1 (menos importante) até 10 (mais importante), por favor indique o peso relativo dos seguintes fatores.

	menos imp.							mais imp.		
Suas declarações e promessas	1	2	3	4	5	6	7	8	9	10
A organização de seu partido	1	2	3	4	5	6	7	8	9	10
O apoio de interesses econômicos	1	2	3	4	5	6	7	8	9	10
Suas possibilidades de êxito	1	2	3	4	5	6	7	8	9	10
O desgaste de outros concorrentes ou siglas	1	2	3	4	5	6	7	8	9	10
O apoio de grupos de base	1	2	3	4	5	6	7	8	9	10
A campanha eleitoral que o Sr. fez	1	2	3	4	5	6	7	8	9	10

Tradição familiar / lealdades históricas   1   2   3   4   5   6   7   8   9   10

Seu carisma pessoal   1   2   3   4   5   6   7   8   9   10

Quando há um conflito entre as necessidades da sua região e as posições partidárias, o Sr. vota, a maioria das vezes:

_____ com o partido

_____ de acordo com as necessidades da região

_____ divide as votações pela metade

Finalmente, gostaria de saber se o senhor concorda ou discorda com as seguintes frases. Por favor, use um dos seguintes códigos para indicar sua opinião:

> 1 = concorda, plenamente
> 2 = concorda, em termos
> 3 = discorda, em termos
> 4 = discorda, plenamente

Em geral, ocupar um cargo executivo é melhor do que ter um mandato parlamentar.
1   2   3   4

Em geral, os presidentes da República têm influência demais sobre as decisões do Congresso.   1   2   3   4

Os regimes autoritários têm mais condições de estimular o crescimento econômico que os regimes democráticos.   1   2   3   4

Na América Latina, tem sido mais difícil para os governos democráticos manter a ordem social que para os governos autoritários.   1   2   3   4

A cobertura jornalística do Poder Legislativo é injustamente negativa.   1   2   3   4

No Brasil, é preciso dar ao presidente da República o poder das medidas provisórias.   1   2   3   4

Em vez de ter vários ministérios militares, o Brasil deve ter um único Ministério da Defesa.   1   2   3   4

Se for criado o Ministério da Defesa, o Ministro deve ser um civil.   1   2   3   4

Um partido político deveria expulsar um parlamentar que vota contra as determinações do partido.   1   2   3   4

Apesar de o clientelismo ser muito criticado, às vezes os eleitores exigem que o parlamentar atue desta maneira.   1   2   3   4

Um parlamentar deve perder o mandato se trocar de partido depois das eleições.   1   2   3   4

Bibliography

Abranches, Sérgio, and Glaucio Ary Dillon Soares. 1972. "Las funciones del poder legislativo." *Revista Latinoamericana de Ciencia Política* 3, no. 2 (August): 256–80.

Abreu, Alzira Alves de, and José Luciano de Mattos Dias, eds. 1995. *O futuro do Congresso brasileiro*. Rio de Janeiro: Editora Fundação Getúlio Vargas.

Agor, Weston, ed. 1971. *Latin American Legislatures: Their Role and Influence*. New York: Praeger Publishers.

Agüero, Felipe. 1995. *Soldiers, Civilians, and Democracy: Post-Franco Spain in Comparative Perspective*. Baltimore: Johns Hopkins University Press.

Alves, Maria Helena Moreira. 1985. *State and Opposition in Military Brazil*. Austin: University of Texas Press.

Ames, Barry. 1995a. "Electoral Strategy under Open-List Proportional Representation." *American Journal of Political Science* 39, no. 2 (May): 406–33.

———. 1995b. "Electoral Rules, Constituency Pressures, and Pork Barrel: Bases of Voting in the Brazilian Congress." *Journal of Politics* 57, no. 2 (May): 324–43.

Assembléia Nacional Constituinte. 1987. *Repertório biográfico dos membros da Assembléia Nacional Constituinte de 1987*. Brasília: Câmara dos Deputados, Centro de Documentação e Informação, Coordenação de Publicações.

Astiz, Carlos Alberto. 1973. "The Decay of Latin American Legislatures." In Allan Kornberg, ed., *Legislatures in Comparative Perspective*, 114–26. New York: David MacKay Company.

———. 1975. "O papel atual do Congresso brasileiro." In Cândido Mendes, ed., *O legislativo e a tecnocracia*, 5–30. Rio de Janeiro: Imago.

Baaklini, Abdo I. 1977. "Legislative Reforms in the Brazilian Chamber of Deputies, 1964–1975." In Abdo I. Baaklini and James J. Heaphey, eds., *Comparative Legislative Reforms and Innovations*. Albany: State University of New York Press.

———. 1989. "Continuidade e mudança no Congresso Nacional: Brasil 1970–1986." In Alexandrina Sobreira de Moura, ed., *O Estado e as políticas públicas na transição democrática*, 42–63. São Paulo: Vértice.

———. 1992. *The Brazilian Legislature and Political System*. Westport, Conn.: Greenwood Press.

Baaklini, Abdo I., and James J. Heaphey. 1976. *Legislative Institution Building in Brazil, Costa Rica, and Lebanon*. Sage Professional Papers in Administrative and Policy Studies, vol. 1, series 03-027. Beverly Hills and London: Sage Publications.

Benevides, Maria Victoria de Mesquita. 1981. *A UDN e o udenismo*. Rio de Janeiro: Paz e Terra.

Blondel, Jean. 1973. *Comparative Legislatures.* Englewood Cliffs, N.J.: Prentice-Hall.

Borón, Atilio A. 1992. "Becoming Democrats? Some Skeptical Considerations on the Right in Latin America." In Douglas Chalmers, Maria do Carmo Campello de Souza, and Atilio Borón, eds., *The Right and Democracy in Latin America,* 68–98. New York: Praeger Publishers.

Bresser Pereira, Luiz Carlos Bresser. 1984. *Development and Crisis in Brazil, 1930–1983,* trans. Marcia Van Dyke. Boulder: Westview Press.

———. 1985. *Pactos políticos: do populismo à redemocratização.* São Paulo: Brasiliense.

Burton, Michael G., and John Higley. 1987. "Elite Settlements." *American Sociological Review* 52, no. 3: 295–307.

Câmara dos Deputados. 1979. *Deputados brasileiros: repertório biográfico dos membros da Câmara dos Deputados, nona legislatura (1979–1983).* Brasília: Centro de Documentação e Informação, Coordenação de Publicações.

———. 1983. *Deputados brasileiros: repertório biográfico dos membros da Câmara dos Deputados, 47ª legislatura (1983–1987).* Brasília: Centro de Documentação e Informação, Coordenação de Publicações.

———. 1991. *Deputados brasileiros: repertório biográfico dos membros da Câmara dos Deputados, 49ª legislatura (1991–1995).* Brasília: Centro de Documentação e Informação, Coordenação de Publicações.

———. 1993. "Leis de 1964 a 1992" (mimeo). Brasilia: Seção de Sinopse.

———. 1995. *Deputados brasileiros: repertório biográfico dos membros da Câmara dos Deputados, 50ª legislatura (1995–1999).* Brasília: Centro de Documentação e Informação, Coordenação de Publicações.

Cammack, Paul. 1982. "Clientelism and Military Government in Brazil." In Christopher Clapham, ed., *Private Patronage and Public Power: Political Clientelism in the Modern State,* 53–75. New York: St. Martin's Press.

Cardoso, Fernando Henrique, and Bolivar Lamounier, eds. 1978. *Os partidos e as eleições no Brasil.* Rio de Janeiro: Paz e Terra.

Cardoso, Fernando Henrique, and Mário Soares. 1998. *O mundo em português: um diálogo.* São Paulo: Paz e Terra.

Carneiro, Luiz. 1990. "Uma Câmara desproporcional." *Jornal do Brasil,* July 26, p. 11.

Cavarozzi, Marcelo. 1986. "Political Cycles in Argentina since 1955." In Guillermo O'Donnell, Philippe C. Schmitter, and Laurence Whitehead, eds., *Transitions from Authoritarian Rule: Latin America,* 19–48. Baltimore: Johns Hopkins University Press.

CEBRAP (Centro Brasileiro de Análise e Planejamento). 1994. "O desafio do Congresso Nacional: Mudanças internas e consolidação institucional." *Cadernos de Pesquisa* 3 (November).

Chalmers, Douglas. 1977a. "Parties and Society in Latin America." In Steffen Schmidt et al., eds., *Friends, Followers, and Factions: A Reader in Political Clientelism,* 401–21. Berkeley and Los Angeles: University of California Press.

———. 1977b. "The Politicized State in Latin America." In James Malloy, ed., *Au-

thoritarianism and Corporatism in Latin America, 23–45. Pittsburgh: University of Pittsburgh Press.

Cintra, Antônio Otávio. 1979. "Traditional Brazilian Politics: An Interpretation of Relations between Center and Periphery." In Neuma Aguiar, ed., *The Structure of Brazilian Development*, 127–66. New Brunswick: Transaction Books.

Close, David. 1995a. "Introduction: Consolidating Democracy in Latin America— What Role for Legislatures?" In David Close, ed., *Legislatures and the New Democracies in Latin America*, 1–15. Boulder: Lynne Rienner Publishers.

———, ed. 1995b. *Legislatures and the New Democracies in Latin America*. Boulder: Lynne Rienner Publishers.

Coelho, João Gilberto Lucas. 1989. "O processo legislativo brasileiro após a Constituinte: reformulações regimentais." Brasília: INESC (mimeo).

Coelho, João Gilberto Lucas, and Antônio Carlos Nantes de Oliveira. 1989. *A nova Constituição: avaliação do texto e perfil dos constituintes*. Rio de Janeiro: Editora Revan.

Collier, David, and Deborah L. Norden. 1992. "Strategic Choice Models of Political Change in Latin America." *Comparative Politics* 24, no. 2: 229–43.

Collier, Ruth Berins, and David Collier. 1991. *Shaping the Political Arena: Critical Junctures, the Labor Movement, and Regime Dynamics in Latin America*. Princeton: Princeton University Press.

Conniff, Michael L., ed. 1982. *Latin American Populism in Comparative Perspective*. Albuquerque: University of New Mexico Press.

Constitution of Brazil, 1967. In *Constituições do Brasil: de 1824, 1891, 1934, 1937, 1946 e 1967 e suas alterações*. 2 vols. Brasília: Senado Federal, Subsecretaria de Edições Técnicas, 1986.

Constitution of Brazil, 1988. In *Constitution of the Federative Republic of Brazil* (English translation published by the Federal Senate). Brasília: Senado Federal, 1990.

Coppedge, Michael. 1994. *Strong Parties and Lame Ducks: Presidential Partyarchy and Factionalism in Venezuela*. Stanford: Stanford University Press.

———. 1995. "Freezing in the Tropics: Explaining Party-System Volatility in Latin America." Paper presented at the Midwest Political Science Association meetings, Chicago, April 6–8.

Dahl, Robert. 1971. *Polyarchy: Participation and Opposition*. New Haven: Yale University Press.

DaMatta, Roberto. 1991. *Carnival, Rogues, and Heroes*. Notre Dame: University of Notre Dame Press.

Dassin, Joan, ed. 1986. *Torture in Brazil: A Report by the Archdiocese of São Paulo*, trans. Jaime Wright. New York: Vintage Books.

Diamond, Larry, Juan J. Linz, and Seymour Martin Lipset. 1989. *Democracy in Developing Countries*. 4 vols. Boulder: Lynne Rienner Publishers.

Diário da Assembléia Nacional Constituinte. 1987–88. Brasília: Assembléia Nacional Constituinte.

Dimenstein, Gilberto, José Negreiros, Ricardo Noblat, Roberto Lopes, and Roberto Fernandes. 1985. *O complô que elegeu Tancredo*. Rio de Janeiro: Editora JB.

Dimenstein, Gilberto, and Josias de Souza. 1994. *A Histórica Real: Trama de uma sucessão*. São Paulo: Editora Atica.

DIAP (Departamento Intersindical de Assessoria Parlamentar). 1988. *Quem foi quem na Constituinte nas questões de interesse dos trabalhadores*. São Paulo: Cortez/Oborê.

Diniz, Eli. 1982. *Voto e máquina política: patronagem e clientelismo no Rio de Janeiro*. Rio de Janeiro: Paz e Terra.

———. 1989. "Transição, partidos e regimes políticos: algumas considerações." In Aspásia Camargo and Eli Diniz, eds., *Continuidade e mudança na Nova República*, 84–108. São Paulo: Vértice.

———. 1990. "O ciclo autoritário: a lógica partidário-eleitoral e a erosão do regime." In Olavo Brasil de Lima Júnior, ed., *O balanço do poder: formas de dominação e representação*, 73–86. Rio de Janeiro: Rio Fundo Editora.

Dreifuss, René. 1989. *O jogo da Direita na Nova República*. Petrópolis: Vozes.

Duverger, Maurice. 1954. *Political Parties: Their Organization and Activity in the Modern State*, trans. Barbara and Robert North. New York: John Wiley and Sons.

Faoro, Raymundo. 1958. *Os donos do poder*. 2 vols. Porto Alegre: Editora Globo.

Figueiredo, Marcus. 1977. "A política de coação no Brasil pós-64." M.A. thesis, Instituto Universitário de Pesquisas do Rio de Janeiro.

Figueiredo, Argelina, and Fernando Limongi. 1994a. "Mudança constitucional, desempenho do Legislativo e consolidação institucional." Paper presented to the XVIII conference of the Associação Nacional de Pós-Graduação e Pesquisa em Ciências Sociais (ANPOCS), Caxambu, Minas Gerais, Brazil, October.

———. 1994b. "A Câmara por seus membros: Imagem e realidade." Mimeo, Centro Brasileiro de Análise e Planejamento (CEBRAP), São Paulo.

———. 1995a. "Partidos políticos na Câmara dos Deputados: 1989–1994." *Dados* 38, no. 3: 497–525.

———. 1995b. "Poderes legislativos e o poder do Congresso." *Monitor Público* 2, no. 5 (March–May): 33–38.

———. 1996. "Presidencialismo e apoio partidário no Congresso." *Monitor Público* 3, no. 8 (January–March): 27–36.

Fleischer, David V., ed. 1981. *Os partidos políticos no Brasil*. 2 vols. Brasília: Editora Universidade de Brasília.

———. 1984. "Constitutional and Electoral Engineering in Brazil: A Double-Edged Sword." *Inter-American Economic Affairs* 37 (spring): 3–36.

———. 1988. "Perfil sócio-econômico e político da Constituinte." In Milton Guran, ed., *O processo constituinte 1987–1988*, 29–40. Brasília: AGIL.

———. 1994. "Political Corruption and Campaign Financing in Brazil: The Distraction Finesse of Impeachment, Congressional Inquests, Ceremonious Sackings, and Innocuous Legislation." Paper presented to the XVI World Congress of the International Political Science Association, Berlin, August 21–25.

Flynn, Peter. 1974. "Class, Clientelism, and Coercion: Some Mechanisms of Internal Dependency and Control." *Journal of Commonwealth and Comparative Politics* 12, no. 2 (July): 133–56.

Geddes, Barbara. 1994. *Politicians' Dilemma: Building State Capacity in Latin America*. Berkeley and Los Angeles: University of California Press.
——. 1995. "A Comparative Perspective on the Leninist Legacy in Eastern Europe." *Comparative Political Studies* 28, no. 2 (July): 239–74.
Geddes, Barbara, and Artur Ribeiro Neto. 1992. "Institutional Sources of Corruption in Brazil." *Third World Quarterly* 13, no. 4: 641–661.
Gibson, Edward L. 1990. "Democracy and the New Electoral Right in Argentina." *Journal of Interamerican Studies and World Affairs* 32, no. 3 (fall): 177–228.
——. 1992. "Conservative Electoral Movements and Democratic Politics: Core Constituencies, Coalition Building, and the Latin American Electoral Right." In Douglas Chalmers, Maria do Carmo Campello de Souza, and Atilio Borón, eds., *The Right and Democracy in Latin America*, 13–42. New York: Praeger Publishers.
——. 1996. *Class and Conservative Parties: Argentina in Comparative Perspective*. Baltimore: Johns Hopkins University Press.
Goertzel, Ted G. 1999. *Fernando Henrique Cardoso: Reinventing Democracy in Brazil*. Boulder: Lynne Rienner Publishers.
Gunther, Richard. 1992. "Spain: The Very Model of the Modern Elite Settlement." In John Higley and Richard Gunther, eds., *Elites and Democratic Consolidation in Latin America and Southern Europe*, 38–80. New York: Cambridge University Press.
Gunther, Richard, P. Nikiforos Diamandouros, and Hans-Jürgen Puhle, eds.. 1995. *The Politics of Democratic Consolidation: Southern Europe in Comparative Perspective*. Baltimore: Johns Hopkins University Press.
Hagopian, Frances. 1986. "The Politics of Oligarchy: The Persistence of Traditional Elites in Contemporary Brazil." Ph.D. diss., Massachusetts Institute of Technology.
——. 1990. " 'Democracy by Undemocratic Means?' Elites, Political Pacts, and Regime Transition in Brazil." *Comparative Political Studies* 23, no. 2 (July): 147–70.
——. 1992. "The Compromised Consolidation: The Political Class in the Brazilian Transition." In Scott Mainwaring, Guillermo O'Donnell, and J. Samuel Valenzuela, *Issues in Democratic Consolidation*, 243–93. Notre Dame: University of Notre Dame Press.
——. 1996. *Traditional Politics and Regime Change in Brazil*. New York: Cambridge University Press.
Hagopian, Frances, and Scott Mainwaring. 1987. "Democracy in Brazil: Problems and Prospects." *World Policy Journal* 4, no. 3: 485–514.
Hall, Peter A. 1986. *Governing the Economy: The Politics of State Intervention in Britain and France*. New York: Oxford University Press.
Hermet, Guy, Richard Rose, and Alain Rouquié, eds. 1978. *Elections Without Choice*. London: Macmillan Publishers.
Higley, John, Judith Kullberg, and Jan Pakulski. 1996. "The Persistence of Post-Communist Elites." *Journal of Democracy* 7, no. 2 (April): 133–47.
Hippolito, Lucia. 1985. *De raposas e reformistas: o PSD e a experiência democrática brasileira, 1945–1964*. Rio de Janeiro: Paz e Terra.

Hunter, Wendy. 1997. *Eroding Military Influence in Brazil: Politicians Against Soldiers*. Chapel Hill: University of North Carolina Press.

Huntington, Samuel. 1968. *Political Order in Changing Societies*. New Haven: Yale University Press.

———. 1989. "The Modest Meaning of Democracy." In Robert Pastor, ed., *Democracy in the Americas: Stopping the Pendulum*, 11–28. New York: Holmes and Meier.

———. 1996. "Democracy for the Long Haul." *Journal of Democracy* 7, no. 2 (April): 3–13.

Hutchinson, Bertram. 1966. "The Patron-Dependant Relationship in Brazil: A Preliminary Examination." *Sociologia Ruralis* 6, no. 1: 3–30.

Isaacs, Anita. 1993. *Military Rule and Transition in Ecuador, 1972–1992*. Pittsburgh: University of Pittsburgh Press.

Jenks, Margaret Sarles. 1979. "Political Parties in Authoritarian Brazil." Ph.D. diss., Duke University.

Jowitt, Ken. 1992. *New World Disorder: The Leninist Extinction*. Berkeley and Los Angeles: University of California Press.

Karl, Terry Lynn. 1986. "Petroleum and Political Pacts: The Transition to Democracy in Venezuela." In Guillermo O'Donnell, Philippe C. Schmitter, and Laurence Whitehead, eds., *Transitions from Authoritarian Rule: Latin America*, 196–219. Baltimore: Johns Hopkins University Press.

Karl, Terry Lynn, and Philippe C. Schmitter. 1991. "Modes of Transition and Types of Democracy in Latin America, Southern and Eastern Europe." *International Social Science Journal* no. 128 (May): 269–84.

Kaufman, Robert R. 1967. "The Chilean Political Right and Agrarian Reform: Resistance and Moderation." Political Study no. 2, Institute for the Comparative Study of Political Systems.

Keck, Margaret. 1992. *The Workers' Party and Democratization in Brazil*. New Haven: Yale University Press.

Kingstone, Peter R. 1999. *Crafting Coalitions for Reform: Business Strategies, Political Institutions, and Neoliberal Reform in Brazil*. University Park: Pennsylvania State University Press.

Kinzo, Maria D'Alva Gil. 1988. *Legal Opposition Politics Under Authoritarian Rule in Brazil*. New York: St. Martin's.

———. 1989. "O quadro partidário e a Constituinte." *Revista Brasileira de Ciência Política* 1, no. 1: 91–124.

———. 1993. *Radiografia do quadro partidário brasileiro*. São Paulo: Fundação Konrad-Adenauer-Stiftung.

Kitschelt, Herbert. 1992. "The Formation of Party Systems in East Central Europe." *Politics and Society* 20, no. 1: 7–50.

Krieger, Gustavo, Fernando Rodrigues, and Elvis Cesar Bonassa. 1994. *Os donos do Congresso: a farsa na CPI do Orçamento*. São Paulo: Editora Ática.

Lamounier, Bolivar. 1984. "Opening Through Elections: Will the Brazilian Case Become a Paradigm?" *Government and Opposition* 19, no. 2 (spring): 167–77.

———. 1989. "Authoritarian Brazil Revisited: The Impact of Elections on the Abertura." In Alfred Stepan, ed., *Democratizing Brazil*, 43–79. New York: Oxford University Press.

———. 1990. *Partidos e utopias: o Brasil no limiar dos anos 90.* São Paulo: Edições Loyola.

———. 1994. "Brazil: Towards Parliamentarism?" In Juan J. Linz and Arturo Valenzuela, eds., *The Failure of Presidential Democracy*, 179–219. Baltimore: Johns Hopkins University Press.

Lamounier, Bolivar, and Rachel Meneguello. 1986. *Partidos políticos e consolidação democrática.* São Paulo: Brasiliense.

Leal, Victor Nunes. 1977. *Coronelismo: The Municipality and Representative Government in Brazil*, trans. June Henfrey. London: Cambridge University Press.

Leeds, Anthony. 1977. "Brazil as a System." Occasional Papers Series no. 5, Program in Latin American Studies, University of Massachusetts at Amherst.

Leoni, Brigitte Hersant. 1997. *Fernando Henrique Cardoso: o Brasil do possível.* Rio de Janeiro: Editora Nova Fronteira.

Levine, Daniel. 1973. *Conflict and Political Change in Venezuela.* Princeton: Princeton University Press.

———. 1988. "Paradigm Lost: Dependency to Democracy." *World Politics* 40, no. 3 (April): 377–94.

Levine, Daniel, and Miriam Kornblith. 1995. "Venezuela: The Life and Times of the Party System." In Scott Mainwaring and Timothy Scully, eds., *Building Democratic Institutions: Parties and Party Systems in Latin America*, 33–71. Stanford: Stanford University Press.

Lima Júnior, Olavo Brasil de. 1983. *Os partidos políticos brasileiros: a experiência federal e regional, 1945–1964.* Rio de Janeiro: Graal.

———, ed. 1990. *O balanço do poder: formas de dominação e representação.* Rio de Janeiro: Rio Fundo Editora.

———, ed. 1991. *Sistema eleitoral brasileiro: teoria e prática.* Rio de Janeiro: Rio Fundo Editora.

———. 1993. *Democracia e instituições políticas no Brasil dos anos 80.* São Paulo: Edições Loyola.

Lijphart, Arend. 1977. *Democracy in Plural Societies.* New Haven: Yale University Press.

———. 1984. *Democracies: Patterns of Majoritarian and Consensus Government in Twenty-One Countries.* New Haven: Yale University Press.

Linz, Juan J. 1973. "The Future of an Authoritarian Situation or the Institutionalization of an Authoritarian Regime: The Case of Brazil." In Alfred Stepan, ed., *Authoritarian Brazil: Origins, Problems, and Future*, 233–54. New Haven: Yale University Press.

———. 1976. "An Authoritarian Regime: Spain." In Douglas Payne, ed., *Politics and Society in Twentieth-Century Spain*, 160–207. New York: New Viewpoints.

———. 1978. *The Breakdown of Democratic Regimes: Crisis, Breakdown, and Reequilibration.* Baltimore: Johns Hopkins University Press.

Linz, Juan J., and Alfred Stepan. 1996. *Problems of Democratic Transition and*

Consolidation: Southern Europe, South America, and Post-Communist Europe. Baltimore: Johns Hopkins University Press.

Longley, Lawrence D., ed. 1994. *Working Papers on Comparative Legislative Studies.* Appleton, Wis.: Research Committee of Legislative Specialists.

Mainwaring, Scott. 1986a. "The Consolidation of Democracy in Latin America: A Rapporteur's Report." Working Paper no. 73, Helen Kellogg Institute for International Studies, University of Notre Dame.

———. 1986b. "The Transition to Democracy in Brazil." *Journal of Interamerican Studies and World Affairs* 28, no. 1 (spring): 149–79.

———. 1988. "Political Parties and Democratization in Brazil and the Southern Cone: A Review Essay." *Comparative Politics* 21, no. 1 (October): 91–120.

———. 1991a. "Clientelism, Patrimonialism, and Economic Crisis: Brazil since 1979." Paper prepared for the XVI International Congress of the Latin American Studies Association, Washington, April 4–7.

———. 1991b. "Politicians, Parties, and Electoral Systems: Brazil in Comparative Perspective." *Comparative Politics* 24, no. 1 (October): 21–43.

———. 1992. "Transitions to Democracy: Theoretical and Comparative Issues." In Scott Mainwaring, Guillermo O'Donnell, and J. Samuel Valenzuela, eds., *Issues in Democratic Consolidation,* 294–342. Notre Dame: University of Notre Dame Press.

———. 1992–93. "Brazilian Party Underdevelopment in Comparative Perspective." *Political Science Quarterly* 107. no. 4: 677–707.

———. 1993. "Democracia presidencialista multipartidária: o caso do Brasil." *Lua Nova* 28–29: 21–74.

———. 1995. "Brazil: Weak Parties, Feckless Democracy." In Scott Mainwaring and Timothy Scully, eds., *Building Democratic Institutions: Parties and Party Systems in Latin America,* 354–98. Stanford: Stanford University Press.

———. 1998. "Electoral Volatility in Brazil." *Party Politics* 4, no. 4 (October): 523–45.

———. 1999. *Rethinking Party Systems in the Third Wave of Democratization: The Case of Brazil.* Stanford: Stanford University Press.

Mainwaring, Scott, and Timothy Scully, eds. 1995. *Building Democratic Institutions: Party Systems in Latin America.* Stanford: Stanford University Press.

Mainwaring, Scott, Guillermo O'Donnell, and J. Samuel Valenzuela, eds. 1992. *Issues in Democratic Consolidation: The New South American Democracies in Comparative Perspective.* Notre Dame: University of Notre Dame Press.

Maravall, José Maria, and Julián Santamaría. 1986. "Political Transition and the Prospects for Democracy in Spain." In Guillermo O'Donnell, Philippe C. Schmitter, and Laurence Whitehead, eds., *Transitions from Authoritarian Rule: Southern Europe,* 71–108. Baltimore: Johns Hopkins University Press.

Martínez-Lara, Javier. 1996. *Building Democracy in Brazil: The Politics of Constitutional Change, 1985–1995.* New York: St. Martin's Press.

Martins, Luciano. 1986. "The 'Liberalization' of Authoritarian Rule in Brazil." In Guillermo O'Donnell, Philippe C. Schmitter, and Laurence Whitehead, eds., *Transitions from Authoritarian Rule: Latin America,* 72–94. Baltimore: Johns Hopkins University Press.

McDonough, Peter. 1981. *Power and Ideology in Brazil*. Princeton: Princeton University Press.

Mendes, Cândido, ed. 1975. "O Congresso brasileiro pós-64: um legislativo para a tecnocracia?" In Cândido Mendes, ed., *O legislativo e a tecnocracia*, 123–56. Rio de Janeiro: Imago.

Mezey, Michael L. 1985. "The Functions of Legislatures in the Third World." In Gerhard Loewenberg, Samuel C. Patterson, and Malcolm E. Jewell, eds., *Handbook of Legislative Research*, 733–72. Cambridge, Mass.: Harvard University Press.

Moisés, José Álvaro. 1993. "Elections, Political Parties, and Political Culture in Brazil: Changes and Continuities." *Journal of Latin American Studies* 25, no. 3: 575–611.

———. 1994. "Political Legitimacy in Brazil in the 1990s: A Study of Public Satisfaction with the Actual Functioning of Democracy." Paper presented to the XVI World Congress of the International Political Science Association, Berlin, August 21–25.

———. 1995. *Os brasileiros e a democracia: bases sócio-políticas da legitimidade brasileira*. São Paulo: Editora Ática.

Moisés, José Álvaro, and Gustavo Venturi. 1990. "Cultura política do povo brasileiro." *Cadernos do CEDESEN*, no. 1. Brasília: Senado Federal.

Monteiro, Brandão, and Carlos Oliveira. 1989. *Os partidos políticos*. São Paulo: Global Editora.

Morgenstern, Scott, and Benito Nacif, eds. Forthcoming. *Legislative Politics in Latin America*. Book manuscript under review.

Munck, Gerardo L. 1994. "Explaining Institutional Choices in Democratic Transitions: Comparative Perspectives on the East European and South American Cases." Paper presented to the XVI World Congress of the International Political Science Association, Berlin, August 21–25.

Needler, Martin C. 1995. "Conclusion: The Legislature in a Democratic Latin America." In David Close, ed., *Legislatures and the New Democracies in Latin America*, 151–59. Boulder: Lynne Rienner Publishers.

Nicolau, Jairo Marconi. 1993. *Sistema eleitoral e reforma política*. Rio de Janeiro: Foglio Editora.

———. 1996a. *Multipartidarismo e democracia: um estudo sobre o sistema partidário brasileiro (1985–94)*. Rio de Janeiro: Editora Fundação Getúlio Vargas.

———. 1996b. "A migração partidária na Câmara dos Deputados (1991–96)." *Monitor Público* 3, no. 10 (July–September): 41–45.

North, Douglass C. 1990. *Institutions, Institutional Change, and Economic Performance*. New York: Cambridge University Press.

Novaes, Carlos Alberto Marques. 1994. "Dinâmica institucional da representação: individualismo e partidos na Câmara dos Deputados." *Novos Estudos,* no. 38: 99–147.

Nunes, Edson de Oliveira. 1978. "Legislativo, política e recrutamento de elites no Brasil." *Dados*, no. 17: 53–78.

Nunes, Edson de Oliveira, and Barbara Geddes. 1987. "Dilemmas of State-Led Modernization in Brazil." In John D. Wirth, Edson de Oliveira Nunes, and

Thomas Bogenschild, eds., *State and Society in Brazil: Continuity and Change*, 103–46. Boulder: Westview Press.

Nylen, William Russell. 1992. " 'Liberalismo para todo mundo, menos eu': Brazil and the Neoliberal Solution." In Douglas Chalmers, Maria do Carmo Campello e Souza, and Atilio Borón, eds., *The Right and Democracy in Latin America*, 259–76. New York: Praeger Publishers.

O'Donnell, Guillermo. 1973. *Modernization and Bureaucratic-Authoritarianism: Studies in South American Politics*. Berkeley: Institute for International Studies, University of California.

———. 1985. "Notes for the Study of Democratic Consolidation in Latin America." Unpublished paper, Helen Kellogg Institute for International Studies, University of Notre Dame.

———. 1992. "Transitions, Continuities, and Paradoxes." In Scott Mainwaring, Guillermo O'Donnell, and J. Samuel Valenzuela, *Issues in Democratic Consolidation*, 17–56. Notre Dame: University of Notre Dame Press.

———. 1993. "On the State, Democratization, and Some Conceptual Problems." *World Development* 21, no. 8: 1355–69.

———. 1994. "Delegative Democracy." *Journal of Democracy* 5, no. 1 (January): 55–69.

———. 1996. "Illusions About Consolidation." *Journal of Democracy* 7, no. 2 (April): 34–51.

O'Donnell, Guillermo, and Philippe C. Schmitter. 1986. *Transitions From Authoritarian Rule: Prospects for Democracy*, vol. 4, *Tentative Conclusions about Uncertain Democracies*. Baltimore: Johns Hopkins University Press.

O'Donnell, Guillermo, and Philippe C. Schmitter, and Laurence Whitehead, eds. 1986. *Transitions from Authoritarian Rule: Prospects for Democracy*. 4 vols. Baltimore: Johns Hopkins University Press.

Packenham, Robert. 1971. "Functions of the Brazilian National Congress." In Weston Agor, ed., *Latin American Legislatures: Their Role and Influence*, 259–92. New York: Praeger Publishers.

Pang, Eul-Soo. 1989. "Debt, Adjustment, and Democratic Cacophony in Brazil." In Barbara Stallings and Robert Kaufman, eds., *Debt and Democracy in Latin America*, 127–42. Boulder: Westview Press.

Payne, Leigh. 1994. *Brazilian Industrialists and Democratic Change*. Baltimore: Johns Hopkins University Press.

Pedone, Luiz, ed. 1993. *Sistemas eleitorais e processos políticos comparados: a promessa de democracia na América Latina e Caribe*. Brasília: Universidade de Brasília.

Peeler, John. 1985. *Latin American Democracies: Colombia, Costa Rica, Venezuela*. Chapel Hill: University of North Carolina Press.

Pereira, Raimundo, Álvaro Caropreso, and José Carlos Ruy. 1984. *Eleições no Brasil pós-64*. São Paulo: Global Editora.

Peterson, Phyllis Jane. 1962. "Brazilian Political Parties: Formation, Organization, and Leadership, 1945–1959." Ph.D. diss., University of Michigan, Ann Arbor.

Petras, James. 1988. "State, Regime, and the Democratization Muddle." *LASA Forum* 18, no. 4 (winter), 9–12.

Pierucci, Antônio Flávio. 1987. "As bases da Nova Direita." *Novos Estudos* no. 19 (December): 26–45.

Porto, Walter Costa. 1995. "A nova lei eleitoral e as sugestões do TSE." *Monitor Público* 2, no. 7 (October–December): 19–25.

Power, Timothy J. 1987. "The Masses and the Critical Mass: A Strategic Choice Model of the Transition to Democracy in Brazil." *Texas Papers on Latin America* 87–11 (May). Institute of Latin American Studies, University of Texas at Austin.

———. 1991. "Politicized Democracy: Competition, Institutions, and 'Civic Fatigue' in Brazil." *Journal of Interamerican Studies and World Affairs* 33, no. 3 (fall): 75–112.

———. 1998. "The Pen is Mightier than the Congress: Presidential Decree Power in Brazil." In John Carey and Matthew Soberg Shugart, eds., *Executive Decree Authority*, 197–230. New York: Cambridge University Press.

———. 2000. "Political Institutions in Democratic Brazil: Politics as a Permanent Constitutional Convention." In Peter R. Kingstone and Timothy J. Power, eds., *Democratic Brazil: Actors, Institutions, and Processes*. Pittsburgh: University of Pittsburgh Press.

Power, Timothy J., and Nancy R. Powers. 1988. "Issues in the Consolidation of Democracy in Latin America and Southern Europe in Comparative Perspective: A Rapporteurs' Report." Working Paper no. 113, Helen Kellogg Institute for International Studies, University of Notre Dame.

Przeworski, Adam. 1986. "Some Problems in the Study of Transitions to Democracy." In Guillermo O'Donnell, Philippe C. Schmitter, and Laurence Whitehead, eds., *Transitions from Authoritarian Rule: Comparative Perspectives*, 47–63. Baltimore: Johns Hopkins University Press.

———. 1992. "The Games of Transition." In Scott Mainwaring, Guillermo O'Donnell, and J. Samuel Valenzuela, *Issues in Democratic Consolidation*, 105–52. Notre Dame: University of Notre Dame Press.

——— et al. 1995. *Sustainable Democracy*. Cambridge: Cambridge University Press.

Rae, Douglas. 1967. *The Political Consequences of Electoral Laws*. New Haven: Yale University Press.

Reis, Fábio Wanderley. 1988. "Partidos, ideologia e consolidação democrática." In Reis and Guillermo O'Donnell, eds., *A Democracia no Brasil: dilemas e perspectivas*, 296–326. São Paulo: Vértice.

Rodrigues, Leôncio Martins. 1987. *Quem É Quem na Constituinte: uma análise sócio-política dos partidos e deputados*. São Paulo: OESP-Maltese.

———. 1995. "As eleições de 1994: uma apreciação geral." *Dados* 38, no. 1: 93–106.

Roett, Riordan. 1984. *Brazil: Politics in a Patrimonial Society*, 3d ed. New York: Praeger Publishers.

Rustow, Dankwart. 1970. "Transitions to Democracy: Toward a Dynamic Model." *Comparative Politics* 2, no. 3 (April): 337–63.

Samuels, David. 1998. "Careerism and Its Consequences." Ph.D. diss., University of California at San Diego.

Santos, Wanderley Guilherme dos. 1977. "Liberalism in Brazil: Ideology and Praxis." In Morris J. Blachman and Ronald G. Hellman, eds., *Terms of Conflict: Ideology in Latin American Politics*, 1–38. Philadelphia: Institute for the Study of Human Issues.

Santos, Wanderley Guilherme dos, Violeta Maria Monteiro, and Ana Maria Lustosa Caillaux. 1990. *Que Brasil É Este? Manual de indicadores políticos e sociais*. São Paulo: Vértice.

Sartori, Giovanni. 1976. *Parties and Party Systems: A Framework for Analysis*. New York: Cambridge University Press.

Schmitter, Philippe. 1971. *Interest Conflict and Political Change in Brazil*. Stanford: Stanford University Press.

———. 1992. "The Consolidation of Democracy and the Representation of Social Groups." *American Behavioral Scientist* 35: 422–49.

———. 1995. "Transitology: The Science or the Art of Democratization?" In Joseph Tulchin and Bernice Romero, eds., *The Consolidation of Democracy in Latin America*, 11–41. Boulder: Lynne Rienner Publishers.

Schneider, Ben Ross. 1995. "Democratic Consolidations: Some Broad Comparisons and Sweeping Arguments." *Latin American Research Review*, 30: 215–34.

Schumpeter, Joseph. 1947. *Capitalism, Socialism, and Democracy*. New York: Harper and Bros.

Schwartzman, Simon. 1982. *Bases do autoritarismo brasileiro*. Rio de Janeiro: Editora Campus.

SEMPREL S.A. 1989. *Anuário Parlamentar Brasileiro: Ano III, 1989*. São Paulo: Editora Três.

Senado Federal. 1991. *Senadores: Dados biográficos, quadragésima nona legislatura 1991–1999*. Brasília: Subsecretaria de Arquivo.

———. 1995. *Senadores: Dados biográficos, qüinquagésima legislatura 1995–1999*. Brasília: Subsecretaria de Arquivo.

Serra, José. 1979. "Three Mistaken Theses Regarding the Connection Between Industrialization and Authoritarian Regimes." In David Collier, ed., *The New Authoritarianism in Latin America*, 61–98. Princeton: Princeton University Press.

Share, Donald, and Scott Mainwaring. 1986. "Transitions Through Transaction: Democratization in Brazil and Spain." In Wayne Selcher, ed., *Political Liberalization in Brazil*, 175–215. Boulder: Westview Press.

Shugart, Matthew, and John Carey. 1992. *Presidents and Assemblies: Constitutional Design and Electoral Dynamics*. New York: Cambridge University Press.

Skidmore, Thomas. 1988. *The Politics of Military Rule in Brazil, 1964–1985*. New York: Oxford University Press.

Smith, William C. 1987. "The Political Transition in Brazil: From Authoritarian Liberalization and Elite Conciliation to Democratization." In Enrique Baloyra, ed., *Comparing New Democracies*, 179–240. Boulder: Westview Press.

Soares, Glaucio Ary Dillon. 1973. *Sociedade e política no Brasil*. São Paulo: DIFEL.

———. 1979. "Military Authoritarianism and Executive Absolutism in Brazil."

Studies in Comparative International Development 14, nos. 3–4 (fall–winter): 104–26.

———. 1984. *Colégio eleitoral, convenções partidárias, e eleições diretas.* Petrópolis: Vozes.

———. 1986. "The Rise of the Brazilian Military Regime." *Studies in Comparative International Development* 21, no. 2 (summer): 34–62.

Souza, Celina. 1997. *Constitutional Engineering in Brazil: The Politics of Federalism and Decentralization.* New York: St. Martin's Press.

Souza, Maria do Carmo Campello de. 1976. *Estado e partidos políticos no Brasil (1930 a 1964).* São Paulo: Alfa-Omega.

———. 1989. "The Brazilian New Republic: Under the Sword of Damocles." In Alfred Stepan, ed., *Democratizing Brazil*, 351–94. Oxford University Press.

———. 1992. "The Contemporary Faces of the Brazilian Right: An Interpretation of Style and Substance." In Douglas Chalmers, Maria do Carmo Campello de Souza, and Atilio Borón, eds., *The Right and Democracy in Latin America*, 99–127. New York: Praeger Publishers.

Stepan, Alfred. 1978. "Political Leadership and Regime Breakdown: Brazil." In Juan Linz and Alfred Stepan, eds., *The Breakdown of Democratic Regimes: Latin America*, 110–37. Baltimore: Johns Hopkins University Press.

———. 1986. "Paths toward Redemocratization: Theoretical and Comparative Considerations." In Guillermo O'Donnell, Philippe C. Schmitter, and Laurence Whitehead, eds., *Transitions from Authoritarian Rule: Comparative Perspectives*, 65–84. Baltimore: Johns Hopkins University Press.

———. 1988. *Rethinking Military Politics: Brazil and the Southern Cone.* New York: Oxford University Press.

Tsebelis, George. 1990. *Nested Games: Rational Choice in Comparative Politics.* Berkeley and Los Angeles: University of California Press.

Valenzuela, Arturo. 1977. *Political Brokers in Chile: Local Government in a Centralized Polity.* Durham: Duke University Press.

———. 1978. *The Breakdown of Democratic Regimes: Chile.* Baltimore: Johns Hopkins University Press.

Valenzuela, J. Samuel. 1992. "Democratic Consolidation in Post-Transitional Settings: Notion, Process, and Facilitating Conditions." In Scott Mainwaring, Guillermo O'Donnell, and J. Samuel Valenzuela, *Issues in Democratic Consolidation*, 57–104. Notre Dame: University of Notre Dame Press.

Verner, Joel G. 1974. "Educational Backgrounds of Latin American Legislators." *Comparative Politics* 6, no. 4 (July): 617–34.

von Mettenheim, Kurt. 1995. *The Brazilian Voter: Mass Politics in Democratic Transition, 1974–1986.* Pittsburgh: University of Pittsburgh Press.

Wallerstein, Michael. 1980. "The Collapse of Democracy in Brazil: Its Economic Determinants." *Latin American Research Review* 15, no. 3: 3–40.

Weber, Max. 1978. *Economy and Society.* 2 vols. Berkeley and Los Angeles: University of California Press.

Wesson, Robert, and David V. Fleischer. 1983. *Brazil in Transition.* New York: Praeger Publishers.

Weyland, Kurt G. 1993. "The Rise and Fall of President Collor and Its Impact on

Brazilian Democracy." *Journal of Interamerican Studies and World Affairs* 35, no. 1 (spring): 1–36.

———. 1996a. *Democracy Without Equity: Failures of Reform in Brazil.* Pittsburgh: Pittsburgh University Press.

———. 1996b. "Neopopulism and Neoliberalism in Latin America: Unexpected Affinities." *Studies in Comparative International Development* 31, no. 3 (fall): 3–31.

———. 2000. "The Brazilian State in the New Democracy." In Peter R. Kingstone and Timothy J. Power, eds., *Democratic Brazil: Actors, Institutions, and Processes,* 36–57. Pittsburgh: University of Pittsburgh Press.

Index